IMAGERY OF HATE ONLINE

Imagery of Hate Online

Edited by
Matthias J. Becker, Marcus Scheiber and Uffa Jensen

OpenBook
Publishers

https://www.openbookpublishers.com

Cover concept and cover image: Matthias J. Becker
Cover design: Jeevanjot Kaur Nagpal

Contents

About the Authors

Dr Carmen Aguilera-Carnerero obtained her degree and Ph.D. at the department of English and German Philology at the University of Granada, Spain, where she currently teaches. Her post-doctoral research focused on the study of extreme speech online, especially on CyberIslamophobia, the online discourse of the post-war ethnic conflict in Sri Lanka, the cyber-rhetoric of the far-right, the semiotics of terrorism and the communicative force of graffiti. She authored the Spanish section of the European Islamophobia report in 2016, 2017, and 2018. She has been a guest speaker at the University of Munich, Charles II University in Prague, Università Cattolica del Sacro Cuore in Milan, at the European Foundation of Arab Studies, Casa Árabe in Madrid and the European Parliament, among others. She has spoken on her research topics for different national and international media.

Web: https://www.ugr.es/en/staff/maria-carmen-aguilera-carnerero

Selected publications:

Aguilera-Carnerero, Carmen and Megara Tegal, 2023. "Multimodal Islamophobia. Gendered Stereotypes in memes". *Journal of Muslim and Media Research*, 16 (2), 201–222.

—, 2022. "From our sisters/To our sisters: the construction of ideal womanhood in the propaganda magazines of the Islamic State". *Pragmatics and Society, Special Issue: The Discourse of Terrorism*, 13 (3), 453–476.

—, 2021. "On heroes and enemies: Visual polarization in the propaganda magazines of the Islamic State". In: L. Fidalgo-Llamas, E. Morales-López and A. Floyd (eds), *Socio-Political Polarization and Conflict: Discursive Approaches*. London: Routledge, 137–152.

—, and Margarita Carretero González, 2021. "The vegan myth: the rhetoric of online anti-veganism". In: L. Wright (ed.), *The Routledge Handbook of Vegan Studies*. London: Routledge, 354–365.

Dr Matthias J. Becker is a linguist specialising in pragmatics, cognitive linguistics, (critical) discourse analysis, and social media studies, with a particular emphasis on researching prejudice and hatred. He studied linguistics, philosophy, and literature at Freie Universität Berlin and has contributed to several research projects focusing on the use of language in political and media campaigns. For over twelve years, his research has focused on the analysis of implicit hate speech—often normalised within mainstream political discourse—and the underlying conditions that enable its emergence. Matthias is the creator and lead of the *Decoding Antisemitism* research project and Postdoc Researcher at the University of Cambridge.

Selected publications:

Becker, Matthias J., Hagen Troschke, Matthew Bolton and Alexis Chapelan (eds), 2024. *Decoding Antisemitism: A Guide to Identifying Antisemitism Online*. London: Palgrave Macmillan/Springer Nature. https://link.springer.com/book/9783031492372.

—, Laura Ascone, Karolina Placzynta and Chloé Vincent (eds), 2024. *Antisemitism in Online Communication: Transdisciplinary Approaches to Hate Speech in the Twenty-First Century*. Cambridge: Open Book Publishers. https://doi.org/10.11647/OBP.0406.

—, and Matthew Bolton, 2024. "Images of Zionism in the Age of the Internet". In: Colin Shindler (ed.), *Routledge Handbook on Zionism*. London: Routledge, 520–537. https://doi.org/10.4324/9781003312352.

—, Laura Ascone and Hagen Troschke, 2022. "Antisemitic comments on Facebook pages of leading British, French, and German media outlets". *Humanities and Social Sciences Communications*, 9, 339. https://doi.org/10.1057/s41599-022-01337-8.

—, 2021. *Antisemitism in Reader Comments: Analogies for Reckoning with the Past*. London: Palgrave Macmillan/Springer Nature. https://link.springer.com/book/10.1007/978-3-030-70103-1.

https://orcid.org/0000-0003-2847-4542

Dr Lisa Bogerts is a Berlin-based independent political scientist and visual culture professional. For eleven years she has been researching, teaching and working practically on political conflicts and protest as well as visual communication and art. She wrote her doctoral thesis at the Goethe University Frankfurt (Cluster of Excellence "Normative Orders") and at the New School for Social Research, New York City.

Web: https://protestinstitut.eu/mitglieder/lisa-bogerts.

Selected publications:

Bogerts, Lisa and David Shim, forthcoming. "Visuality". In: Rhys Crilley (ed.), *Thinking World Politics Otherwise: A Textbook for International Relations Students.* Oxford: Oxford University Press.

—, and Maik Fielitz, 2023. "Fashwave: The Alt-Right's Aestheticization of Politics and Violence". In: Sarah Hegenbart and Mara-Johanna Kölmel (eds), *Dada Data. Contemporary Art Practice in the Era of Post-Truth Politics.* London: Bloomsbury, 230–245.

—, 2022. *The Aesthetics of Rule and Resistance. Analyzing Political Street Art in Latin America.* Protest, Culture & Society Series. New York: Berghahn Books.

—, and Maik Fielitz, 2020. "The Visual Culture of Far-Right Terrorism". In: *Global Network on Extremism & Technology (GNET) and PRIF-Blog (Peace Research Institute Frankfurt)* (31.03.2020).

—, and Maik Fielitz, 2019. "Do You Want Meme War? Understanding the Visual Memes of the German Far Right". In: Maik Fielitz and Nick Thurston (eds), *Post-Digital Cultures of the Far Right. Online Actions and Offline Consequences in Europe and the US.* Bielefeld: Transcript, 137–154.

—, 2017. "Mind the Trap. Visual Literacy, Street Art, and Visual Resistance". *SAUC (Street Art & Urban Creativity) Scientific Journal*, 3, 6–10.

—, 2015. "Bilder und Emotionen in der Sozialen Bewegungsforschung". In: Karl-Rudolf Korte (ed.), *Emotionen und Politik, Veröffentlichungen der Deutschen Gesellschaft für Politikwissenschaft (DGfP)*. Baden-Baden: Nomos, 225–246.

Wyn Brodersen is a sociologist and researcher at the Jena Institute for Democracy and Civil Society. His work examines the influence of digital interactions on radicalisation processes, focusing on digital subcultures, right-wing terrorism, and their intersections. He is part of the editorial team of the online magazine *Machine Against the Rage* (machine-vs-rage.bag-gegen-hass.net).

Web: https://www.idz-jena.de/ueber-das-institut/mitarbeitende/ wyn-brodersen.

Selected publications:

Bogerts, Lisa, Wyn Brodersen and Maik Fielitz, forthcoming. *Digitale Kulturen? Frag doch einfach.* München: UTB, UVK.

Brodersen, Wyn, Maik Fielitz, Holger Marcks, Ann-Kathrin Rothermel and Harald Sick, forthcoming. *Digitaler Hass. Formen, Kontexte und Gegenmaßnahmen*. Bielefeld: UTB, Transcript.

—, and Maik Fielitz, 2024. "The ominous allure of online antisemitism. Ambivalent participation in the practice of digital hate". In: Florian Hartleb (ed.), *The New Wave of Antisemitism. A Comparative Perspective*. Wien: European Institute for Counter Terrorism and Conflict Prevention, 55–67.

—, and Maik Fielitz, 2024. "Hass durch Freude. Memetischer Humor als Gateway zu rechtsextremen Weltbildern". In: Melis Becker, Jessica Maron and Alladin Sarhan (eds), *Hass und Hetze im Netz. Herausforderungen und Reaktionsmöglichkeiten*. Frankfurt am Main: Wochenschau Verlag, 38–52.

Maik Fielitz is a social scientist and conflict researcher. He is the head of the research unit on digital conflict studies at the Jena Institute for Democracy and Civil Society, as well as co-editor of the online magazine *Machine Against the Rage* (machine-vs-rage. net). His research examines the ways in which digital technologies and digital cultures influence the emergence and evolution of right-wing extremism, as well as the strategies employed by liberal democracies to counter authoritarian tendencies in online contexts.

Web: https://www.idz-jena.de/ueber-das-institut/mitarbeitende/ maik-fielitz.

Selected publications:

Bogerts, Lisa, Wyn Brodersen and Maik Fielitz, forthcoming. *Digitale Kulturen? Frag doch einfach*. München: UTB, UVK.

Brodersen, Wyn, Maik Fielitz, Holger Marcks, Ann-Kathrin Rothermel and Harald Sick, forthcoming. *Digitaler Hass. Formen, Kontexte und Gegenmaßnahmen*. Bielefeld: UTB, Transcript.

Fielitz, Maik and Holger Marcks, 2020. *Digitaler Faschismus. Soziale Medien als Motor des Rechtsextremismus*. Berlin: Dudenverlag.

—, and Nick Thurston (eds), 2019. *Post-Digital Cultures of the Far Right. Online Activism and Offline Consequences in Europe and the US*. Bielefeld: Transcript.

Yasmine Goldhorn is a master's graduate in Sociology and a research assistant with the *RelcoDiff* research project. Her research interests broadly concern institutional antisemitism, antisemitism among teenagers, and gender inequality in labour markets.

Web: https://www.uni-frankfurt.de/117681293/ Yasmine_Goldhorn.

Selected publications:

Rensch-Kruse, Benjamin, Saba-Nur Cheema, Yasmine Goldhorn and Isabell Diehm, 2024. "Antisemitismus unter jungen Kindern. Forschungsgrundlagen und -reflexionen im Kontext einer Differenzforschung in Einrichtungen der frühen Kindheit". In: Emra Ilgün-Birhimeoğlu and Seyran Bostancı (eds), *Elementarpädagogik in der postmigrantischen Gesellschaft. Theoretische und empirische Zugänge zu einer rassismuskritischen Pädagogik*. Weinheim: Beltz Juventa, 79–95.

—, and Yasmine Goldhorn, forthcoming. "Antisemitismus in Kindertagesstätten erforschen. Forschungsethische Perspektiven und Reflexionen dilemmatischer Herausforderungen". In: Sabine Andresen, Michael Fingerle and Helge Kminek (eds), *Erziehungswissenschaft und Ethik – zu den Verstrickungen einer Disziplin*. Stuttgart: Kohlhammer.

Otto Halmesvaara (M.Soc.Sci) is a doctoral researcher in social psychology at the University of Helsinki, Finland. Halmesvaara has studied far-right rhetoric, as well as topics such as shame and morality. In his forthcoming doctoral thesis, he addresses lay attitudes towards health information obtained from genetics.

Web: https://researchportal.helsinki.fi/fi/persons/ otto-halmesvaara.

Selected publications:

Halmesvaara, Otto, Ville J. Harjunen, Matthias B. Aulbach and Niklas Ravaja, 2020. "How bodily expressions of emotion after norm violation influence perceivers' moral judgments and prevent social exclusion: A socio-functional approach to nonverbal shame display". *PloS One*, 15 (4), e0232298.

Hakoköngäs, Eemeli, Otto Halmesvaara and Inari Sakki, 2020. "Persuasion Through Bitter Humour: Multimodal Discourse Analysis of Rhetoric in Internet Memes of Two Far-Right Groups in Finland". *Social Media + Society*. https://doi.org/10.1177%2F2056305120921575.

Dr Eemeli Hakoköngäs (D.Soc.Sci, Title of Docent) is a university lecturer in social psychology at the University of Helsinki, Finland. In his research, Hakoköngäs has focused on history politics, political psychology, and visual rhetoric in the Finnish context.

Web: https://researchportal.helsinki.fi/fi/persons/
juho-eemeli-hakok%C3%B6ng%C3%A4s.

Selected publications:

Hakoköngäs, Eemeli and Inari Sakki, 2023. "Multimodal nationalist rhetoric in Finland: From banal to extreme political persuasion". In: W. Wei, and J. Schnell (eds), *The Routledge Handbook of Descriptive Rhetorical Studies and World Languages*. London: Routledge, 234–248. https://doi.org/10.4324/9781003195276.

Sakki, Inari and Eemeli Hakoköngäs, 2022. "Dialogical construction of hate speech in established media and online discussions". In: K. Pettersson and E. Nortio (eds), *The Far-Right Discourse of Multiculturalism in Intergroup Interactions: A Critical Discursive Perspective*. London: Palgrave Macmillan, 85–111. http://doi.org/10.1007/978-3-030-89066-7_4.

Dr Pablo Jost is a communication scientist at the Institute of Journalism at the Johannes Gutenberg University in Mainz, Germany, where he received his Ph.D. in 2022 with a thesis on "Popularity Indicators in Political Communication Research". He is currently a visiting professor at the Department of Journalism and Communication Research at the University of Music, Drama and Media, Hannover.

As co-founder and strategic advisor of the Federal Association for Countering Online Hate, he investigates the communication of radical and extremist protest movements on digital platforms and their offline effects. His research also focuses on the media representation of social controversies, how political actors communicate, and how they adapt to the conditions of digitalization.

Web: https://www.polkom.ifp.uni-mainz.de/pablo-jost.

Selected publications:

Jost, Pablo, 2023. "How politicians adapt to new media logic. A longitudinal perspective on accommodation to user-engagement on Facebook." *Journal of Information Technology & Politics, 20 (*2), 184–197. https://doi.org/10.1080/19331681.2022.2076271.

—, and L. Dogruel, 2023. "Radical Mobilization in Times of Crisis: Use and Effects of Appeals and Populist Communication Features in Telegram Channels." *Social Media + Society, 9 (*3). https://doi.org/10.1177/20563051231186372.

—, A. Heft, K. Buehling, M. Zehring, H. Schulze, H. Bitzmann and E. Domahidi, 2023. "Mapping a Dark Space: Challenges in Sampling and Classifying Non-Institutionalized Actors on Telegram." *Medien & Kommunikationswissenschaft, 71* (3–4), 212–229. https://doi. org/10.5771/1615-634X-2023-3-4-212.

—, M. Maurer and J. Hassler, 2020. "Populism Fuels Love and Anger: The Impact of Message Features on Users' Reactions on Facebook." *International Journal of Communication, 14,* 2081–2102.

Maurer, M., Pablo Jost, M. Schaaf, M. Sülflow and S. Kruschinski, 2023. "How right-wing populists instrumentalize news media: Deliberate provocations, scandalizing media coverage, and public awareness for the Alternative for Germany (AfD)." *The International Journal of Press/ Politics, 28* (4), 747–769. https://doi.org/10.1177/19401612211072692.

Dr Lev Topor is a policy-oriented researcher and a private consultant in the fields of antisemitism and cyber policy. He teaches Cybersecurity at the School of Information Systems at the Academic College of Tel Aviv-Yaffo, Israel. He is a fellow at the Institute for the Study of Global Antisemitism and Policy (ISGAP). Lev is a former visiting ISGAP fellow at the Woolf Institute, Cambridge, United Kingdom, a former Senior Research Fellow at the Center for Cyber Law and Policy (CCLP), University of Haifa, Israel, and a former Visiting Scholar at the International Institute for Holocaust Research, Yad Vashem, Jerusalem.

Lev received his PhD from the Bar Ilan University, Israel (supervised by Prof. Jonathan Rynhold). His works have won several awards like the Honors Award from The Association of Civil-Military Studies in Israel (2020), the Presidential Prize from the President of Bar Ilan University, Israel (2019), and the Robert Wistrich Award from the Vidal Sassoon Center for the Study of Antisemitism (2019). He has published dozens of peer-reviewed journal articles, book chapters, and reports on cyber policies, anonymous communications, racism, antisemitism, and anti-Zionism.

Selected publications:

Fox, Jonathan and Lev Topor, 2021. *Why Do People Discriminate against Jews?* New York: Oxford University Press.

Topor, Lev, 2023. *Phishing for Nazis: Conspiracies, Anonymous Communications, and White Supremacy Networks on the Dark Web.* Abingdon, Oxon; New York: Routledge.

—, 2024. Cyber Sovereignty: International Security, Mass Communication, and the Future of the Internet. Cham, Switzerland: Springer Nature.

Dr Mohamed Salhi is a researcher and lecturer at the institute of Political Science, Goethe University in Frankfurt, specialising in critical discourse analysis, far-right populism, crisis discourse, and visual politics.

Web: https://www.fb03.uni-frankfurt.de/129559823/ Mohamed_Salhi

Selected publications:

Salhi, Mohamed, forthcoming. "Reinventing the Right in Morocco: Right-Wing Populist Discourses and Sentiments in Moroccan Online Spaces." *Middle East Law and Governance, Special Issue on Populism in the Arab World* 17.01

—, 2023. "What Explains the Absence of Transnational Far Right Ties between Lega Nord and AfD?" In: T. Notermans, S. Piattoni, L. Verzichelli and C. Wagemann (eds), *E La Nave Va: Italy and Germany in Turbulent Times*. Lovorno Di Menaggio: Villa Vigoni Editore | Verlag, 63–90.

https://orcid.org/0009-0003-7260-4188.

Prof. Inari Sakki, D.Soc.Sc., is Professor in Social Psychology at the University of Helsinki, Finland. Inari's core interests lie in the field of societal and political social psychology, including research on political discourse, nationalism, populism, political and online hate speech, and discursive, visual, and multimodal methodologies. Inari's work has been published in international peer-reviewed journals and volumes in the fields of social and political psychology, nationalism and memory studies, education, communication, qualitative research methods, and discourse studies. She recently edited the book *Qualitative Approaches to the Social Psychology of Populism: Unmasking Populist Appeal* (2025, Routledge).

Web: https://researchportal.helsinki.fi/fi/persons/inari-sakki.

Marcus Scheiber is a discourse semiotician specialising in critical discourse analysis, internet linguistics, multimodal research and antisemitism research. He started his academic career at the Universities of Heidelberg and Bern, and as a visiting researcher and lecturer at the University of Mumbai. He received his MA from the University of Heidelberg in 2018 with a thesis about internet memes. He is currently working on a Ph.D. project at the University of Vechta and the University of Vienna, in which he is investigating how the communication format of memes is used for antisemitic communication strategies in the digital sphere.

Selected publications:

Scheiber, Marcus, 2024. "Multimodal cognitive anchoring in antisemitic memes." In: Matthias J. Becker, Laura Ascone, Karolina Placzynta and Chloé Vincent (eds), *Antisemitism in Online Communication, Transdisciplinary Approaches*. London: Palgrave, 159–184.

—, Hagen Troschke and Jan Krasni, 2024. "Vom kommunikativen Phänomen zum gesellschaftlichen Problem: Wie Antisemitismus durch Memes viral wird." In: Susanne Kabatnik, Lars Bülow, Marie-Luis Merten and Robert Mroczynski (eds), *Pragmatik multimodal* (Studies for Pragmatics), 7. Tübingen: Narr Francke Attempto Verlag GmbH + Co, 257–284.

Scheiber, Marcus, 2019. "Perspektivistische Setzungen von Wirklichkeit vermittels Memes. Strategien der Verwendung von Bild-Sprache-Gefügen in der politischen Kommunikation." In: Lars Bülow and Michael Johann (eds), *Politische Internet-Memes – Theoretische Herausforderungen und empirische Befunde*. Berlin: Frank & Timme, 143–166.

https://orcid.org/0009-0006-1714-2015

Dr Dimitris Serafis is Assistant Professor at the Faculty of Arts / Center for Language and Cognition (CLCG), Department of Communication and Information Studies, at the University of Groningen, The Netherlands. His research interests lie at the intersection of critical discourse studies, social semiotics and multimodality, and argumentation studies, with his current focus being on topics such as racism, hate speech, populism and authoritarianism.

He has published internationally on these topics in journals such as Discourse & Communication, Critical Discourse Studies, Journal of Language and Politics, Social Semiotics, Topoi, Informal Logic, Journal of Argumentation in Context.

He is the Editor of the *CADAAD Journal – Critical Approaches to Discourse Analysis Across Disciplines* as well as sits at the Editorial Board of academic journals such as *Argumentation* (Springer)

and *Journal of Argumentation in Context* (John Benjamins)
Web: https://www.rug.nl/staff/d.serafis/?lang=en.

Selected publications:

Serafis, Dimitris, 2023. *Authoritarianism on the front page: Multimodal discourse and argumentation in times of multiple crises in Greece.* Amsterdam: John Benjamins.

—, Jolanta Drzewiecka, and Sara Greco, 2021. "Critical perspectives on migration in discourse and communication". *Studies in Communication Sciences*, 21 (2). https://doi.org/10.24434/j. scoms.2021.02.011.

Dr Janina Wildfeuer is a multimodalist with a multi-faceted background in linguistics, semiotics, and discourse analysis. She has more than fifteen years of experience in working with visual and audiovisual communication and has built particular expertise in films and audiovisual data, comics, social media and games.

In her position at the University of Groningen, Janina teaches classes on multimodality, digital communication, visual and audio-visual analysis, and works as programme coordinator of the Communication and Information Studies Master's. She is also the Chief Editor of the journal 'Visual Communication', one of the key journals in the field of visual and multimodal communication, and Associate Editor for the speciality section 'Multimodality of Communication' with Frontiers in Communication.

Janina has contributed to several edited collections and papers focused on the theoretical and methodological development of multimodality studies. Her work also provides valuable insights into corpus-analytical and empirically oriented projects on various media, including film, comics, and social media.

Web: https://www.rug.nl/staff/j.wildfeuer/?lang=en.

Selected publications:

Wildfeuer, Janina, John A Bateman and Tuomo Hiippala, 2020. *Multimodalität: Grundlagen, Forschung und Analyse – Eine problemorientierte Einführung.* Berlin: De Gruyter.

—, Janina Wildfeuer and Tuomo Hiippala, 2017. *Multimodality: Foundations, Research and Analysis – A Problem-Oriented Introduction.* Berlin: De Gruyter.

Wildfeuer, Janina, 2014. *Film Discourse Interpretation: Towards a New Paradigm for Multimodal Film Analysis.* London: Routledge.

List of Figures

List of Tables

1. Introduction

Marcus Scheiber and Matthias J. Becker

In any given society, there are a variety of different propositions that are held to be true at any given time and that guide the actions of the society. These propositions are not constant, but usually present themselves in the form of epistemic competition for claims to validity. Likewise, social actions do not necessarily take place in a consensual manner, as is quickly apparent from the number of divergent views held by a wide range of actors. Only the heterogeneity of social structures forms the basis of our democracy, because only "where heterogeneous use of semiotic acts between competing [...] groups is recognisable, [...] there is a debate and no dictatorial continuation of views of reality, patterns of interpretation and truths" (Niehr 2014: 47). But it is precisely in this everyday competition for claims to validity that the enormous explosiveness of sign actions is revealed: they can polarise, radicalise, and ultimately, they can kill. The Holocaust did not begin with the Nuremberg laws and the construction of crematoria; rather, it was rooted in centuries of persistent use and society-wide normalisation of certain semiotic acts, preserved within the collective reservoir of shared ideas for centuries (Schwarz-Friesel and Reinharz 2017). Today, the visual stereotypes of Jews from the Middle Ages persist, for instance, in the Happy Merchant meme, while accusations of blood libel and conspiracy myths have evolved into distorted representations of Israel as the Jewish state (for the distinction between criticism of Israel and Israel-related antisemitism, see below). Similarly, other hate ideologies—such as racism or misogyny—, reiterated in public communication in often

https://doi.org/10.11647/OBP.0447.01

elaborate ways, gain increased persuasiveness through renewed visual or multimodal patterns that carry related hateful ideas, surpassing their tabooed predecessors.

This volume is dedicated to digital spaces and the unique forms of communication within them, as it is precisely in these contexts that age-old hateful and exclusionary ideas—and their associated communication patterns—are proliferating at an alarming rate in new ways. The communicative reach and influence of individuals who endorse certain hate ideologies (or uncritically propagate them), are expanding like never before. In the early phase of digital communication, known as Web 1.0, only a limited number of users had the ability to create and share media content. With the advent of Web 2.0, however, digital technologies now enable almost anyone to produce and distribute their own (hateful) content.

These developments are particularly problematic, as the erosion of boundaries in digital communication through network connectivity significantly amplifies the spread—and thus normalisation—of hateful discourse in society (Troschke and Becker 2019): network connections allow hateful ideas to gain global validation and be strategically embedded in moderate areas of the digital public sphere (Ebner 2023). In these spaces, repeated exposure to such ideas in familiar contexts gradually imparts a sense of normalcy, leading to their acceptance even within environments previously regarded as moderate.

Moreover, digital communication increasingly relies on visual content, with meanings often conveyed more directly through images than words (Sachs-Hombach 2003, Engelkamp 2004, Nöth 2016). This trend is particularly relevant for hate communication, as hatred and other forms of resentment as well as exclusionary attitudes can be encoded in visual artefacts that make these ideas seem tangible and validated. Such images appear to affirm prejudiced beliefs by invoking traditional stereotypes. For instance, an image that portrays people of colour in a racist manner may, to a racist viewer, seem like an "authentic" depiction of reality, reinforcing their biased perspectives.

Despite their relevance in contemporary digital communication, approaches to the analysis of hate imagery are primarily undertaken from a historical perspective (Hauser and Janáčová 2020, Königseder 2020 and 2022). When examining hate ideologies in digital communication spaces, the focus is usually on verbal forms of communication (for antisemitism studies see Grimm and Kahmann 2018, Schwarz-Friesel 2020, Becker 2021, Becker et al. 2024; for racism studies see HateWatch (Southern Poverty Law Center); for social media studies with regard to various forms of hate communication, see HateLab; for extremism studies, see Hammer, Gerster, and Schwieter 2023 (ISD); for gender hostility, see KhosraviNik and Esposito 2018). This focus is particularly striking, as the pictorial dimension within digital communication—especially on social media platforms—plays a pivotal role in the spread of hateful content (Nagle 2017, Hübscher and von Mering 2022, Ebner 2023, see also Siever 2015). The use of images in everyday online hate communication has become commonplace, as the interplay between pictorial and verbal sign modalities in a concrete language-image relationship evokes its own communicative dynamics: memes, for example, represent a form of communication that constructs a shared sphere of cultural knowledge (Breitenbach 2015) and, as such, function as a communicative template for online social interaction, which is then adapted to advance various hate ideologies.

The interplay of pictorial and verbal signs is not a novelty of digital communication, but rather a natural feature of human communicative action. This phenomenon can be conceptualised through the lens of *multimodality*. On the one hand, multimodality describes the observation that all actions and communicative artefacts (such as antisemitic memes) draw on different sign modalities, interweaving them both productively and receptively in formal, discourse-semantic, and argumentative terms (Stöckl 2019: 50). On the other hand, multimodality refers to the methodological approaches used to analyse the interaction between different sign systems—such as language, image, or even music.

> Understood as an approach to the simultaneous analysis of all
> semiotic resources in an artefact, multimodality is seen [...] as one of
> the most influential concepts for semiotization of diverse forms of
> communications, providing a range of frameworks for the detailed
> analysis of meaning construction within and across several modes
> (Wildfeuer 2015: 14).

Multimodality thus aims to analyse the mutual integration of
different sign potentials of verbal and non-verbal sign modalities.
For as soon as sign modalities are interwoven, their specific qualities
are also merged. This integration gives rise to an emergent meaning
that is not inherent in the sign modalities involved or that can be
derived from them alone. In other words: multimodality seeks to
grasp and explain the fact that within multimodal sign actions the
"sum of all components [...] cannot be determined by the simple
addition of all the separate components—text, image, layout, etc.—
as they often do not acquire an independent meaning of their
own" (Wetzchewald 2012: 129; for a discussion on the principle of
emergence in the context of understanding metaphors, see Skirl
2009); however, this only emerges from the dialectical interaction
of the sign potentials involved in the sense of an overarching
(communicative-semiotic) action structure. With regard to the
mutual integration of verbal and pictorial sign modalities in the
context of digital hate communication, the specific communicative
and semiotic contributions that images and language make to a
specific hate artefact are therefore of particular interest. Through
the strategic placement of hateful, multimodal content, previously
"niche positions can be carried from the margins into the public
digital sphere, where they not only appear highly salient through
mass distribution, but also function successfully as mobilising
agents" (Schulze et al. 2022: 42). Research on contemporary visual
and multimodal expressions of hate in digital communication is
therefore urgently needed in order to understand the phenomena
and their underlying dynamics and to counter them effectively.
However, a multimodal approach to hate communication—like
any other empirical work involving both online and offline
datasets—should not be understood as an instrument for (morally)
evaluating individual statements against a supposed standard of

acceptable communication, as such standards are shaped by the epistemes of a given time and are therefore variable. Instead, the analytical value of a multimodal approach lies in identifying the semiotic contexts within (the specifics of) digital communication that both constitute and reinforce hateful content in all its forms.[1]

In addition to these structural communication-related specifics, it is crucial to offer a precise definition of the underlying conceptual layer when examining hate ideologies. This becomes especially challenging in the case of antisemitism, as the classifications used reveal how expressions related to Israel, as well as anti-capitalist statements and anti-elitist remarks, are framed. The latter two often emerge during online debates about figures like George Soros, Jewish celebrities in Hollywood, or during the COVID-19 pandemic, when anti-Jewish rhetoric was widespread. Antisemitism is a hate ideology that is often surrounded by grey areas. The same applies to anti-Muslim racism, where questions often arise about its relationship to criticism of political Islam, Islamism, Jihadism, and, in extreme cases, religiously legitimised terrorist organisations such as Hamas, al-Qaeda, ISIS, and Hezbollah.

The authors of this introduction, together with the Decoding Antisemitism team, emphasise that legitimate criticism of Israel is not synonymous with antisemitism. In defining antisemitic concepts—whether related to Israel or other contexts—it is crucial to assess claims based on contextual knowledge and to determine the extent of essentialisation and generalisation attributed to a particular characteristic or practice. As outlined once more in our recently published *Lexicon* (Becker et al., 2024)—a comprehensive guide informed by the operationalization of the International Holocaust Remembrance Alliance (IHRA) definition (2016)—clear distinctions exist between criticism of Israel and Israel-related

---

1   In terms of scientific ethics, we, in agreement with Pippa Norris (2017) and Martha C. Nussbaum (2010), regard science as indispensable for upholding democratic values and promoting public discourse, objective and analytical. However, we acknowledge that scientific findings—although they should neither serve as the basis for nor bear responsibility for moral judgments and solutions—do influence moral and political decisions. The responsibility for these matters should instead be entrusted to democratic institutions and public debate.

antisemitism, as well as the other related phenomena mentioned above. Criticism of right-wing populism in the Knesset, structural racism in Israeli society, injustice, loss of life, and destruction in the Gaza strip is legitimate, provided it remains grounded in genuine critique and does not devolve into stereotypical, reality-distorting, one-sided statements that reflect a double standard, which have been a constant feature of many international narratives surrounding the Arab-Israeli conflict since 1948.

We do not wish to suggest that there are no grey areas—indeed, there are. However, our argument is that, for decades, discursive rituals have sought to convince us that the field of Israel-related antisemitism is an impenetrable minefield, beyond any form of analysis. We believe that many of the frequently cited "grey areas" were already thoroughly discussed and academically classified years, if not decades, ago. The current Gaza war does not alter this reality. Rather, some of the discursive responses we observe today in traditional and social media continue to reflect familiar patterns of bias and/or demonisation of Israel that have long been embedded in the antisemitic repertoire, such as in the former Soviet Union or among both left-leaning and conservative circles in Germany, France, Spain, and the UK. Thus, the same classificatory frameworks can still be applied to identify patterns that are immediately recognisable to the informed reader of historical sources (for claims of genocide and apartheid, see Bolton et al. 2023, Bolton 2024; for claims of Nazism and colonialism, see Becker 2021). What remains lacking, however, is broader recognition of these classifications by other sectors of the academic community, politics, the media, and civil society.

As previously mentioned, definitional precision is equally crucial when critiquing Muslim or Islamist individuals and organisations (and here it is important to clarify that we do not equate these entities with the Israeli government, as these are fundamentally different entities). Such statements cross the boundary of legitimate discourse when the inherent patterns reflect derogatory, racist attitudes toward all Muslims (see Henzell-Thomas 2001, Pintak et al. 2021, and Aguilera-Carnerero et al. in chapter 5 of this volume). This kind of distorted demonisation of all Muslims lacks any basis in truth and compels those targeted by such rhetoric to answer for terrorist attacks like those of October 7 or September 11, or for other acts committed in the name of Islamism.

Any research project on hate speech, or more broadly on hate communication, whether in online or offline contexts, must clearly define the conceptual characteristics of the phenomenon being studied. Based on empirical data, these definitions should be expanded with inductive categories, enabling the systematic and consistent classification of the multimodal communication strategies employed by hateful actors, as demonstrated in this book. Our edited volume also seeks to operationalise the contexts in which hate manifests by offering a multidisciplinary overview of the range of theoretical and methodological approaches to the study of visual and multimodal hate communication. The aim is to gain insights and provide an overview of established research practices and the challenges they face. As part of the analysis of multimodal dimensions, several contributions will further illuminate how the findings from these case studies relate to broader public discourse.

In chapter 2, Uffa Jensen explores the affective dimension of the use of images and attributes independent agency to images. He illustrates this affective dimension by analysing the "visual markers" of the "Happy Merchant" meme.

Lev Topor in chapter 3 outlines how antisemitic users employ a variety of memes, drawing on established antisemitic patterns to spread antisemitism. The chapter provides insight into why antisemitic, or more generally radical and hateful, content becomes normalised within digital communication, drawing on the knowledge of an insider community.

Chapter 4 by Eemeli Hakoköngäs and Otto Halmesvaara provides an overview of qualitative rhetorical analysis of Internet memes created and disseminated by various extremist groups. They show that memes possess strategic potential for right-wing extremist actors, which they are aware of and therefore actively use for their communicative purposes.

Carmen Aguilera-Carnerero, Matthias J. Becker, and Marcus Scheiber in chapter 5 explore how the same mechanisms that enable the spread of hate speech can be repurposed to promote counter-speech, specifically focusing on memes combating Islamophobia.

Chapter 6 by Mohamed Salhi and Yasmine Goldhorn presents a fine-grained analysis of antisemitic communication in coded form on all semiotic levels, showing how multimodal resources are used in different ways and how they differ in their use to convey an antisemitic meaning.

Inari Sakki's chapter 7 presents a fine-grained analysis of right-wing populist communication strategies within TikTok, drawing on multimodal critical discursive psychology analysis to show how populist groups use multimodal communication to propagate hate and hostility.

In their study in chapter 8, Lisa Bogerts, Wyn Brodersen, Maik Fielitz, and Pablo Jost analyse the visual propaganda of far-right and conspiratorial actors using computational and interpretive methods. They reveal significant differences in how these actors target specific groups or audiences, focusing on polarising issues in current public debates in ways that amplify divisions.

Chapter 9 by Dimitris Serafis and Janina Wildfeuer outlines an integration of approaches from multimodality studies and argumentation theory to provide a systematic approach to the analysis of online forms of soft hate speech that is also generally applicable to other forms of (online) communication.

Marcus Scheiber in chapter 10 outlines the epistemic danger of antisemitic deepfakes and presents a qualitative approach that promises to complement existing quantitative AI-based approaches to deepfake identification with a discourse-semiotic perspective.

References

Becker, Matthias J., 2021. *Antisemitism in Reader Comments: Analogies for Reckoning with the Past.* London: Palgrave Macmillan.

—, Hagen Troschke, Matthew Bolton and Alexis Chapelan (eds), 2024. *Decoding Antisemitism: A Guide to Identifying Antisemitism Online.* London: Palgrave Macmillan.

Bolton, Matthew, 2024. "'More Like Genocide'. The Use of the Concept of Genocide in UK Online Debates About Israel". In: Matthias J. Becker,

Laura Ascone, Karolina Placzynta and Chloé Vincent (eds), 2024. *Antisemitism in Online Communication: Transdisciplinary Approaches to Hate Speech in the Twenty-First Century*. London: Open Book Publishers, 107–136. https://doi.org/10.11647/OBP.0406.

—, Matthias J. Becker, Laura Ascone, and Karolina Placzynta, 2023. "Enabling concepts in Hate Speech: The Function of the Apartheid Analogy in Antisemitic Online Discourse about Israel". In: Isabel Ermida (ed.), *Hate Speech in Social Media: Linguistic Approaches*. London: Palgrave Macmillan, 253–286. https://doi.org/10.1007/978-3-031-38248-2.

Breitenbach, Patrick, 2015. "Memes. Das Web als kultureller Nährboden". In: Patrick Breitenbach, Christian Stiegler and Thomas Zorbach (eds), *New Media Culture. Mediale Phänomene der Netzkultur*. Bielefeld: Transcript, 29–49. https://doi.org/10.14361/9783839429075-002.

Ebner, Julia, 2023. *Going Mainstream: How Extremists Are Taking Over*. London: Bonnier.

Engelkamp, Johannes, 2004. "Gedächtnis für Bilder". In: Klaus Sachs-Hombach and Klaus Rehkämper (eds), *Bild – Bildwahrnehmung – Bildverarbeitung*. Wiesbaden: Deutscher Universitätsverlag, 227–242.

Grimm, Marc and Bodo Kahmann (eds), 2018. *Antisemitismus im 21. Jahrhundert*. Berlin: De Gruyter.

Hammer, Dominik, Lea Gerster and Christian Schwieter, 2023. *Inside the Digital Labyrinth – Right-Wing Extremist Strategies of Decentralisation on the Internet and Possible Countermeasures*. 2022 Annual Report for the Research Project "Countering Radicalisation in Right-Wing Extremist Online Subcultures". Institute for Strategic Dialogue (ISD). https://www.isdglobal.org/isd-publications/inside-the-digital-labyrinth.

Hauser, Jacub and Eva Janáčová (eds), 2020. *Visual Antisemitism in Central Europe*. Berlin: De Gruyter.

Henzell-Thomas, Jeremy, 2001. "The Language of Islamophobia. Paper presented at the 'Exploring Islamophobia' Conference at The University of Westminster School of Law". London, 29 September. http://www.masud.co.uk/ISLAM/misc/phobia.htm.

Hübscher, Monika and Sabine von Mering (eds), 2022. *Antisemitism on Social Media*. London: Routledge.

IHRA (International Holocaust Remembrance Alliance), 2016. "Working Definition of Antisemitism". https://www.holocaustremembrance.com/resources/working-definitions-charters/working-definition-antisemitism

KhosraviNik, Majid and Eleonora Esposito, 2018. "Online Hate, Digital Discourse and Critique: Exploring Digitally-Mediated Discursive

Practices of Gender-Based Hostility". *Lodz Papers in Pragmatics*, 14 (1), 45–68. https://doi.org/10.1515/lpp-2018-0003

Königseder, Angelika, 2020. "In eigener Sache: Arthur Langermans Sammlung visueller Antisemitika am Zentrum für Antisemitismusforschungl". *Jahrbuch für Antisemitismusforschung*, 29, 17–25. https://doi.org/10.14279/depositonce-15580

—, 2022. "Arthur Langerman's Collection of Visual Antisemitica at the Center for Research on Antisemitism, Technische Universität Berlin". In: Kazerne Dossin (ed.), *#FakeImages. Unmask the Dangers of Stereotypes*. Berlin: Metropol, 108–112.

Nagle, Angela, 2017. *Kill All Normies: Online Culture Wars from 4Chan and Tumblr to Trump and the Alt-Right*. Winchester: Zero Books.

Niehr, Thomas, 2014. *Einführung in die Politolinguistik. Gegenstände und Methoden*. Göttingen: Vandenhoeck und Ruprecht.

Norris, Pippa, 2017. *Democratic Deficits: Critical Citizens Revisited*. Cambridge: Cambridge University Press.

Nöth, Winfried, 2016. "Verbal-Visuelle Semiotik". In: Nina-Maria Klug and Hartmut Stöckl (eds), *Handbuch Sprache im multimodalen Kontext*. Berlin: De Gruyter, 190–216.

Nussbaum, Martha C., 2010. *Not for Profit: Why Democracy Needs the Humanities*. Princeton: Princeton University Press.

Pintak, Lawrence, Brian J. Bowe and Jonathan Albright, 2021. "Influencers, Amplifiers, and Icons: A Systematic Approach to Understanding the Roles of Islamophobic Actors on Twitter". *Journalism & Mass Communication Quarterly*, 99, 1–25. https://doi.org/10.1177/10776990211031567

Sachs-Hombach, Klaus, 2003. *Das Bild als kommunikatives Medium. Elemente einer allgemeinen Bildwissenschaft*. Köln: Herbert von Halem.

Schwarz-Friesel, Monika, 2020. "Antisemitism 2.0 – The spreading of Jew-hatred on the World Wide Web". In: Armin Lange, Kerstin Mayerhofer, Dina Porat and Lawrence H. Schiffman (eds), *Comprehending and confronting antisemitism. A multi-faceted approach*. New York/Boston: De Gruyter, 311–338.

—, and Jehuda Reinharz, 2017. *Inside the Antisemitic Mind: The Language of Jew-Hatred in Contemporary Germany*. Waltham: Brandeis University Press.

Schulze, Heidi, Simon Greipl, Julian Hohner and Diana Rieger, 2022. "Zwischen Furcht und Feindseligkeit: Narrative Radikalisierungsangebote in Online-Gruppen". In: Uwe Kemmesies, Peter Wetzels, Beatrix Austin, Christian Buscher, Axel Dessecker,

Sven Hutter and Diana Rieger (eds), *Motra-Monitor 2022*. Wiesbaden: MOTRA Bundeskriminalamt – Forschungsstelle Terrorismus/ Extremismus, 40–67.

Siever, Christina, 2015. *Multimodale Kommunikation im Social Web. Forschungsansätze und Analysen zu Text-Bild-Relationen*. Frankfurt am Main: Lang.

Skirl, Helge, 2009. *Emergenz als Phänomen der Semantik am Beispiel des Metaphernverstehens. Emergente konzeptuelle Merkmale an der Schnittstelle von Semantik und Pragmatik*. Tübingen: Gunter Narr (Tübinger Beiträge zur Linguistik).

Southern Poverty Law Center, 2023, "Hatewatch". https://www.splcenter. org/hatewatch.

Stöckl, Hartmut, 2019. "Linguistic Multimodality – Multimodal Linguistics: A State-of-the-Art Sketch". In: Janina Wildfeuer, Jana Pflaeging, John Bateman, Ognyan Seizov and Chiao-I Tseng (eds), *Multimodality. Disciplinary Thoughts and the Challenge of Diversity*. Berlin: De Gruyter, 41–68.

Troschke, Hagen and Matthias J. Becker, 2019. "Antisemitismus im Internet. Erscheinungsformen, Spezifika, Bekämpfung". In: Günther Jikeli and Olaf Glöckner (eds), *Das neue Unbehagen. Antisemitismus in Deutschland und Europa*. Baden-Baden: Georg Olms, 151–72.

Wetzchewald, Marcus, 2012. *Junktoren zwischen Text und Bild – dargestellt anhand der Unternehmenskommunikation im Internet*. Duisburg: Rhein-Ruhr.

Wildfeuer, Janina, 2015. "Bridging the Gap between Here and There: Combining Multimodal Analysis from International Perspectives". In: Jens Runkehl, Peter Schlobinski and Torsten Siever (eds), *Building Bridges for Multimodal Research. International Perspectives on Theories and Practices of Multimodal Analysis*. Frankfurt am Main: Lang, 13–33.

Williams, Matthew, 2019. *Hatred Behind the Screens: A Report on the Rise of Online Hate Speech*. Cardiff University and Mishcon de Reya. https:// hatelab.net/wp-content/uploads/2019/11/Hatred-Behind-the-Screens. pdf.

2. The "Happy Merchant" as an antisemitic hate picture: A historical perspective on visual antisemitism

Uffa Jensen

Abstract

The "Happy Merchant" serves as a prominent example of visual antisemitism, reflecting a long and complex history of anti-Jewish imagery distinct from textual traditions. While antisemitic texts date back to late antiquity, the visual representation of Jews began to emerge significantly in the 9th and 10th centuries, and evolved into more aggressive forms by the 13th century. This chapter explores the historical development of the "Happy Merchant" and its role in contemporary digital communication. The image, which combines various antisemitic markers—such as stereotypical physical features and behaviour—aims to evoke negative emotions towards Jews, thereby reinforcing harmful stereotypes. This contribution highlights the need to understand the affective dimensions of hate imagery and its impact on contemporary antisemitic discourse.

Keywords: *Happy Merchant, Internet memes, hate pictures, affective agency, historical visual analysis*

https://doi.org/10.11647/OBP.0447.02

Introduction

The long and complex history of anti-Jewishness and antisemitism has produced a long and complex tradition of visual material.[1] However, this tradition of images, while certainly closely related, is not identical with the textual one. Anti-Jewish texts go back at least as far as the Christian polemics of late antiquity—and some scholars assume that the beginnings reach back even further into the ancient world (see Schäfer 1997). Yet, the visual tradition emerged much later. The first examples—mostly juxtapositions of the figures of Synagoga and Ecclesia in Christian art—appeared in the 9th and 10th century (see Jochum 1993). By the 13th century, the visual representation of Jews had already reached a rather aggressive level, with the emergence of the "gothic Jewish face" (see Lipton 2014). Moreover, the textual and visual traditions diverged not only at this early stage, but also during the second half of the 20th century. While antisemitic texts and statements were fundamentally transformed in Central Europe after the Holocaust, they continued to exist. From all we know, this was not the case with the rich visual culture of prewar antisemitic imagery. In the immediate postwar era, these images seemed to have vanished from the public eye, at least in Central Europe. Obviously, this has changed again with the advent of the digital age and especially with communication on social media formats. Here, antisemitism has attained again a very visual quality.

Given the observation that antisemitic textual and visual traditions have different trajectories, how can we understand such differences? Do we need to treat these distinct forms as related or as separate entities? Do antisemitic text and images work entirely

---

1　　However, this visual tradition is much less discussed in the historiography and the study of antisemitism which remains in many ways oriented and fixated on text. Consequently, many of the available overviews of the history of antisemitism rarely discuss visual sources, including: Schäfer 2020; Eriksen, et al. 2019; Nirenberg 2013. Certainly, an old, important and impressive body of literature exists that has examined anti-Jewish motifs in Christian art. See i.e. Blumenkranz (1965); Schreckenberg (1988); Schreckenberg (1966). Among medieval historians, there exists a fruitful discussion about the importance of racist and antisemitic imagery: Kaplan (2014); Lipton (2014); Strickland (2003); Mellinkoff (1993).

differently or are they essentially similar? As I will argue in this chapter, the answer is both. Answering such questions, in my view, involves interrogating the complex issue of what we believe images do. I propose, in order to do so, to rethink their affective dimension.

For this, I suggest using the concept of hate pictures. The antisemitic version of such pictures, I argue, mobilise specific forms of visuality against Jews in order to create, nurture and sustain negative emotions about them.[2] The connection between image and emotion is particularly important for such an approach, and we should consider three different levels of this connection. First, we can question the emotions that play a role for the image producers. Here, it is often implied that these producers visualise such emotions in the image because they are also moved by them and/or because they want to convey them through this image. Secondly, we might also ask what emotions arise during the reception of an antisemitic image, i.e. whether viewers resonate emotionally with the image that they see. Sometimes we can learn about such reception directly, i.e. through ego-documents like diaries, memoirs etc. Sometimes we can study the reception through the ways in which the recipients use the image or react to it, as is often the case in online communication. The final dimension is, arguably, the most controversial: in my understanding, we need to also ask about the affective quality of these images. Here, the assumption is that images can have a direct – and possibly different, in comparison to text – effect on our emotions. Thus, I would propose to carefully ascribe an affective agency to these hate pictures.[3]

---

2   By using the word 'hate'—much as in 'hate speech'—I do not imply that this is the only meaningful emotion in such images. On the contrary, it is an important step in any study of such images to explore their specific emotional logic, which can involve various emotions. For the concept of negative emotions, I have used the—frequently forgotten—phenomenological works by Aurel Kolnai (see Kolnai 2004). However, a historical adaptation is necessary, as I have explained in Jensen (2017).

3   An important indicator for the power of such images is our own ambivalent usage of them. I have observed in many different contexts that people have many reservations about showing these images, e.g. in exhibitions, because they ascribe considerable potency to them. However, in order to explore this

Currently, a prominent example of visual antisemitism in online communication is the "Happy Merchant". This image has a suggestive history and is conceptually significant, which is why I would like to use it as a point of departure for my discussion of hate pictures.

Fig. 2.1 Image known today as the "Happy Merchant"[4]

Today, it is relatively certain that the cartoonist Nick Bougas produced this image and published it under the pseudonym "A. Wyatt Mann."[5] The American neo-Nazi and white supremacist, Tom Metzger, began publishing such caricatures in his newsletter "WAR: White Aryan Resistance" from 1989 onwards.[6] In general, Metzger very skilfully used many different media formats: radio and television shows, videos, booklets, stickers, an early website and even an early computerised bulletin board.[7] Thus, it is not surprising that he started to use caricatures as a particularly

---

thoroughly, a complex discussion about image theory, phenomenological studies of perception, the nature of stereotypes, the nature of projection etc. would necessarily have to follow: I cannot provide this at this point. But I have been working on these issues for several years, together with my late friend and scholar Jan Plamper. For now, it must suffice to refer to a growing body of literature that stresses the specific agency of images. See Bredekamp (2010); Mitchell (2005). However, there exist also important warnings about visual essentialism that any reasonable description of the agency of images needs to take into account. See Bal (2003).

4   For more about the image, see https://www.adl.org/resources/hate-symbol/happy-merchant

5   It was first argued that Bougas was "A. Wyatt Mann" by Bernstein (2015). As far as I know, Bougas never protested against or refuted this claim.

6   On Metzger, see Ezekiel (1995); Hamm (1993).

7   See the ADL-dossier on Metzger in: https://web.archive.org/web/20070826114712/http://www.adl.org/learn/Ext_US/Metzger.asp

aggressive method of visual communication. Already in the second edition to which A. Wyatt Mann contributed, he was allowed to design an entire page full of cartoons: an "A. Wyatt Mann collection". It contained "honest depictions of conditions that exist!" and the reader was asked to: "Post 'em... Copy 'em... Color 'em... Spread 'em around!"[8]

All of the images published in WAR are deeply disturbing, radically racist or antisemitic. In addition, "A. Wyatt Mann" also used aggressively homophobic, anti-Mexican, anti-immigration and sexist images. Moreover, the image later known as "Happy Merchant" originally did not stand alone, but was combined with an equally vicious, racist, anti-Black image. Both figures were dehumanised with comparisons to rats and vermin.

Fig. 2.2 Cartoon by "A. Wyatt Mann" (1992)[9]

At least one commentator has suggested that Bougas was not a white nationalist and that his original intention was to protest against political correctness, as it emerged in the early 1990s in the United States (see Bernstein 2015, appendix). However, it must be stressed that "A. Wyatt Mann" regularly contributed the most aggressive and derogative images to WAR, which declared itself

8   See WAR—White Aryan Resistance. 8/2 (1989), p. 11. After a while, WAR offered stickers with cartoons by "A. Wyatt Mann" to be purchased and, thus, the readers could distribute them on their own.
9   See WAR 11/5 (1992), p. 7.

to be the "most racist and hateful newspaper on this planet".[10] To be sure, it is important to understand that, in their aggressive language, these images were meant to be satirical attacks—and, thus, to be "funny".[11] Still, if one looks at all the images by "A. Wyatt Mann" in WAR, one cannot convincingly acquit Bogas of the charge of radical racism and antisemitism.

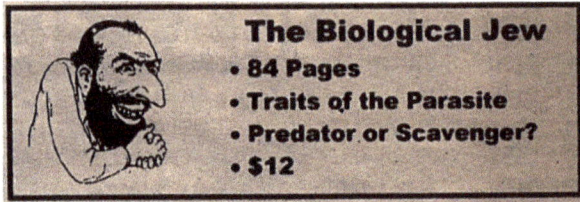

Fig. 2.3 Advertisement in "WAR" (2001)[12]

Eventually, the antisemitic part of the original image became separated from the anti-Black image. While it is not entirely clear when this happened, we have some indicators. In later years, adverts appeared in WAR for little booklets with collections of A. Wyatt Mann's cartoons, which its readers were encouraged to order.[13] Some of his caricatures were also turned into stickers that were available on Metzger's website. In July 2001, one of the advertisements for these publications in WAR featured the separate antisemitic image.

In the same year, this version also appeared for the first time in an online context, when it was used on "JRBooksOnline", an antisemitic, racist website and online bookshop.

---

10 See WAR, April 1997, appendix.

11 In the modern history of antisemitic images, this function is well-known. In fact, much of the proliferation of antisemitic imagery cannot be understood without the element of aggressive humour. While contemporary observers may not perceive these images as funny or humorous in any way, this was not necessarily the perspective of many historical subjects—and, even today, such an understanding may result from a certain well-mannered notion of what is not meant to be funny. By contrast, there exists a well-established form of humour to denigrate others who are, thus, turned into outsiders by the laughing community. See Freud's description of the aggressive joke in Freud (1904/1960).

12 See WAR, July 2001, appendix.

13 The back pages of WAR increasingly contained endless lists of items to order and receive through the mail, among them books, and audio and video tapes.

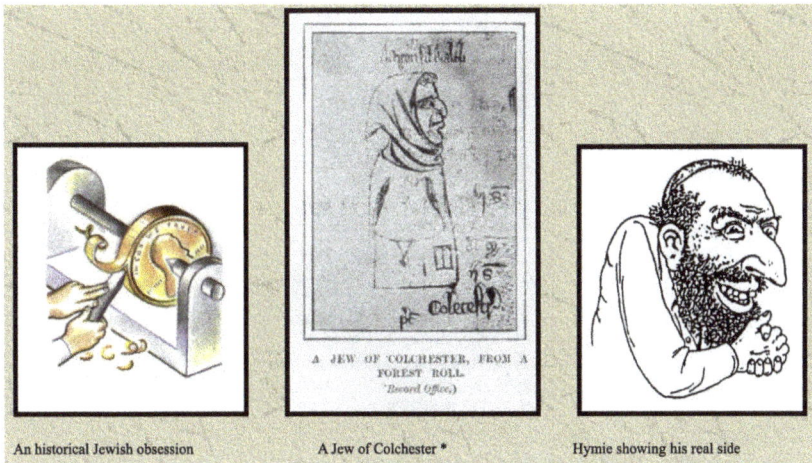

Fig. 2.4 Use of the "Happy Merchant" on "JRBooksOnline" (2001)[14]

This specific combination also related the contemporary image to the long history of anti-Jewish imagery. The image later known as "Happy Merchant" was juxtaposed with a historical image from 13th-century England in the centre.

Fig. 2.5 Image called "Aaron, Son of the Devil" (1277)[15]

This historically informed antisemitic website frequently stressed the long tradition of antisemitic slander and, thus, tried to give its

---

14 For the image see https://knowyourmeme.com/memes/happy-merchant
15 For the image see https://upload.wikimedia.org/wikipedia/commons/c/c7/ Aaron%2CSonOfDevil.jpg

users a sense of the permanence of visual antisemitism. The caption under the "Happy Merchant" in this version reads "Hymie showing his real side". The implication is that Jews—for whom "hymie" is a derogatory term—are usually hiding their 'real' nature which, therefore, must be disclosed through such images. Ever since the high medieval period, anti-Jewish image production has revealed an obsession with Jewish invisibility—either that of the individual Jewish person or of the Jews' 'real' intentions.[16] Such anti-Jewish and antisemitic images were thus intended to make Jews and, by implication, their evilness visible. Ever-present as contrasts, but not observable, were non-Jews who were simply different by implication from what was revealed as Jewish. In the following two decades since 2001, the "Happy Merchant" has become one of the most influential hate pictures in the digital age. It is significant that it was this antisemitic image, and less the complete image with the racist cartoon included, that became popular.

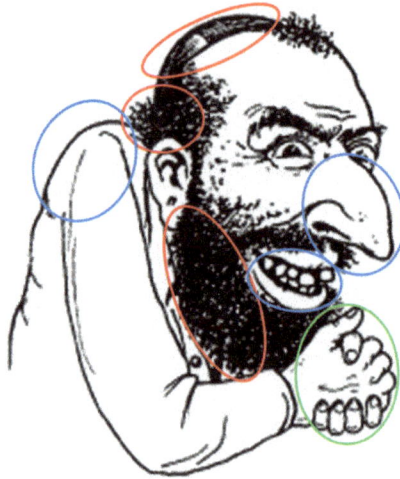

Fig. 2.6 Markers on the image of the "Happy Merchant"

16 It is usually believed that Jewish invisibility only became an issue with the emancipation and acculturation of Jews in the course of the 19th century, although there exist convincing arguments that earlier forms of anti-Jewish imagery performed a similar function of making Jews and their supposed character visible. See esp. Lipton (2014).

To examine this image from the point of view of visual history, it is helpful to use the concept of the visual marker.[17] The image of the "Happy Merchant" includes several different kinds of markers. One category of markers relates to dress and/or physical qualities which are usually associated with Jewish religious practices: in this case (red), these often include beards, payot, or various kinds of headgear such as a kippah etc. Another denotes behavioural patterns that are associated with typical Jewish conduct. In the case of the "Happy Merchant", the rubbing of hands (green) can be classified in this way, as I will discuss later. The final category of markers is connected to physiognomic characteristics, which have become associated with Jews over a long period of time.[18] In the "Happy Merchant", we can detect such elements (blue), i.e. the distorted body with a hump, the bad, large teeth, the puffy lips, the piercing eyes and the hooked nose. While all of these groups of markers contribute to the overall negative and aggressive impression of the image, the last set is arguably the most problematic, because it attaches essentializing features to the body. By dissecting the different markers in this way, we attain a better perspective on why the "Happy Merchant" is a particularly aggressive image, for two reasons. First, the sheer number of markers in this image is remarkable. Thus, the Jewishness of the "Happy Merchant" seems overdetermined by them. Second, it contains several markers of the particularly problematic physiognomic category, which helps to explain the aggressive appearance of the image. Such bodily features contribute substantially to the unpleasant, ugly, and alien expression of the figure. We can certainly speculate about the influence of this threatening appearance on the spectacular success of the "Happy Merchant" once it entered the digital world. Arguably, its aggressive nature helped to make it popular, because much of its usage relies on this quality.

Some of these markers play a role in the later history of the image. Eventually, the image became known as "Jew-bwa-ha-ha.

---

17   In a similar fashion, Ruth Mellinkoff has suggested using the term "signs" (Mellinkoff 1993). However, the term "marker" relates more specifically to bodily features and aspects of identity, whereas the concept of the "sign" can also imply the specific theory of semiotics.

18   Many of these (alleged) physiognomic qualities were established during the medieval period. On the beginnings of the science of physiognomy see Ziegler (2009). See also Erb (1985).

gif", a usage that again stressed its humorous dimension. Surely, with this name an unmistakeable identification with its subject—a distorted Jewish person—was also established. This is significant because it is at least possible to imagine a viewer who is ignorant of the history of antisemitism and who, thus, cannot identify the depicted person as Jewish. As far as we know, the image became known as "Happy Merchant" by 2012.[19] In many ways, this change narrowed the possible interpretations of the image and, at the same time, placed it into an additional visual tradition. With the new name, the image now could be read as depicting a particular economic behaviour that was often assumed to be Jewish. The term "merchant" associated the image with a long tradition of vilifying Jews as deceitful traders and bankers.[20] The word "happy" underscored the dimensions of greed and malice. The visual tradition of antisemitism is full of such examples, e.g. the numerous portrayals of the figure Shylock in William Shakespeare's *The Merchant of Venice*. Thus, the behavioural marker of the rubbing of hands gained even more force with the new name.

Fig. 2.7 E. Goodwyn Lewis, *The Merchant of Venice* (1863)

19   The earliest example in which the image was called "Le Happy Merchant" is from a post on 4chan in May 2012. See https://knowyourmeme.com/memes/happy-merchant
20   See, for this tradition, Bonnell (2008); Penslar (2001).

Fig. 2.8 John Hamilton Mortimer, *Merchant of Venice* (ca. 1750)

What is the function of these different markers in the image? Overall, they aspire to induce negative emotions against Jews by illustrating their fundamentally alien and aggressive nature. Primarily, this alien look is established aesthetically, as well as morally. The fact that this image was also called "Jew face" underlines these aspects[21] because, in general, the visual representation of the face has long been described as the essential location to discern the emotional qualities of the depicted individual.[22] This is certainly illustrated by the history of visual representations of Jews: since the high medieval period, the 'Jewish face' has been the site for the denigration of Jews. Thus, it became a convention to portray the 'Jewish face' in profile, which helped to accentuate those characteristics considered to be ugly. As the face was described as the site of truth, beauty and trustworthiness, the Jewish face appeared as ugly and evil, warning any observers to affectively keep at a distance.

While it is necessary to study the use of the "Happy Merchant" in order to understand its visual and affective qualities, the

---

21   See https://www.adl.org/resources/hate-symbol/happy-merchant

22   See the long tradition of the representation of the face in film studies: Balázs (2019).

markers of the image themselves establish the figure as alien in his religious, behavioural and physiognomic traits. Thus, the image is quite a radical example of a hate picture. However, the visual logic of the image implies more than hate; it includes several different emotions such as greed, malice, disgust and revulsion. Some of the markers are especially responsible for certain negative emotions; for example the physiognomic markers of the mouth, nose and the hump are relevant to disgust and revulsion, because they paint the figure in a particularly ugly fashion. The "Happy Merchant" stands in a long tradition in which an unpleasant appearance is associated with moral dubiousness and a bad, evil and deceiving character— see for example the many depictions of Judas, a crucially negative Jewish figure, in the Christian artistic canon.

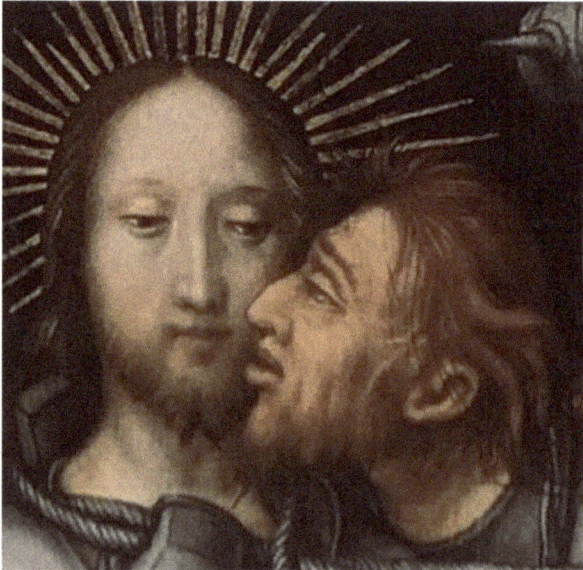

Fig. 2.9 Holbein the Elder, *The Kiss of Judas* (1494-1500)

Moreover, the behavioural markers in the "Happy Merchant" portray the emotional repertoire of greed and malice. However, we might feel hard-pressed to claim that all of these specific emotional reactions are necessarily implied by the image, or, in other words, that they are caused by its agency. Yet, I would argue that these markers taken together cause the clearly negative and disgusting appearance of this image. In this sense, we might describe the "Happy Merchant" as an essentially antisemitic image which will always be used in a negative way and, in this sense, works without context. Of course, individual recipients of the image might not be able to relate the image to Jews if they are not familiar with the visual history of antisemitic stereotypes. Yet, it seems to me that an individual reading of the figure as positive, attractive or trustworthy is necessarily precluded. While we cannot fix any inevitable reading of the image or even an emotional reaction to it, we can nevertheless assert that the nature of the image suggests certain readings and reactions and renders others unlikely, or even impossible. To put it—possibly too—drastically: the agency of the "Happy Merchant" imposes its negativity onto the reception.

To return to the image's production, I would argue that the hyper-antisemitism and racism of the images that "A. Wyatt Mann" published in WAR further supports the visual agency of the "Happy Merchant". Without a doubt, "A. Wyatt Mann" intended to produce very ugly, humiliating, and aggressive images of Jews, Black people and homosexual men. Unsurprisingly, the "most racist and hateful newspaper on this planet" featured such hate pictures. Thus, on the level of production, the antisemitic (and racist) intention behind the creation of the image is more than obvious, whatever we might think about Nick Bougas' individual beliefs. The publication of these images in WAR and their alignment with other images of the same nature also created a publication context which, given the later uses of the image, prefigured much of the reception and made an antisemitic and racist understanding almost inevitable.

But how was the "Happy Merchant" used and what does this reveal about the image and its reception? Significantly, the image became popular online as a reaction image, at least initially.[23] In online communication, such images function as responses to a previous act of communication, commenting on what was said by using the content of the image. Such reaction images usually add meaning to the initial content and often hold emotional

---

23   https://knowyourmeme.com/memes/happy-merchant

significance.[24] Yet, the use of such reaction images in the context of social media communication is complex: by commenting on something with an image—e.g. with the classical image of Michael Jackson eating popcorn while watching a movie in a cinema with excitement—we reveal a certain amount of self-reflexivity. We know that we are employing a staged image in order to present our emotional reaction to something for others. This ironic, self-reflective act has been described as "metawitnessing".[25] At the same time, we trust that this image will create an—emotional—effect on those we communicate with online, e.g. they might think that our posting of the Jackson image is funny. Thus, the use of such reaction images amounts to a self-reflective way of representing and producing emotions in online communication.[26]

How was the "Happy Merchant" used as a reaction image? Of course, more data and examples of such practices are required to fully answer this question. Observers have, however, reported that posts with the "Happy Merchant" often took "the form of sardonically roleplaying a Jew who gleefully and transparently manipulates the 'good goyim' who are duped by his deceptions [...]."[27] Such a use reveals a certain level of self-reflexivity, as well. Moreover, these users seem to claim the Jewish position for themselves, only to portray it as manipulative and deceiving. The other position that they temporarily leave behind belongs to the betrayed individuals, the "good goyim", who turn out to be the users themselves all along. This roleplay is funny in an aggressive way, which is best described by the German word 'Häme' that combines malice and wit. Certainly, the dimension of 'Häme' lies in the extremely negative and antisemitic portrayal, but the roleplay adds to it.

---

24 See, for a study of such "reaction images", Schankweiler (2020).
25 See ibid, p. 254.
26 I would stress the productive nature of emotions in this context. See e.g. Scheer (2012). Schankweiler, like many others in media and visual studies, relies on affect theory in the tradition of Silvan Tomkins, which usually implies a fixated, biological concept of affects (instead of a historical concept of emotions, as I prefer it and as Scheer has developed).
27 https://knowyourmeme.com/memes/happy-merchant

But what can we say about the emotional position involved? In contrast to the normal use of reaction images, the idea is not that the user of the image produces the emotion that he means to display with the image—and, consequently, wants to instil in the observer who receives the image. The intended communication scenario to which this reaction image is applied presupposes two non-Jews reassuring themselves that they do not possess the qualities depicted in the figure of the "Happy Merchant". Structurally, this is a joke at the expense of the Jewish other. The transgression of the communicator who plays this Jewish figure for a split second adds to the joke, but it also—implicitly—verifies the truth and credibility of the negative Jewish character in the image. The communicator seems to say: for this split second, I act as deceitfully as this Jew does—and such shameful deceitfulness really exists, in those Jews. Thus, the emotional logic of using the "Happy Merchant" as a reaction image is not, as is usual, to induce the emotions in the recipient that are shown in the image. One is not supposed to be excited in the same way as Michael Jackson is portrayed to be in a cinema. But what, then, is the logic of this reaction image? Possibly, it aims to produce the adequate emotional reaction to deceit, fraud and evilness, which are on display as the 'Jewish' qualities. Candidates for such a legitimate reaction would be outrage, anger and revulsion against such (alleged) moral wickedness. Certainly, this may be the case. But, first of all, I would claim that this creates 'Häme', that the immediate emotional reaction is a form of laughter, a mocking laughter aimed at Jews. This substantially qualifies the understanding of reaction images. The metawitnessing of such usage lies less in the self-reflexive sharing of an emotion that is communicated through the image, but in the sharing of the emotional rejection of Jews' evil emotionality.

However, at a certain, still unknown, point in time, the "Happy Merchant" began to transcend this function of a reaction image. It started an independent online life of its own. The usage of the image, most likely, continued to be a 'funny' gesture that proliferated its antisemitic message through mocking laughter. But it also became a display of—alleged—Jewish character traits that were meant to directly induce emotional rejection in the audience.

The "Happy Merchant" thus seems to have attained a new role: it is increasingly used for the allegation of Jewish conspiracy. Here is one example.

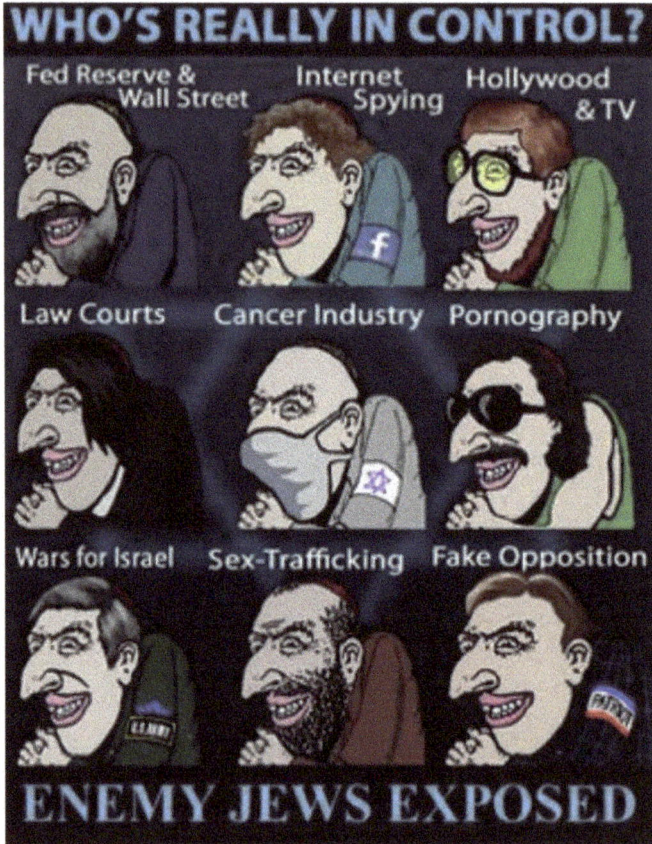

Fig. 2.10 "Happy Merchant" variations

In such versions, the initial economic dimension of the "Happy Merchant"—its greedy and deceitful behavioural qualities—is expanded. It turns into a depiction of Jewish secretiveness.[28] It thus takes part in the tradition of visualising a Jewish world conspiracy,

---

28 For example, in 2017, a study related the use of the image on 4chan to a missile strike by the USA on a Syrian target. It showed that users of the image on this website "use the image to express their belief that the Jews are 'behind this attack'". See Zannettou et al. (2019).

which it also renews. In its classical form, such as Charles Lèandre's image of Rothschild, the visual markers are also at work, although slightly differently.

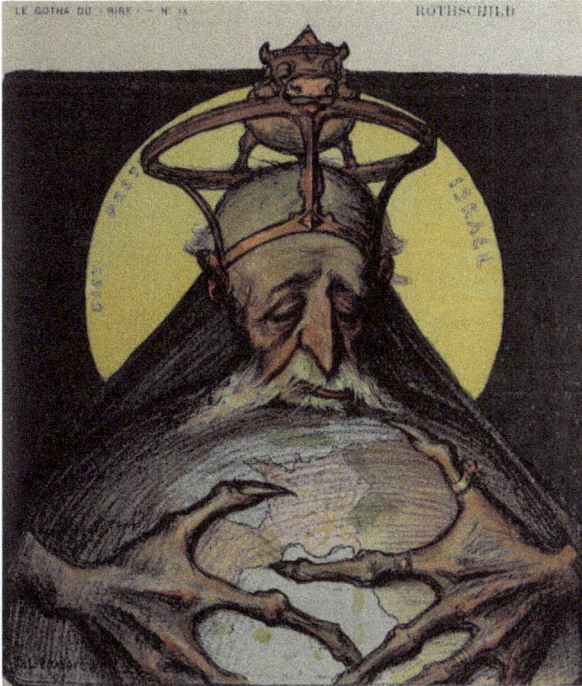

Fig. 2.11 Charles Lèandre, *Rothschild* (1898)

Such images, which became increasingly widespread around the turn to the 20th century, concentrated on the allegation of Jewish influence, control and power. While these themes are retained, the new images of the "Happy Merchant" add malice and deceitfulness.

Today, the "Happy Merchant" has become one of the most significant hate pictures against Jews in our world that is dominated by digital and online communication. The image has been reproduced multiple times by numerous users in all kinds of contexts. In 2018, it appeared consistently in alt-right contexts and media, e.g. on 4chan or Gab (Zannettou et al. 2019). Subsequently, it spread to more mainstream platforms like Reddit and Twitter/X. It has also started to be combined with other images, e.g. with "Pepe the frog." (Ibid.)

In the last two decades of online and social media communication, we have encountered a veritable explosion of antisemitic texts as well as the proliferation of such images like the "Happy Merchant". In general, it seems that the visual and textual traditions of antisemitism have converged again, for the first time since World War II. As scholars of antisemitism, we must analyse the visual forms in their own right, not least because people obviously use them in very specific ways that are not easily replicated with texts in the same fashion. One of the important aspects of visual communication is the way in which emotions are evoked by images—and for this purpose, hate pictures are particularly effective. To be able to describe this dimension more thoroughly, we must think more deeply about the particular visual agency of such hate pictures as the "Happy Merchant."

References

Bal, Mieke, 2003. Visual Essentialism and the Object of Visual Culture. *Journal of Visual Culture,* 2 (1), 5–32.

Balázs, Béla, 2019. *Der sichtbare Mensch oder die Kultur des Films (1924).* Frankfurt am Main: Suhrkamp.

Bernstein, Joseph, 2015. "The Surprisingly Mainstream History Of The Internet's Favorite Anti-Semitic Image". *BuzzFeed News.* https://www.buzzfeednews.com/article/josephbernstein/ the-surprisingly-mainstream-history-of-the-internets-favorit.

Blumenkranz, Bernhard, 1965. *Juden und Judentum in der mittelalterlichen Kunst.* Stuttgart: Kohlhammer.

Bonnell, Andrew, 2008. *Shylock in Germany: Antisemitism and the German Theatre From the Enlightenment to the Nazis.* London: Tauris.

Bredekamp, Horst, 2010. *Theorie des Bildakts. Frankfurter Adorno-Vorlesungen 2007.* Frankfurt am Main: Suhrkamp.

Erb, Rainer, 1985. "Die Wahrnehmung der Physiognomie der Juden: Die Nase". In: Heinrich Pleticha (ed.), *Das Bild des Juden in der Volks- und Jugendliteratur vom 18. Jahrhundert bis 1945.* Würzburg: Könighausen & Neumann, 107–126.

Eriksen, Trond Berg, Hakon Harekt and Einhart Lorenz, 2019. *Judenhass. Die Geschichte des Antisemitismus von der Antike bis zur Gegenwart.* Göttingen: Vandenhoeck & Ruprecht.

Ezekiel, Raphael S., 1995. *The Racist Mind. Portraits of American Neo-Nazis and Klansmen.* New York: Viking.

Freud, Sigmund, 1960. *Jokes and their Relation to the Unconscious* (1904). *The Standard Edition of the Complete Psychological Works of Sigmund Freud*, ed. by James Strachey and Anna Freud. Vol. 8 London: Hogarth.

Hamm, Mark S., 1993. *American Skinheads: The Criminology and Control of Hate Crime.* Westport: Praeger.

Jensen, Uffa, 2017. *Zornpolitik.* Berlin: Suhrkamp.

Jochum, Herbert (ed.), 1993. *Ecclesia und Synagoga. Das Judentum in der christlichen Kunst.* Ottweiler: Ottweiler Verlag.

Kaplan, Lindsay M., 2019. *Figuring Racism in Medieval Christianity.* New York: Oxford University Press.

Kolnai, Aurel, 2004. *On Disgust*, ed. by Carolyn Korsmeyer and Barry Smith. Chicago: Open Court.

Lipton, Sara, 2014. *Dark Mirror. The Medieval Origins of Anti-Jewish Iconography.* New York: Metropolitan.

Mellinkoff, Ruth, 1993. *Outcasts: Signs of Otherness in Northern European Art of the Late Middle Ages.* Berkeley: University of California Press.

Mitchell, William J. Thomas, 2005. *What Do Pictures Want? The Lives and Loves of Images.* Chicago: University of Chicago Press.

Nirenberg, David, 2013. *Anti-Judaism. The Western Tradition.* New York: Norton.

Penslar, Derek, 2001. *Shylock's Children: Economics and Jewish Identity in Modern Europe.* Berkeley: University of California Press.

Schäfer, Peter, 1997. *Judeophobia. Attitudes Toward the Jews in the Ancient World.* Cambridge: Harvard University Press.

—, 2020. *Kurze Geschichte des Antisemitismus.* Munich: Beck.

Schankweiler, Kerstin, 2020: "Reaction Images and Metawitnessing". *Parallax*, 26 (3), 254–270. https://doi.org/10.1080/13534645.2021.1883299

Scheer, Monique, 2012. "Are Emotions a Kind of Practice (and Is That What Makes Them Have a History)? A Bourdieuan Approach to Understanding Emotion". *History and Theory*, 51 (2), 193–220. https://doi.org/10.1111/j.1468-2303.2012.00621.x

Schreckenberg, Heinz, 1988. *Die christlichen Adversus-Judaeos-Texte (11.-13. Jahrhundert). Mit einer Ikonographie des Judenthemas bis zum 4. Laterankonzil.* Frankfurt am Main: Lang.

—, 1996. *Die Juden in der Kunst Europas. Ein historischer Bildatlas.* Göttingen: Vandenhoeck & Ruprecht.

Strickland, Debra Higgs, 2003. *Saracens, Demons, and Jews. Making Monsters in Medieval Art.* Princeton: Princeton University.

Zannettou, Savvas, Tristan Caulfield, Jeremy Blackburn, Emiliano De Cristofaro, Michael Sirivianos, Gianluca Stringhini and Guillermo Suarez-Tangil, 2018. *On the Origins of Memes by Means of Fringe Web Communities.* Proceedings of IMC '18. ACM. New York.

—, Joel Finkelstein, Barry Bradlyn and Jeremy Blackburn, 2019. "A Quantitative Approach to Understanding Online Antisemitism". *arXiv* preprint, 1–14.

Ziegler, Joseph, 2009. "Physiognomy, Science, and Proto-Racism 1200–1500". In: Miriam Eliav-Feldon, Benjamin Isaac and Joseph Ziegler (eds), *The Origins of Racism in the West.* Cambridge: Cambridge University, 181–199.

3. Memetic antisemitism: How memes teach age-old hatred

Lev Topor

Abstract

This chapter explores the concept of memetic antisemitism, a phenomenon in which internet memes are used to propagate age-old antisemitic tropes, conspiracy theories, and stereotypes. The research highlights how far-right groups, neo-Nazis, Islamists, and other actors disseminate antisemitic messages via platforms like Telegram and social media, repackaging historical hate into visually engaging and easily shareable content. Through qualitative analysis, this study demonstrates how these memes, ranging from explicit imagery to covert optical illusions generated by AI, are designed to normalize antisemitic rhetoric, fostering a climate of prejudice and enabling real-world harm. The chapter also examines the historical roots of visual antisemitic propaganda, from Nazi Germany to Soviet anti-Zionism, and connects these historical precedents to contemporary digital hate culture. It underscores the urgency of addressing memetic antisemitism through content moderation, education, and critical media literacy to counter its widespread impact.

Keywords: *antisemitism, social media, Telegram, Internet, memes, online behaviour*

https://doi.org/10.11647/OBP.0447.03

Introduction

A meme is a unit of cultural information that is spread by imitation (the term "meme" comes from the Greek word *mimema*, meaning imitated). While we humans have imitated each other throughout history, passing cultural, religious, ideological, and behavioral characteristics from one generation to another, and from one group to another, this art of mimicry is a double-edged sword. On the one hand, we mimic our culture and pass it on; on the other hand, during this process we also pass negative aspects like hate and discriminatory worldviews. In the digital age, a meme is a piece of content that spreads rapidly from one internet user to another, passing through cultural, behavioral, religious, and ideological ideas. Such internet memes can be of any form, including an image, a GIF,[1] a video, or even a sound. People usually tend to share memes with friends or like-minded people, and they mainly use memes to strengthen an example or an argument by presenting some light-hearted material that is not text. People use memes online to express themselves more effectively. Meme usage is a very important tool of communication; the problem is, however, that many internet users—hatemongers—create or share memes for negative reasons like hate, misogyny, racism, xenophobia, or antisemitism.[2]

Before the vast majority of people, mainly in the developed world, began using the internet, hate, misogyny, racism, xenophobia, or antisemitism were spread by radio, television, printed text and illustrations, and, of course, rumors (Wike et al. 2022). In this chapter, I intend to discuss the relationship between internet memes and antisemitism. Cultural, religious, ideological, and behavioral mimicry predates anti-Judaism and antisemitism, but, in the 21st century, internet memes are regularly employed as a tool by many antisemites. Illustrative and informative memes are mainly used by neo-Nazi antisemites from the right but also by Islamist antisemites. Further, such memes are also used and consumed by leftists or centrists who, being raised within the same

---

1   GIF: Graphics Interchange Format. It is an image file that can also contain a short animation. The format is widely used on the internet for simple images, logos, and basic animations.

2   See "Meme," in the Britannica Dictionary. https://www.britannica.com/topic/meme

societies as extremists, also understand this memetic information perfectly well (Topor 2023). As Jordan McSwiney, Michael Vaughan, Annett Heft, and Matthias Hoffmann argue, among others, memes play a significant role in the far right's digital culture online. Now, they do not simply share hateful text and long manifestos but are increasingly sharing memes (McSwiney et al. 2021; Nagle 2017).

The purpose of this chapter is to demonstrate how the far right, mainly neo-Nazis and white supremacists, use memes to disseminate antisemitism. Interestingly, as we found out in this study, while the platform and method of dissemination are new—i.e. illustrative online material shared on social media and messaging applications—the antisemitic ideas being spread are not new at all and they reflect age-old hatred. Jews are still portrayed stereotypically, conspiracy theories and blood libels are used to explain that Jews, as those antisemites argue, are abandoned by God, spread disease, control the media and global finances, and are the orchestrators of wars and other global disasters. While memes are shared on websites like 4chan, dark websites, fringe social media, and even, still, on mainstream social media, they are also disseminated on Secure Messaging Applications (SMAs) like Telegram. In this study, and after examining several websites, social media pages and Telegram channels, the main focus is on the Telegram channels "Holohoax Memes and Info,"[3] "🏴 WLM MEME'S Ƶ,"[4] and, one particularly interesting channel, "/BMW/— The Bureau of Memetic Warfare."[5] As it seems, the Western far right has their special bureau, just as the Nazi regime had its Ministry of Propaganda—the *Propagandaministerium.*

Methodology

Conducting qualitative research on illustrations and memes gathered from online sources requires a systematic approach to

---

3   See "Holohoax Memes and Info" on Telegram. https://t.me/holohoax_
      memes1 (Channel is archived for analysis).

4   See "🏴 WLM MEME'S Ƶ" on Telegram. https://t.me/WLMmemes (Channel is
      archived for analysis).

5   See "/BMW/—The Bureau of Memetic Warfare" on Telegram. https://t.me/
      TheBureauOfMemeticWarfareOG (Channel is archived for analysis).

ensure data collection, analysis, and interpretation are rigorous and meaningful. The approach we have taken is also an exploratory one, as it is useful to gather a diverse range of memes from various online platforms and not to be bound to a single specific platform. The nature of this study is qualitative, and here, I aim to focus on the nuances, themes, and cultural significance embedded within the collected memes and, of course, to interpret them according to the common definitions and explanations of antisemitism, as outlined in the next section. This random sampling methodology is applied to explore a variety of sources, including websites, dark websites, and Telegram channels. After the first exploration, I decided to focus on the Telegram messaging application due to its ease of use and reachability but also due to its privacy and anonymity. Mainly, Telegram offers End-to-end Encryption (E2EE), which ensures that only the sender and receiver can read the messages. It also allows for anonymous account creation, and it is registered in the British Virgin Islands and Dubai, making it almost inaccessible to Western law enforcement agencies. It also has many privacy-oriented features like anonymous postings or account self-destruction. In such a case, users often feel protected and are more likely to share hateful content such as antisemitic memes. Users do often share such antisemitic content on more public social media platforms such as X or Facebook; however, and usefully for the purpose of analysis, Telegram allows one to download and review a large number of images, even several thousands of them, instantly.

The analysis of data was done thematically to identify recurring patterns, themes, motifs, and cultural references within the collected material. The qualitative analysis is very beneficial for understanding deeply rooted concepts like antisemitism, and it may provide a background for future large-scale research on the topic of memes and hate. However, such research should be grounded in contextual analysis of memes in consultation with experts in the fields of antisemitism, racism, Holocaust denial, and hate in general.

Antisemitism and its illustrative demonstration

What is antisemitism? According to the International Holocaust Remembrance Alliance (IHRA) working definition of antisemitism, it is: "… a certain perception of Jews, which may be expressed as hatred toward Jews. Rhetorical and physical manifestations of antisemitism are directed toward Jewish or non-Jewish individuals and/or their property, toward Jewish community institutions and religious facilities."[6]

Antisemitism is the belief, and accusation, that Jews are the source of all evil, that they were abandoned by God, and that they control or attempt to control the world. Topor, in a study about antisemitism on the dark web and Telegram, demonstrated that contemporary examples of antisemitism include these accusations (Topor 2023, 95-116):

> Jews and/or Israel control the Federal Reserve, Wall Street, and global finances.
>
> Jews control internet surveillance.
>
> Jews control media and control Hollywood and television productions.
>
> Jews control law courts.
>
> Jews control the cancer industry.
>
> Jews made, and controlled, pornography.
>
> Jews manage and promote wars for Israel.
>
> Jews control sex trafficking.
>
> Jews make and control fake political oppositions.
>
> Visual methods also abuse these perceptions and accusations.

Throughout history, racist and antisemitic regimes have weaponized visual imagery to spread their ideologies, dehumanize targeted groups, and consolidate power. From the caricatures of Nazi propaganda to the graphic posters of American white supremacists, pictures, illustrations, and art have served not just as aesthetic tools, but as instruments of hate with devastating consequences. One such example is Nazi propaganda. Perhaps the

---

6   "Working definition of antisemitism." *International Holocaust Remembrance Alliance (IHRA)* (adopted on 26 May 2016). https://holocaustremembrance. com/resources/working-definition-antisemitism

most chilling example of visual propaganda serving a genocidal agenda is Nazi Germany's use of antisemitic imagery. Posters depicting Jews with exaggerated features, hooked noses, and greedy expressions fueled popular hatred and dehumanized the targeted group. Julius Streicher's infamous newspaper, *Der Stürmer*, relied heavily on such caricatures to demonize Jews and incite violence. Nazi films like *Jud Süss* (The Jew, 1940) further perpetuated harmful stereotypes, justified persecution, and paved the way for the Holocaust. In fact, Joseph Goebbels (and later Werner Naumann) served as the chief Nazi propagandist while the Reich had its own Ministry for Public Enlightenment and Propaganda (Reichsministerium für Volksaufklärung und Propaganda) (Herf 2006, 2005; Giesen 2008: 118–143; Narayanaswami 2011). The purpose of such Propagandaministerium was to brain-wash people into believing Nazi ideology, including antisemitism. *Der Ewige Jude* (The Eternal Jew) is perhaps one of the most well-known examples of such posters or films (see Figures 3.1 and 3.2).[7]

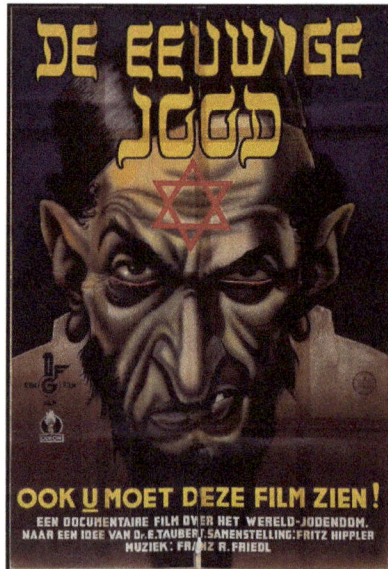

Fig. 3.1 A poster advertising the antisemitic *Der Ewige Jude* film, The Netherlands, 1942. Source: United States Holocaust Memorial Museum, courtesy of Samuel (Schrijver) Schryver.

---

7   Figures 3.1 and 3.2, as well as many other such examples, can be found on the online Holocaust Encyclopedia of the United States Holocaust Memorial Museum: https://encyclopedia.ushmm.org/tags/en/tag/propaganda

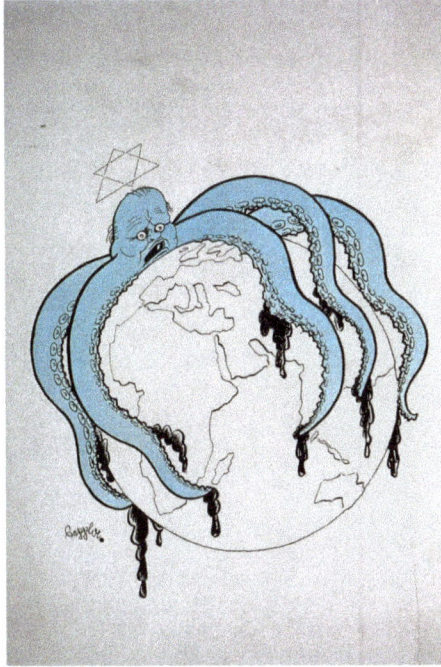

Fig. 3.2 Nazi propaganda cartoon by Seppla (Josef Plank), a political cartoonist. Germany, date uncertain [probably during World War II]. Source: United States Holocaust Memorial Museum.

After the Holocaust, during the Cold War, the Soviet Union employed visual propaganda to attack Zionism and delegitimize the State of Israel. This was done for antisemitic reasons, but also as a way to downgrade global support for the emerging Jewish state that shifted, politically, towards the United States and the West. Posters portrayed Israelis as imperialist aggressors, often conflating them with Western powers. Antisemitic tropes resurfaced once more, with images of Jews controlling global finance or manipulating world affairs. This visual narrative demonized Israel on the international stage and contributed to rising antisemitism within the Soviet bloc. As Izabella Tabarovsky has demonstrated, Soviet antisemitic and/or anti-Zionist visual propaganda owes many, if not most, of its similarities to Nazi antisemitic propaganda. In the example of Figure 3.3, a—or the—Jew appears as an octopus dominating the world. Words such as "aggression", "provocation", "terror" and others appear on each of its tentacles (in Russian), hinting that Jews dominate the world without using too many words to do so. This is an example of an old Soviet meme, published in *Krokodil* in 1972 (Tabarovsky 2019, 2022; Korey 1972).

Fig. 3.3 An antisemitic poster by the Soviet magazine *Krokodil*, 1972. Source: Secondary source, by the journal *Fathom*. This can also be viewed in the archives of *Krokodil* (further information in: Tabarovsky 2019, 2022).

Another example of visual antisemitic and anti-Zionist propaganda is the Arab, Persian (Iranian), and Turkish anti-Israel propaganda that grew tremendously from the late 1940s onwards due to the Arab conflict with Israel, and from the 1979 Iranian Islamic revolution onwards. The roots of such antisemitism lie in radical Islamist ideologies. In such visual propaganda, Israel and/or Jews are often portrayed as colonialists, threatening Arabs and Muslims. In his book *Cartoons and Extremism: Israel and the Jews in Arab and Western Media*, Joël Kotek (2009) describes antisemitic and anti-Zionist cartoons used by the Arab world and by Arab state supporters to portray Jews as evil, along similar lines as the Soviet and Nazi propaganda. Such visual antisemitism is used to vilify Israel, a geopolitical adversary of many Arab countries, but also to spread antisemitism, following the growth of radicalized Islamism (Kotek 2009, Aviv 2020, Antisemitism Policy Trust 2020). In Figure 3.4, collected by the Anti-Defamation League (ADL 2023), the figure of Death wearing a Star of David on its back is seen while the background presents a clock, the world, and the Gaza strip, hinting that Jews are gradually killing Gaza.

Fig. 3.4 The killing of Gaza by Jews. Source: Al-Quds, 14 October 2023 (Palestinian Authority)

In the United States of America, Russia, and Europe, white supremacist groups have long used visual imagery to spread racist ideology and intimidate Jewish, Muslim, Asian, and Black communities. From the Ku Klux Klan's burning crosses to white nationalist groups' appropriation of historical symbols, visual propaganda serves as a potent tool for recruitment, intimidation, and the perpetuation of racial hierarchies. Using visual hate, nowadays mainly using racist and antisemitic memes online, neo-Nazis and white supremacists spread their propaganda. They rely on old Nazi and Soviet propaganda and borrow from Islamists, but they also create their propaganda using the online domain, with free and easy-to-use editing tools, even with Artificial Intelligence (AI) tools (Topor 2023). Every single antisemitic internet user can now become the editor, author, and publisher of such hateful content. They create, as it is demonstrated in the next section, memetic antisemitism.

Memetic antisemitism

Antisemitism is not just a concept in people's minds; it is spread by text, film, sound, and images. It leads, gradually, to radicalization and it nudges people to harm Jews. This visual antisemitism now spreads on the internet, social media platforms, the dark web, and SMAs like Telegram. Evidence suggests that anonymous antisemitic internet users, either independent or affiliated with some group or country, spread tens of thousands of antisemitic memes with a single click using their computers and smartphones (Topr 2023). In this section, the evolution of visual antisemitic material into "memetic antisemitism" is explained and demonstrated. Memetic antisemitism is the spread of antisemitism by memes, imitating age-old hatred and utilizing the ease of information-sharing in the digital age to spread it. To demonstrate and explain, the Telegram channels "Holohoax Memes and Info,"[8] "🏴 WLM MEME'S Z,"[9] and, "/BMW/— The Bureau of Memetic Warfare" are examined.[10]

Antisemitic memes can be found all over the internet; some are even printed and used as stickers that include barcodes that lead to antisemitic channels or websites. By spreading memes as online material but also as real-world stickers (which can also be considered memes) or pamphlets, antisemites close the gap between the digital and the kinetic. Antisemitism is spread everywhere. A widespread sticker on social media and SMAs is that of the "Happy Merchant" which depicts a heavily stereotyped Jewish man rubbing his hands in a "greedy" manner.[11] In an example from the Telegram channel "White Lives Matter Official Chat," such antisemitic memes and stickers are often propagated.[12] In Figure 3.5, the "Happy Merchant" sticker is shared by an

---

8	See "Holohoax Memes and Info" on Telegram. https://t.me/holohoax_memes1 (Channel is archived for analysis).

9	See "🏴 WLM MEME'S Z" on Telegram. https://t.me/WLMmemes (Channel is archived for analysis).

10	See "/BMW/ — The Bureau of Memetic Warfare" on Telegram. https://t.me/TheBureauOfMemeticWarfareOG (Channel is archived for analysis).

11	"The Happy Merchant." ADL. https://www.adl.org/resources/hate-symbol/happy-merchant

12	See "White Lives Matter Official Chat" on Telegram. https://t.me/WhiteLivesMatterOfficialChat (Channel is archived for analysis).

anonymous user. Such stickers can be easily shared on SMAs like Telegram, WhatsApp, Signal, and others.

Fig. 3.5 The "Happy Merchant" sticker from the "White Lives Matter Official Chat" Telegram channel

"Holohoax Memes and Info"[13] is a particularly interesting example, as it is a whole Telegram channel dedicated to Holocaust denial and distortion. The channel itself is based on banned channels and its anonymous creator(s) also guide the actions that must be taken if the channel is banned (again). The anonymous creator(s) of the channel share extremely offensive antisemitic material with texts, sound messages and files, videos, GIFs, and, of course, memes. The vast majority of this channel is antisemitic and racist but, one particular example, seen in Figure 3.6, is the "Keep on Hoaxin'..." meme. It depicts a Jewish man, with the face of the "Happy Merchant", holding a bag of money and the United States Capitol Hill building, stepping on a person. Below Capitol Hill, "Zionist Lobbyists" is written. Other motifs include Holocaust denial, and below the term "White Genocide" is written. This particular

---

13   See "Holohoax Memes and Info" on Telegram. https://t.me/holohoax_memes1 (Channel is archived for analysis).

example describes many of the antisemitic conspiracy theories that accuse Jews of being responsible for the evil of the world.

Fig. 3.6 "Keep on Hoaxin'..." meme from "Holohoax Memes and Info" Telegram channel

Another example is the "☠ WLM MEME'S Ƶ" channel.[14] The creator(s) of this channel create and share antisemitic and racist content in the Russian language. Other affiliated channels are shared by the creator(s) of this channel, leading to more such antisemitic and racist material which together are called (by the creators) the "Maurov Project", including the "MAUROV" telegram channel which has the link https://t.me/MAUROV1488, referring to the 1488 combination of two white-supremacist numeric symbols. The first symbol, the number 14, refers to the "14 words" slogan: "We must secure the existence of our people and a future for white children." The second number—88—refers to "Heil Hitler" (H being the eighth letter of the alphabet).

There are thousands of antisemitic memes on "☠ WLM MEME'S Ƶ", but one particular example is the world-dominating octopus

---

14   See "☠ WLM MEME'S Ƶ" on Telegram. https://t.me/WLMmemes (Channel is archived for analysis).

which, as presented in the previous section, is a direct continuation from Nazi and Soviet antisemitic propaganda. The octopus shared on this antisemitic channel is, interestingly, borrowed from the promoted works of anti-Zionist and antisemitic organizations from the United Kingdom, including the British Muslim Initiative (BMI) organization and the terror-supporting Friends of Al-Aqsa organization. This octopus, as presented in Figure 3.7, draws similarities from other such octopuses but this one is shown as if attempting to destroy the Al Aqsa mosque (NGO Monitor 2019). The " WLM MEME'S Ƶ" channel promotes antisemitism, racism but also Islamophobia. Why then, is this Islamist meme shared by those who also promote Islamophobia? A logical answer is that the meme promotes antisemitic ideas, regardless of the religious or geo-political context. The "Jewish octopus" has transferred ideas from generation to generation and from one group to another exactly as a meme should. As the saying goes, "The enemy of my enemy is my friend" and, in this case, the enemies of neo-Nazis and Islamists are the Jews.

Fig. 3.7 The "Jewish Octopus" shared on " WLM MEME'S Ƶ" Telegram channel (it includes a watermark from Dvatch as well, unlike the original BMI from 2 June 2013)[15]

---

15 The "Jewish octopus" shared on " WLM MEME'S Ƶ" Telegram channel has the watermark of Dvatch (in Russian: Двач, meaning two-chans, or 2ch). Dvatch is the largest anonymous imageboard in the Russian language and

Another example from this channel is a visual or optical illusion that users created online, using graphical manipulations. In it, the antisemitic feature is hidden from those not familiar with antisemitic memes and material. Figure 3.8 presents a man hugging a woman, a harmless scene to the naked eye. Yet, when looking at this illustration from far away, or at its thumbnail (a smaller version of the image) the "Happy Merchant" is revealed. This is demonstrated in Figure 3.9, with a screenshot of the many memes and photos shared on the "☠ WLM MEME'S Ƶ" channel (unfocusing your eyes might help you to see the "Happy Merchant").

Fig. 3.8 A seemingly harmless hug

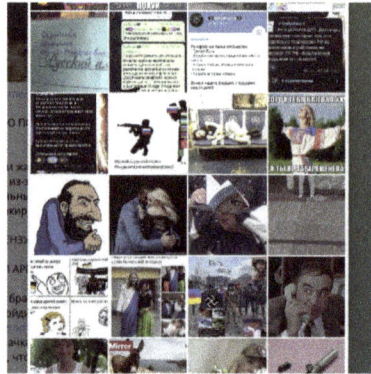

Fig. 3.9 The "Happy Merchant" optical illusion

Another example of memetic antisemitism is the Telegram channel "/BMW/—The Bureau of Memetic Warfare."[16] This channel, as the name suggests, is dedicated to memes and it facilitates the sharing of antisemitic, racist, misogynistic, xenophobic material. By early February, it had over 6,000 subscribers and had facilitated over 11,000 photos as well as thousands of videos, links, and other material. Its creator(s) seem to understand perfectly well the power of memes. Of course, the "Happy Merchant" and the "Jewish Octopus" have a presence on this channel. Another optical illusion

---

its Telegram channel (https://t.me/dvachannel) has over 810,000 subscribers and millions of views.

16 See "/BMW/—The Bureau of Memetic Warfare" on Telegram. https://t.me/TheBureauOfMemeticWarfareOG (Channel is archived for analysis).

was shared there—an illusion created using a snake, an apple, and some tree branches. Again, to those unaware of such antisemitic memes, the illustration might seem harmless. However, looking from a distance, the snake, apple, and tree branches create, together, the image of the "Happy Merchant" (see Fig. 3.10).

Fig. 3.10 The "Happy Merchant" optical illusion, another version, shared on the "/BMW/—The Bureau of Memetic Warfare" Telegram channel

Jews did it!

Fig. 3.11 "Jews did it!" octopus, shared on the "/BMW/—The Bureau of Memetic Warfare" Telegram channel

The "Jewish octopus" is also shared on this channel; for example, it was shared there as a doll, referring to the octopus doll that Greta Thunberg, the environmental activist, had previously shared on a social media post while protesting against the war in Gaza that followed the 7/10 terrorist attack by Hamas on Israel (Curiel 2023). As presented in Figure 3.11, the meme shared on the channel has the writing "Jews did it!" above it, referring to the criticism, made by some, of Thunberg and also referring to the Nazi, Soviet, and Islamist illustrations of the octopus (this is not to suggest that Thunberg is antisemitic, but in reference to the fact that she removed the doll from her image following public criticism).

What can be learned from the use of memes by antisemites? It has been theorised that memes could be considered examples of multimodal metaphors. Memes often combine various modes of communication, including text, images, symbols, and sometimes sound or video, to convey a humorous, satirical, or culturally relevant message and, in our context, hate. In addition, pragmatics provides a useful framework to understand how memes operate within the realm of communication. While memes are often characterized by their humorous, hateful, or viral nature, they also rely heavily on pragmatic principles to convey meaning effectively, including implicature and context (Scott 2021). As Shifman notes, an internet meme is: "(a) a group of digital items sharing common characteristics of content, form and/or stance, which (b) were created with awareness of each other, and (c) were circulated, imitated, and/or transformed via the internet by many users" (Shifman 2014).

As shown throughout this chapter, antisemitic memes have common characteristics of content and stance, were created with an awareness of each other, and were circulated online. They are also generated, spread, mixed, and reshaped or remodeled for further dissemination while keeping very similar characteristics. As Wiggins and Bowers (2015) suggest, such memes are a genre of their own.

The next stage of memes: Memes for "people of culture"

The internet, once hailed as a haven for free expression and connection, has morphed into a fertile ground for the spread of hatred and prejudice. Within this landscape, "memetic antisemitism" has emerged as a concerning phenomenon, utilizing conciseness, humor, irony, and virality as well as skilled graphic editing to perpetuate age-old hatred against Jews. At its core, memetic antisemitism repackages centuries-old antisemitic tropes into easily digestible online formats. From the greedy "Happy Merchant" caricature to the blood libel conspiracy theory repurposed or the "Jewish octopus", these memes rely on pre-existing biases and prejudices, normalizing hate through less hateful presentations. The anonymity and detachment offered by online platforms further embolden antisemites, who often hide behind the veil of anonymity, but also behind explanations like "just kidding" or "it's just a meme."

Memes thrive on virality, spreading rapidly through social media feeds and online communities. This rapid dissemination fuels the normalization of antisemitic rhetoric, exposing unsuspecting individuals to harmful stereotypes and narratives. Algorithms that prioritize engagement often amplify these hateful memes, creating echo chambers where prejudice resonates and festers (Goel 2023). Three main characteristics describe memetic antisemitism. Firstly, it is based on conciseness, humor, irony, and contextual complexity. As Becker, Ascone, and Troschke have previously demonstrated through linguistic analysis, antisemitism is contextual and not just direct (Becker and Troschke 2023), meaning that the memes can be promoted in a more palatable manner. In other words, while a mainstream internet user might be appalled by hardcore antisemitic material, such memes can help mitigate the gap between weak antisemitic worldviews and strong ones. Secondly, memetic antisemitism is based on the repetition and mimicry of historical tropes, stereotypes, and conspiracy theories, as demonstrated earlier in this chapter. Further, as Fox and Topor found out, belief in conspiracy theories is a major cause of anti-Jewish discrimination and antisemitism, and memes spread these conspiracies (Fox and Topor 2021). Thirdly, memetic antisemitism is also based on virality, meaning that the more widespread such memes are, online but also offline, the greater their impact on society. This virality enables antisemitic content to reach a broad audience quickly, contributing to the normalization of discriminatory beliefs among online communities.

Memetic antisemitism contributes to the normalization of hatred by presenting discriminatory beliefs in a seemingly light-hearted and casual manner. This normalization poses a threat as it desensitizes individuals to the seriousness of antisemitic ideologies. Yet, the online propagation of memetic antisemitism can have real-world consequences, contributing to an increase in violent hate crimes, discrimination, and the marginalization of Jewish communities. The boundary between online rhetoric and offline actions is blurred nowadays, making it imperative to address this form of hatred (Topor 2023).

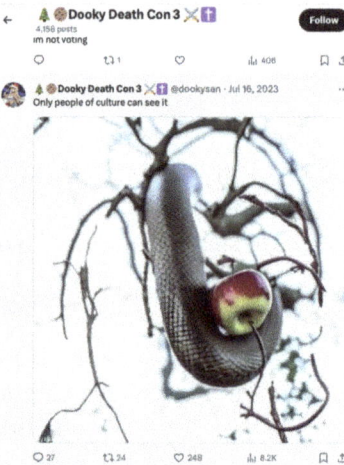

Fig. 3.12 "Only people of culture can see it", as shared on X by @ dookysan (16 July 2023). The post is no longer available.

Fig. 13.3 "i just love Christian imagery", as shared on X by @DeathAngelUSA (16 December 2022), https://x. com/DeathAngelUSA/ status/1603786517595422720

Explicit and implicit memes can serve the same purpose. Explicit memes can be shared by antisemitic users on antisemitic websites, groups, and channels. Implicit memes can be shared by antisemitic users on regulated, monitored, and mainstream websites, groups, and channels. For instance, as presented in Figures 3.12 and 3.13, some X (Twitter) users have published the "Happy Merchant" meme on their X account. While many people will just see a snake and a tree, or a nun and some stars, "only people of culture" will see the "Happy Merchant." This phrase of "people of culture" suggests that understanding and appreciating certain memes requires a deep understanding of the cultural context, references, or subtext they contain. X user @DeathAngelUSA had published this meme with the text: "i just love Christian imagery", suggesting that the meme is harmless.

These examples may seem harmless to those unaware of the hidden antisemitic nature of such memes. Since they appear harmless, they are shared on various websites, social media platforms and SMAs, and such memes might then become viral and be shared with ease by many users. In fact, a simple search with Google Lens or any other image search engine reveals that such photos are spread on X, Facebook, YouTube, 9Gag, and many other websites. Furthermore, the impact of memetic antisemitism extends far beyond the digital realm. It emboldens extremists, normalizes hate speech, and contributes to real-world violence against Jewish communities. Additionally, it can have a chilling effect on Jewish individuals online, silencing their voices and creating a climate of fear and intimidation (Topor 2023).

Conclusion

A meme is a unit of cultural, religious, or ideological information that is spread by imitation. By spreading internet memes, people spread their cultural beliefs and ideas. This is done instead, or alongside, other forms of information such as text, videos, or sound recordings. The relationship between internet memes and antisemitism is a complex and concerning issue. Antisemitic content has been observed on various internet and social media platforms, as well as on SMAs, where memes, as a form of cultural communication or information, have played a significant role in its propagation. Memes, as a ubiquitous form of communication in the digital age, have the potential to influence society, politics, and the human mind. While they can serve as a tool for social commentary and connect people, it is crucial to acknowledge that they can also be used to perpetuate harmful stereotypes, spread misinformation, and promote hate. In the context of antisemitism, memes have been employed to disseminate and reinforce deeply rooted perceptions that diminish the human value of Jewish people or portray them as dangerous and manipulative. The power of memes to distill complex ideas into simple, relatable formats has been harnessed to propagate antisemitic narratives, often exploiting cultural references and symbols to convey harmful messages.

Thus, memetic antisemitism is the spread of antisemitism by memes that propagate and imitate age-old hatred, and utilize the ease of information-sharing in the digital age to spread it. While some social media platforms do regulate and monitor content, some might disregard such graphical illusion memes as presented in this chapter. Countering memetic antisemitism requires a multi-layered approach. Platforms must implement stricter content moderation policies that address antisemitic tropes and symbols effectively, and update their information as memes constantly evolve. Further, educational initiatives can empower users to critically analyze online content and recognize the harmful intent behind seemingly harmless memes. Counter-speech campaigns can challenge hateful narratives with humor, facts, and personal stories. Ultimately though, addressing memetic antisemitism necessitates tackling the root causes of antisemitism itself. Debunking conspiracy theories, fostering empathy, understanding, and interfaith dialogue are crucial steps in dismantling the foundations of prejudice. Promoting media literacy and critical thinking skills can empower individuals to become responsible consumers, moderators, and creators of online content. Being aware of such memetic antisemitism can help in eradicating the phenomenon.

References

2020. "Antisemitic Imagery and Caricatures". *Antisemitism Policy Trust*. https://antisemitism.org.uk/wp-content/uploads/2020/07/Antisemitic-imagery-May-2020.pdf

2023. "Antisemitism in Arab Cartoons during the Israel-Hamas War: A Chronology of Dehumanization of Jews and Demonization of Zionism and Israel". *ADL*, December. https://www.adl.org/resources/report/antisemitism-arab-cartoons-during-israel-hamas-war-chronology-dehumanization-jews

2019. "Palestine Expo 2019's Promotion of BDS and Hatred". *NGO Monitor*, 16 July. https://www.ngo-monitor.org/reports/palestine-expo-2019s-promotion-of-bds-and-hatred/

Aviv, Efrat, 2017. *Antisemitism and Anti-Zionism in Turkey: From Ottoman Rule to AKP*. Abingdon: Routledge, 140–211.

Becker, Matthias J. and Hagen Troschke. 2023. "Decoding implicit hate speech: The example of antisemitism". In: Christian Strippel, Sünje Paasch-Colberg, Martin Emmer, and Joachim Trebbe (eds), *Challenges and Perspectives of Hate Speech research*. Berlin, 335–352. https://doi.org/10.48541/dcr.v12.0.

Curiel, Ilana, 2023. "Why did the octopus doll disappear from Greta Thunberg's anti-Israel tweet?" *Ynet News*, 21 October.

Fox, Jonathan and Lev Topor, 2021. *Why Do People Discriminate Against Jews?* Oxford: Oxford University Press.

Giesen, Rolf, 2008. *Nazi Propaganda Films: A History and Filmography*. Jefferson: McFarland & Company Inc., 118–143.

Goel, Vasu, Dhruv Sahnan, Subhabrata Dutta, Anil Bandhakavi, and Tanmoy Chakraborty. 2023. "Hatemongers ride on echo chambers to escalate hate speech diffusion". *PNAS nexus*, 2 (3), pgad041. https://doi.org/10.1093/pnasnexus/pgad041

Herf, Jeffrey, 2005. "The 'Jewish war': Goebbels and the antisemitic campaigns of the Nazi propaganda ministry". *Holocaust and Genocide Studies*, 19 (1), 51–80.

—, 2006. *The Jewish Enemy: Nazi Propaganda During World War II and the Holocaust*. Harvard: Harvard University Press.

Korey, William, 1972. "The origins and development of Soviet anti-Semitism: An analysis". *Slavic Review*, 31 (1), 111–135.

Kotek, Joël, 2009. *Cartoons and Extremism: Israel and the Jews in Arab and Western Media*. London: Vallentine Mitchell.

McSwiney,
Jordan, Michael Vaughan, Annett Heft and Matthias Hoffmann. 2021. "Sharing the hate? Memes and transnationality in the far right's digital visual culture". *Information, Communication & Society*, 24 (16), 2502–2521. https://doi.org/10.1080/1369118X.2021.1961006

Nagle, Angela, 2017. *Kill All Normies: Online Culture Wars from 4chan and Tumblr to Trump and the Alt-Right.* London: Zero Books.

Narayanaswami, Karthik, 2011. "Analysis of Nazi propaganda". *HIST E-1572: The Holocaust in History, Literature, and Film.*

Scott, Kate, 2021. "Memes as multimodal metaphors: A relevance theory analysis". *Pragmatics & Cognition*, 28 (2), 277–298. https://doi.org/10.1075/pc.21010.sco

Shifman, Limor, 2014. *Memes in Digital Culture.* Cambridge: MIT Press, 41-42.

Tabarovsky, Izabella, 2022. "Demonization Blueprints: Soviet Conspiracist Antizionism in Contemporary Left-Wing Discourse". *Journal of Contemporary Antisemitism*, 5 (1), 1–20. https://doi.org/10.26613/jca/5.1.97

—, 2019. "Soviet Anti-Zionism and Contemporary Left Antisemitism". *Fathom*, May 2019.

Topor, Lev, 2023. *Phishing for Nazis: Conspiracies, Anonymous Communications and White Supremacy Networks on the Dark Web.* London: Routledge, 95–116.

Wiggins, Bradley E., and G. Bret Bowers, 2015. "Memes as genre: A structurational analysis of the memescape". *New Media & Society*, 17 (11), 1886–1906. https://doi.org/10.1177/1461444814535194

Wike, Richard, Laura Silver, Janell Fetterolf, Christine Huang, Sarah Austin, Laura Clancy and Sneha Gubbala, 2022. "Social Media Seen as Mostly Good for Democracy Across Many Nations, But U.S. is a Major Outlier". *Pew Research Center*, 6 December. https://www.pewresearch.org/global/2022/12/06/social-media-seen-as-mostly-good-for-democracy-across-many-nations-but-u-s-is-a-major-outlier

Sources

"/BMW/ - The Bureau of Memetic Warfare" on Telegram. https://t.me/TheBureauOfMemeticWarfareOG (Channel is archived for analysis).

"🖼 WLM MEME'S Ƶ" on Telegram. https://t.me/WLMmemes (Channel is archived for analysis).

"Holohoax Memes and Info" on Telegram. https://t.me/holohoax_memes1 (Channel is archived for analysis).

"White Lives Matter Official Chat" on Telegram. https://t.me/ WhiteLivesMatterOfficialChat (Channel is archived for analysis).

4. Extremist internet memes as a means of persuasion: A visual rhetorical approach

Eemeli Hakoköngäs and Otto Halmesvaara

Abstract

This chapter provides an overview of a qualitative rhetorical analysis of internet memes created and disseminated by various extremist groups. We will address the rhetorical nature of memes and provide practicable steps for applying visual rhetorical analysis to unravel their persuasive content, form, and functions. Our approach will be illustrated through the analysis of a communication by the Finnish branch of the Nordic Resistance Movement (NRM). With a view to providing tools for future researchers studying internet memes, we will consider the limitations of rhetorical analysis and the ethical and copyright issues associated with the gathering and use of internet memes as research material.

As its key message, this chapter suggests that paying attention to the visuality of communication is necessary in order to unravel the persuasive nature of memes. While internet memes are typically bound to a certain cultural context (e.g. Finland, Scandinavia), they can simultaneously act as an intercultural means of persuasion (e.g. across European extremist movements). Understanding the immediate rhetorical function of memes requires placing them in the specific context of political and societal discussion in which

    https://doi.org/10.11647/OBP.0447.04

they were published. Defining the broader ideological work carried out by memes requires delving into their roots and their use in different contexts.

Keywords: *Internet memes, visual rhetorical analysis, qualitative research, research ethics*

Internet memes as a means of persuasion

The concept of a meme, referring to various "cultural units" spreading from person to person and explaining cultural change, was established well before the internet era (Dawkins, 1976). Following Richard Dawkins' original conceptualization, Limor Shifman (2013) defined memes on digital platforms as "cultural information that passes along from person to person, yet gradually scales into a shared social phenomenon... [and] reproduces by various means of imitation" (pp. 364–365). She also emphasized their intertextual nature and shared characteristics in terms of content and form when defining memes on the internet (Shifman 2014). However, Shifman has aptly noted that the term has several ambiguous meanings. Internet users have adopted the term to refer to a form of virtual object such as an image or video clip, regardless of whether the "social phenomenon" conditions are met.

In new media, memes are commonly understood as user-generated online content in the form of images, videos, or animations that circulate from person to person, particularly on social media and other digital platforms. Memes are considered to be characterized by humor, with the primary goal of amusing users (e.g. Yoon 2016). Recent researchers have widely adopted this vernacular definition. For example, Davis, Glantz, and Novak (2016) broadly define memes as "ideas and images as they spread throughout new media environments" (p. 66). The widespread use of memes, encompassing both harmless amusement and intentional persuasion, has established conventions of expression and interpretation. For example, Huntington (2013, 2016) posits that the widespread presence of internet memes establishes them as a distinctive mode of communication, forming digital discourses.

Memes are, by definition, the results of social interaction, meaning they do not exist without the audience, their users. The term "audience," drawing from classic communication and (mass) media studies, is only partly applicable to social media, particularly when addressing memes. The advantage of memes is that they can reach large "audiences" with minimal investment and without censorship. A number of people who see a meme in their social media feed are likely to be passive and meet the old definition of an audience receiving the message (but not necessarily accepting it). However, in social media in particular, the effectiveness of memes is bound to the audience's participation. Positive and negative reactions towards the shared content are likely to increase its visibility and facilitate the message's memefication, whereby it becomes a social phenomenon. In this sense, it is more appropriate to speak about "users" rather than "audience" (see Livingstone, 2003).

As the popularity of meme-like content has risen as a prominent means of communication, researchers' interest in its various roles has steadily increased over the past decade (e.g. Huntington 2013, 2016; Jenkins 2014). New media environments have allowed various movements to amplify their agendas in social spheres and the memes can serve social functions for the group. For example, for minorities, memes can function as tools for fostering positive ingroup identity (Gal et al. 2016). However, the reverse is also possible, including defaming outgroups and disseminating extreme political arguments and ideologies, such as antisemitism (Hakoköngäs et al. 2020; Hübscher 2023; Knobel and Langshear 2006; Yoon 2016).

Memes shared anonymously and quickly disseminated across platforms have become an attractive tool for extremist rhetoric due to their elusive nature and the challenge of monitoring their content on the internet (Horsti 2015; Hatakka 2020). From a political rhetoric perspective, memes are tools used to crystallize arguments into easily shareable, concise, and often visual forms. This feature makes them valuable in the context of busy and congested everyday interactions (Hahner 2013). While memes often offer innocent or inconsequential entertainment, their humorous nature also provides opportunities for disseminating hateful rhetoric (Gal 2019; Hakoköngäs et al. 2024; Kelly 2023). When employed as a rhetorical tool, humor can camouflage derogatory messages as mere jokes, legitimizing racist discourse (Malmqvist 2015). In general, it has been noted that visual communication in online environments has facilitated the transmission of derogatory language in a socially acceptable manner (Forchtner and Kolvraa 2017). Furthermore, anonymity and the absence of face-to-face social barriers have reduced the normative threshold for expressions of hatred and resentment (Bilewicz and Soral 2020; Burke and Goodman 2012). These shifts in the culture of discourse have expanded the boundaries of what is deemed acceptable in public speech, leading to increased scrutiny of the concept of hate speech (Sakki and Hakoköngäs 2022).

Finnish extremist movements employing internet memes

Far-right and other extremist groups are increasingly leveraging social media as a platform to disseminate their ideas and ideology (Ekman 2018; Hatakka 2020). In the Finnish context, Horsti (2015) has argued that the transformation of the media landscape partially explains the shift of anti-immigration movements from marginal political entities to a prominent societal position. In Finland, the presence of extremist movements in new media dates back to the 2010s when conflicts in Syria, Afghanistan and other regions led to a temporary increase in asylum seekers in Finland. This, in turn, triggered the emergence of various radical anti-immigration groups that opposed immigrants, refugees, and the existing political system. These groups employed diverse modes of communication to organize and propagate their agenda and rally supporters. These modes included street patrolling, demonstrations, and the sharing of various materials on the internet, including memes, which was a relatively novel approach in the Finnish political landscape at that time (e.g. Ekman 2018).

Internet memes were not the only, and not necessarily the most important, tool in the groups' rhetoric, but their analysis made it possible to gain insight into the core of the different groups' agendas and illustrated how they employed memes to appeal to various audience and user groups (Hakoköngäs et al. 2020; Hakoköngäs and Sakki 2023; Hakoköngäs et al. 2024). In this chapter, we will focus on how the most radical of the groups that emerged, the Nordic Resistance Movement (NRM), communicated its message. The rhetoric of NRM was explicitly fascist and antisemitic compared with that used by the other extremist groups at that time. The Finnish legal system abolished the group by court order in 2020.

An overview of the forms of communication used by the group showed that the vernacular concept of the internet meme has itself become 'memeised' in the sense that extremists determinedly strove to adopt forms of communication that were considered typical of internet memes (see Yoon 2016; Davis et al. 2016). The material shared on the group's website (NRM) resembled the common understanding of memes as humorous digital (still) images with embedded text. The Swedish branch of the NRM provided instructions on how to create memes for rhetorical purposes. The humor and irony associated with memes were argued to be a powerful tool for breaking down the mental barriers of 'ordinary people' and encouraging them to adopt the movement's fascist ideology: "When a person has laughed at a 'Holocaust joke,' the first barrier is broken" ("Har en person skrattat åt ett 'förintelse'-skämt är första barriären bruten"), it argued (Nordfront, 27 May 2017). The Finnish branch of NRM followed this example and introduced "memes of the week" posts on its website in 2017 (NRM, 24 August 2018).

The contents of the Finnish extremist internet memes revolved around themes such as mythology, xenophobia, antisemitism, and symbols explicitly tied to fascist ideology. Across the material, quirky humor and satire were the most pervasive means of rhetoric. Humor in the memes included cartoon-like images, caricatures, exaggerated alignment of images, hyperbole, parody, pastiche, and image manipulation. The humor was targeted at Islam or Muslims, asylum seekers, refugees, and Jews, as well as ideological opponents (e.g. 'liberals') and politicians. The memes constructed an image of the ingroup, Finns or Europeans, exploited by foreigners and greedy politicians. The activists, i.e. members of the group, constituted the core of the ingroup, 'true believers' who wanted to help 'pure'

Finns, Nordics, and Europeans against outside invaders (refugees, immigrants) and internal traitors (liberals, politicians, Jews) (Hakoköngäs et al. 2020; Hakoköngäs et al. 2024).

A common thread across various rhetorical tropes was the reliance on everyday knowledge—the symbolic repository of shared knowledge and collective memories (Hakoköngäs and Sakki, 2023). Selective historical awareness characterized the memes. In the 20th century, fascist aesthetics utilized imagery from Christianity, ancient Greece and Rome, and medieval anti-Semitic motifs (Ranta 2016, 2017; Young 2007). Twenty-first-century memes, in turn, incorporate elements from early 20th-century fascist imagery and contemporary popular culture (Thorleifsson 2021). Historical visual references can be interpreted as expressing not only the continuity of fascist ideology but also the nostalgic attitude towards the past typical of fascism (DeCock 2018). The 'palingenetic myth', the idea of society's decline due to multiculturalism and the democratic system, and the rebirth of society through the efforts of an extremist movement, were underlying themes across the analyzed memes.

Analyzing internet memes: Visual rhetorical analysis

Rhetorical analysis examines the means and goals of persuasion, providing a better understanding of the ideology and agenda of extremist movements. The central role of both textual and visual elements in memes warrants the application of visual rhetorical analysis as a method of exploring their content, forms, and functions (Foss 2005). Rhetorical analysis itself has a long history, but its focus on everyday modes of communication is relatively new. The emergence of new rhetoric in the 1960s, as highlighted by Perelman (1979), shifted the focus towards more vernacular forms of persuasion, expanding the understanding of rhetoric beyond text and spoken words to include photographs, videos, sonic features, and their interconnected use. The evolution of rhetoric in the internet era can be viewed as a continuation of this trend (Mihelj and Jiménez-Martínez 2021), and thus the analysis of memes can be placed in the tradition of 'new rhetoric' (Hakoköngäs and Sakki 2023).

In practice, visual rhetorical analysis of internet memes can be divided into three steps, namely: content analysis, compositional analysis, and socio-semiotic analysis. Content analysis, based on systematic content classification, allows the elements (e.g. people, objects, environments) constituting the memes to be examined and the contents characteristic of the research material to be explored. Compositional analysis, exploring visual expression, leads to a description of the form of memes. Regarding the composition, it is useful to pay attention to details such as color, size, font, perspective, and distance, and to interpret their meaning in the cultural context where communication happens. (Rose 2016.) Finally, through socio-semiotic analysis (Kress and van Leeuwen 2006), it is possible to interpret the rhetorical functions targeted through strategic choices regarding the particular content and form. Kress and van Leeuwen emphasize that content and form dynamically interrelate with each other to pursue the objective(s) of communication. However, they add that to be able to interpret the intended goal of rhetoric, it is also necessary to consider the interpersonal aspect of communication, including the "audience's or participants" actions in producing and viewing the message. As discussed above, users' reactions and participation in sharing and constructing the message are an inseparable part of internet memes, a form of communication that is becoming a social phenomenon (Shifman 2013).

Memes are inherently intertextual, drawing from various sources and referencing the previous meme culture and beyond. Visual rhetorical analysis provides a means to interpret images based on the culturally preferred meanings of the visual elements. (Kress and van Leeuwen 2002, 2006.) Askanius and Keller (2021) underscore the importance of intertextuality when examining the ideological message of memes. In practice, in order to understand the life cycle and historical context of memes, employing electronic archives such as the Know Your Meme website (https://knowyourmeme.com/), which specializes in meme culture, is beneficial. Also, conducting so-called reverse image searches on various search engines may provide helpful contextual information on the evolution of the memes. Reverse image search identifies visually similar images on the internet and can be considered the primary method of investigating the digital roots of memes. At the same time, electronic archives and search engines have limitations regarding what can be inferred from their results: some content may have been removed and search engines cannot find material that is not available on the open web (e.g. it is located in closed forums or on the dark web).

Applying visual rhetorical analysis

Fig. 4.1 Boss vs. Leader (Nordic Resistance Movement in Finland). (2018). Retrieved from https://www.vastarinta.com/viikon-meemit-1/

To illustrate a process by which the above-mentioned tools are employed, we present an analysis of a meme published by the Finnish branch of the Nordic Resistance Movement (NRM). Following a content analysis of NRM's memes, we noticed that the ingroup's actions were identified as repetitive content, making these a potential focus for interpreting the forms and functions of rhetoric. The next steps—compositional analysis and socio-semiotic analysis—were applied to explore the forms and functions of individual memes. For example, the composition of the meme depicted in Figure 4.1 consists of two parallel images, with the upper "boss" face belonging to Juha Sipilä, who served as the Prime

Minister of Finland at the time of the memes publication in 2018, and the lower "leader" face to Simon Lindberg, a prominent figure in the NRM's Swedish branch.

Through the reverse image search tool, we were able to delve into the socio-semiotic dimension of the meme by approximating a crude evolution of it from a rather uncontroversial work-related image, to one advocating for the ideology of a neo-Nazi organization. A reverse image search using Google, Bing, TinEye and Yandex indicates that earlier versions of the meme appeared mainly in work-related publications, where it was used to illustrate the ideas of leading by example and the difference between a boss and a leader. The oldest-found version of the meme was published in 2013 and followed by (at least) three other versions published in 2016 and 2018.

Figure 4.2 illustrates a feature typical of meme culture, where users layer new elements on top of old ones: the edit from the 2013 'original' to the 2016 fascist meme is relatively clean and depicts quite a unified visual look, where all the swapped faces are from posters, drawings, or other stylized art. In the 2018 memes, however, the added elements are from photographs, and the sizing seems out of proportion compared to other figures in the image. Most tellingly, the flag of the Soviet Union used in the 2016 meme is still partly visible in the 2018 memes under the party logo clumsily added below the "boss" figure sitting behind the desk.

As a starting point of the analysis, in the Finnish meme, the face of the 'boss' punishing his subordinates has been replaced by the face of the Prime Minister, with the Centre Party logo appearing below. The face of the 'leader' participating in the work has been replaced by the face of the NRM representative and the movement's flag. In a nod to the original work-related meme, the Prime Minister, a democratically elected politician, is portrayed as a boss exploiting the workforce, while Lindberg is represented as a leader putting himself on the line. Dates on the images found through reverse search indicated that the Swedish branch of NRM had published a previous version of the meme more than six months earlier, in 2018. In that meme the rhetorical tension was created through a comparison between the Swedish Prime Minister Stefan

Löfven (Social Democratic Party), who appears as the 'boss', and Lindberg who again appears as the leader figure. Both the Finnish and Swedish memes relied on the assumption that the recipient was familiar with the Prime Minister and NRM leader, or at least their group symbols, and was thus able to interpret the intended meaning of the juxtaposition of these two individuals.

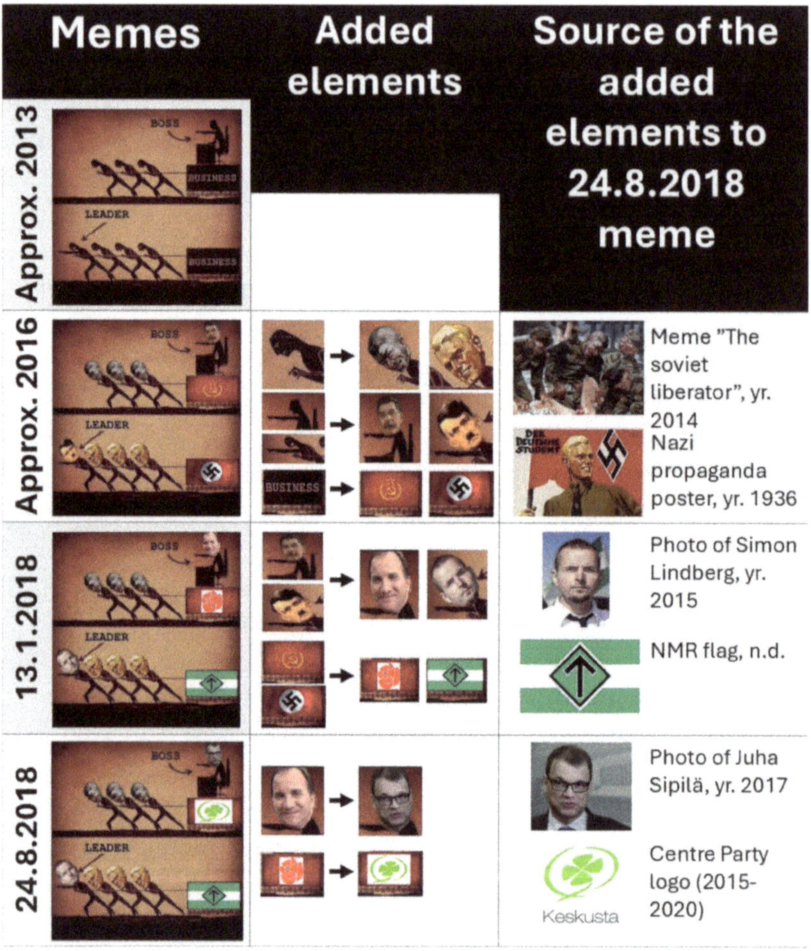

Fig. 4.2 The evolution of the Boss vs. Leader meme between 2013 and 2018, with a particular focus on the source of the components of the 24.8.2018 version of the meme.

The Swedish meme was also preceded by a version of a fascist meme published by the Swedish branch of the NRM circa 2016. This version was based on a comparison between Josef Stalin and Adolf Hitler and the related flags. Using this version as a basis, a reverse image search also enabled us to delve deeper into the different components used in the meme. In the upper image of the 2016 meme shown above, the faces of the figures pulling the load were from a 1940s German propaganda poster depicting the cruelty of Russian soldiers during World War II. In meme culture, these faces are known as "the Soviet Liberator" (Le Liberator Face), and they have been used predominantly in memes mocking Russians (https://knowyourmeme.com/memes/the-soviet-liberator-le-liberator-face). In the lower image, the faces of the figures pulling the load are from a 1930s German propaganda poster advertising a national socialist student association, representing the Aryan ideal typical of fascist aesthetics.

This is fitting imagery for fascist propaganda in general, but its significance becomes even more evident when considering that, in the context of the 2016 memes, Josef Stalin and Adolf Hitler were juxtaposed with one another. Given the context, the subsequent 2018 Swedish meme hints that the NRM sees itself as the Nazi Party's successor and equates Löfven's Social Democratic Party with Soviet socialism or perhaps with what the threat of socialism represents for far-right actors. The same applies to the Finnish 2018 version, which is almost a carbon copy of the Swedish meme (interestingly, the Finnish branch did not include a picture of a leader figure from their ranks but used the same picture of the Swedish leader Simon Lindberg, perhaps to signal the seniority of the parent organization).

When examining the visual form of the meme in light of the previous literature on fascist aesthetics and rhetoric, our attention is drawn to the utilization of historical visual elements. The reddish-brown color scheme and the ornamental nature of the background image resemble ancient Greek vase paintings (Kracauer 1995/1963). The visual form of the upper and lower images uses pun-like repetition (antanaclasis), where the structure of the image remains the same, but meaningful symbols change

(Sipilä–Lindberg; Center Party–Nordic Resistance Movement's symbol). The relationships between the figures in the image express a hierarchy typical of the visual aesthetics of fascism in the early 20th century (Young 2007). Using the same faces to represent the people depicts them as a homogeneous mass and emphasizes their distance from the leader. The appearance of a fair-skinned idealized male figure in the lower image (Mosse 1999; Ranta 2017) also contributes to building a connection to fascist aesthetics.

While the 2016 meme's rhetorical goal can be interpreted as highlighting the difference between the unequal and exploitative nature of Soviet Socialism and the equal and cooperative nature of National Socialism, the rhetorical goal of the 2018 memes can be interpreted as criticizing the Nordic democratic system and its democratically elected political leaders. The replacement of the party symbol with the movement's symbol refers to a palingenetic myth also employed in other movements' memes, suggesting that the rise of fascism would change established power relations and improve people's lives (Hakoköngäs et al. 2024). The rhetorical play, drawing on the images' identical visual structure and symbolism, constructs a humorous framework where the idealization of the movement's own actions and goals is central.

Defining 'a meme' for analysis

When planning the research, it should be considered that not all digital content visually representing the common understanding of memes (e.g. 'image with embedded text') is necessarily a meme in the strict sense of the message being socially known and shared. However, it can sometimes be difficult to pinpoint exactly when the image is 'shared enough' to become a meme in this sense. Moreover, it might be enough to determine that the intention behind the posted material was for it to become a meme rather than quantify how well this intention materialized (although this may also be of crucial interest). For example, the NRM created specific instructions for its members on how to create memes to gain popularity for the movement's agenda, thus establishing a clear intention of what was to be communicated (Hakoköngäs et al.

2024). Another issue is whether the material became a successful meme (i.e. whether it was widely circulated). In terms of the validity of the visual rhetorical analysis of the material, the latter question seems less important.

However, the popularity of certain content can obviously be used as a practical criterion to focus research on a limited number of accounts. For example, in the Finnish context, when analyzing the social media communications of two extremist groups, we noted that different kinds of meme-like posts prompted different user reactions. Memes arousing strong emotions (anger towards refugees or pride towards national heroes) were popular themes, gaining hundreds of reactions and shares from users and clearly meeting the definition of a meme. At the same time, posts that were relatively similar from a visual standpoint but presented less emotional content (e.g. the movements' logos) were clearly less attractive. Thus, the former appeared more practically relevant for the rhetorical analysis (Hakoköngäs et al. 2020). On the other hand, it is often useful to contrast popular and recurring content with unpopular and sporadic content to identify what is of central importance in the research material.

Furthermore, the researcher should note that memefication, i.e. becoming a social phenomenon, can either happen organically, when internet users react to attention-grabbing content, or be artificially fabricated when the 'speaker' pays for the visibility of their content (e.g. King et al. 2017; Lu and Pan 2020). Regarding the analysis of rhetoric, both methods of gaining visibility for the persuasive message are relevant but lead the researcher to different research questions. Organic memefication begs the question as to why a certain message grabs the attention of users, while fabricated visibility invites the researcher to examine why the 'speaker' wants to increase the visibility of particular content.

Copyrights and research ethics

Lastly, we wish to address a number of practical issues related to reporting and publishing research on internet memes. The first issue is technical and concerns the appropriate ways of referencing memes. As a result of researchers' increased interest in memes, several publication manuals (e.g. APA 2020) have recently updated their instructions for referring to memes. A reference should now provide a title, information on the publisher, the publication date and/or year and the URL of the website from which the meme was sourced. For example, for the meme published by the Finnish section of the Nordic Resistance Movement, the citation would look as follows (Fig. 4.3):

Fig. 4.3 The resistance movement opposes the police. (2018). Retrieved from https://www.vastarinta.com/viikon-meemit-6-kielto-edition/

The meme presented above includes cartoon-like sequential squares showing how the blue character first puts a symbol into the trash and how the black character then puts the blue character into the trash and takes the first symbol out. The meme form refers to common infographics requesting that rubbish be put in the bin. The head of the blue symbol refers to the Finnish police force, while the other symbol is an emblem of the NRM. APA's reference guideline does not require the publication date to be reported. However, for the purposes of analysis, the exact date may be key to understanding the meaning of the meme in context. The above meme was originally published on 28.9.2018 as a reaction to the Court of Appeal's recent decision to ban the NRM movement in Finland. The date provides contextual information for interpreting the meme as rhetorically arguing that the NRM will not accept the court's decision and continues to operate.

Figure 4.3 also demonstrates the benefits of presenting visual excerpts to demonstrate the analysis. The reader can evaluate the credibility and relevance of the researcher's interpretation, for example, the similarity of the meme to the 'put your rubbish in the bin' infographic. This leads to our second observation regarding the fact that the researcher may face difficulties publishing excerpts from internet meme material. Copyright laws, citation rights, and fair use principles differ from country to country, and researchers may find it challenging to establish which country's legislation is observed by the publisher of the research article. In the case of internet memes, copyrights are also complicated, as both the user creating the memes and the artist who made the original image (into which the user embedded the text) may be the copyright owners. The user whose meme is being studied may not necessarily be either of these parties. As memes are often created and shared by anonymous users, the rights-holder's identity is typically unclear, and it may be practically impossible to request permission to use the image. Researchers should be prepared for the publisher to refuse to reprint a visual excerpt. In such cases, despite its limitations, a tight verbal description is the primary solution, but other means should also be developed to overcome this issue. The researcher can edit the original meme for research purposes so that it constitutes a new unit, the copyright of which belongs to the researcher. Original color images can be reproduced in monochrome, resized, or incorporated into researcher-created collages (see Figure 4.2.) that are directly discussed in the text (Merrill 2023). In difficult cases, copyright issues might be avoided by reconstructing visually very similar memes using Creative Commons (CC) licensed material to demonstrate the crucial details of the original meme.

Finally, presenting examples of the material may also raise ethical concerns, as the researcher may not want to reprint a visual excerpt. Some internet memes created and shared by extremist groups may include graphical content or explicit hate that should be considered by researchers, as presenting excerpts might indirectly support preserving and disseminating this material. Likewise, internet memes may include personal information about private individuals, such as recognizable photographs of refugees and immigrants presented as objects of harsh humor and hate. In such cases, choosing not to publish a meme or anonymizing individuals using image processing is a responsible decision (see Hakoköngäs et al. 2020 for examples).

Regarding ethical principles, researchers may also need to preserve the anonymity of users participating in 'memefication'. Even though the memes were collected from public platforms or groups, individual users reacting and commenting on them may not be aware of the extent to which their actions are visible to other internet users. With search engines, a single comment can easily be linked to a user later, even if their name was not published in the research report. Furthermore, researchers should bear in mind that accessing social media data has become increasingly difficult, as many services have limited researchers' access to data, for example, by tying all data collection to the use of APIs (application programming interfaces) with restrictive usage terms (Davidson et al. 2023). Also, the terms and conditions of commercial platforms change regularly and those applicable at the time when research is published may differ from those in force when material was compiled from the platform.

Conclusions

In this chapter, we presented insight gained from previous research analyzing how internet memes are used as a rhetorical vehicle by the fascist Nordic Resistance Movement in Finland. The examples taken from the research illustrated that the movement intentionally used memes to convey an ideological message, for instance, questioning the established democratic political system. The deliberate blending of ironic humor typical of youth cultures with social media communication (Forchtner and Kølvraa 2017) serves a purpose in extremist group communication. Despite comprising only a few elements, the memes result in nuanced visual rhetoric. Exploiting satirical humor in social media communication can be seen as an adaptation of rhetoric to attract new audiences and communicate to like-minded supporters.

The virtual arenas have made it necessary for extremist groups to adapt to the trends and preferences of virtual communities (Forchtner and Kølvraa 2017). However, the results from Finland illustrate that this adaptation mainly addresses the form of the communication, while the content and intended rhetorical functions have remained relatively similar to those observed in the past. In the 20ᵗʰ century, racist, antisemitic, and xenophobic messages were conveyed in a manner inspired by antiquity and characterized by an elevated level of aesthetics. In the 21ˢᵗ century, the same messages are conveyed in a more "homemade" and vernacular form (DeCock 2018; Young 2007), for example, by means of internet memes. However, according to Mosse (2019), the elevated and vernacular forms used in communication serve the same goal, i.e. to engage broad audiences by concealing the cruelty at the core of the extremist agenda. This observation of simultaneous change and continuity in extremist rhetoric has also been noted in communication other than social media (Sakki et al. 2018).

Visual rhetorical analysis is suitable when the researcher wants to examine the content, form, and functions of internet memes. However, it is not the only method suitable for analyzing rhetoric in memes. Researchers may find, for example, a combination of multimodal discourse analysis (MDA) and critical discursive psychology (CDP) particularly useful, forming an approach that could be termed multimodal critical discourse analysis (MCDA) (Kilby and Lennon 2021). While visual rhetorical analysis leans more towards persuasive strategies and agrees with different epistemological perspectives, multimodal discourse analysis allows the complexity of nationalist rhetoric to be identified and unpacked as discursive, affective, and performative acts that construct social reality (Hakoköngäs and Sakki, 2023).

Examining the social media discussions sparked by provocative humor would enhance our understanding of the interpersonal metafunctions (Kress and van Leeuwen 2006) of visual rhetoric and the formation of delegitimizing discourses (Davis et al. 2016). An important aspect of internet memes that partially sets them apart from traditional forms of persuasive communication is their social aspect. Users can react to and comment on posts, enabling them to participate in defining their meaning. Investigating how individuals respond to visual (and multimodal) messages and what rhetorical strategies contribute to supporting and sharing extremist material should be a focus for future research.

References

APA, 2020. "Publication manual of the American psychological association". *American Psychological Association.*

Askanius, T. and Nadine K., 2021. "Murder fantasies in memes: fascist aesthetics of death threats and the banalization of white supremacist violence". *Information, Communication & Society* 24 (16), 2522–2539. https://doi.org/10.1080/1369118X.2021.1974517

Bilewicz, M. and W. Soral, 2020. "Hate speech epidemic: The dynamic effects of derogatory language on intergroup relations and political radicalization". *Political Psychology*, 41 (S1), 3–33. https://doi.org/10.1111/pops.12670

Burke, S. and S. Goodman, 2012. "'Bring back Hitler's gas chambers': Asylum seeking, Nazis and Facebook–a discursive analysis". *Discourse and Society*, 23 (1), 19–33.

Davidson, B. I., D. Wischerath, D. Racek, D. A. Parry, E. Godwin, J. Hinds and A. G. Cork, 2023. "Platform-controlled social media APIs threaten open science". *Nature Human Behaviour*, 7 (12), 2054–2057. https://doi.org/10.1038/s41562-023-01750-2

Davis, C., M. Glantz and D. Novak, 2016. "'You Can't Run Your SUV on Cute. Let's Go!': Internet Memes as Delegitimizing Discourse". *Environmental Communication*, 10 (1), 62–83.

Dawkins, R., 1976. *The Selfish Gene.* Oxford University Press.

DeCook, J. R., 2018. "Memes and symbolic violence: #proudboys and the use of memes for propaganda and the construction of collective identity". *Learning, Media and Technology*, 43 (4), 485–504. https://doi.org/10.1080/17439884.2018.1544149

Ekman, M., 2018. "Anti-refugee mobilization in social media: The case of soldiers of Odin". *Social Media + Society*, 4, 1–11. https://doi.org/10.1177/2056305118764431

Forchtner, B., and C. Kølvraa, 2017. "Extreme right images of radical authenticity: Multimodal aesthetics of history, nature, and gender roles in social media". *European Journal of Cultural and Political*

Sociology, 4 (3), 252–281. https://doi.org/10.1080/23254823.2017.13229 10

Foss, S. K., 2005. "Theory of visual rhetoric". In: K. Smith, S. Moriarty, G. Barbatsis and K. Kennedy (eds), *Handbook of Visual Communication: Theory, Methods, and Media.* Routledge, 141–152.

Gal, N., 2019. "Ironic humor on social media as participatory boundary work". *New Media and Society,* 21 (3), 729–749. https://doi. org/10.1177/1461444818805719

—, Shifman L. and Z. Kampf, 2016. "'It gets better': Internet memes and the construction of collective identity". *New Media & Society,* 18, 1698–1714. https://doi.org/10.1177/1461444814568784

Hahner, L. A., 2013. "The riot kiss: Framing memes as visual argument". *Argumentation and Advocacy,* 49, 151–166.

Hakoköngäs, E. and Inari Sakki, 2019. "The past as a means of persuasion: Visual political rhetoric in Finnish dairy product advertising". *Journal of Social and Political Psychology,* 7, 507–524. https://doi.org/10.5964/ jspp.v7i1.1107.

—, and Inari Sakki, 2023. "Multimodal nationalist rhetoric in Finland: From banal to extreme political persuasion". In: W., Wei, and J., Schnell (eds), *The Routledge Handbook of Descriptive Rhetorical Studies and World Languages.* London: Routledge, 234–248. https://doi. org/10.4324/9781003195276.

—, O. Halmesvaara, J. Martikainen, and Inari Sakki, 2024. "Meemit ja fasismin estetiikka: Visuaalinen retorinen analyysi Pohjoismaisen Vastarintaliikkeen viestinnästä Suomessa. [Memes and the aesthetics of fascism: A visual rhetorical analysis of the Internet memes of the Finnish branch of the Nordic Resistance Movement]". *Kulttuurintutkimus,* 1 (41), 41–59.

—, O. Halmesvaara, and Inari Sakki, 2020. "Persuasion through bitter humor: Multimodal discourse analysis of rhetoric in internet memes of two far-right groups in Finland". *Social Media + Society,* 6 (2), 2056305120921575. https://doi.org/10.1177/2056305120921575

Hatakka, N., 2020. "Expose, debunk, ridicule, resist! Networked civic monitoring of populist radical right online action in Finland". *Information, Communication & Society,* 23 (9), 1311–1326. https://doi. org/10.1080/1369118X.2019.1566392.

Horsti, K., 2015. "Techno-cultural opportunities: The anti-immigration movement in the Finnish mediascape". *Patterns of Prejudice,* 49 (4), 343–366.

Huntington, H. E., 2013. "Subversive memes: Internet memes as a form of visual rhetoric". *AoIR Selected Papers of Internet Research*, 3. https://journals.uic.edu/ojs/index.php/spir/article/view/8886.

—, 2016. "Pepper spray cop and the American dream: Using synecdoche and metaphor to unlock internet memes' visual political rhetoric". *Communication Studies,* 67 (1), 77–93. https://doi.org/10.1080/10510974.2015.1087414

Hübscher, M., 2023. "Algorithmic Antisemitism on Social Media". In: M. Weitzman, R. J. Williams and Wald, J. (eds), *The Routledge History of Antisemitism*. London: Routledge, 364–372.

Jenkins, E., 2014. "The modes of visual rhetoric: Circulating memes as expressions". *Quarterly Journal of Speech*, 100 (4), 442–466.

Kelly, N., 2023. "A Critical Analysis: Key Strategies of Far-Right Online Visual Propaganda". In: R. Montasari (ed.), "Applications for Artificial Intelligence and Digital Forensics in National Security". *Springer*, 127–141.

Kilby, L. and H. Lennon, 2021. "When words are not enough: Combined textual and visual multimodal analysis as a critical discursive psychology undertaking". *Methods in Psychology*, 5. https://doi.org/10.1016/j.metip.2021.100071

King, G., J. Pan, and M. E. Roberts, 2017. "How the Chinese government fabricates social media posts for strategic distraction, not engaged argument". *American Political Science Review*, 111 (3), 484–501. https://doi.org/10.1017/S0003055417000144

Knobel, M. and C. Lankshear, 2006. "Online memes, affinities and cultural production". In: C. Bingum and M. Peters (eds), *A new literacy sampler*. Frankfurt am Main: Lang, 199–227.

Kracauer, S., 1995. *The mass ornament. Weimar essays* [Ornament der Masse, 1963]. Translated by Thomas Y. Levin. Cambridge: Harvard University Press.

Kress, G. and T. van Leeuwen, 2006. *Reading Images: The grammar of visual design*. London: Routledge.

—, and T. van Leeuwen, 2002. "Colour as a semiotic mode: Notes for a grammar of colour". *Visual Communication*, 1 (3), 343–368. https://doi.org/10.1177/147035720200100306

Livingstone, S., 2003. *The changing nature of audiences: From the mass audience to the interactive media user. A companion to media studies*. New York: Wiley & Sons, 337–359.

Lu, Y. and J. Pan, 2021. "Capturing clicks: How the Chinese government uses clickbait to compete for visibility". *Political Communication*, 38 (1–2), 23–54. https://doi.org/10.1080/10584609.2020.1765914

Malmqvist, K., 2015. "Satire, racist humour and the power of (un) laughter: On the restrained nature of Swedish online racist discourse targeting EU-migrants begging for money". *Discourse and Society*, 26 (6), 733–753.

Martikainen, J. and Inari Sakki, 2021. "Myths, the Bible, and Romanticism as ingredients of political narratives in Finns Party election video". Discourse, *Context & Media* 39, 1–11. https://doi.org/10.1016/j. dcm.2021.100466.

Merrill, S., 2023. "Memory, Iconicity, and Virality in Action: Exploring Protest Photos Online". In A. Rigney and S. Thomas (eds), The Visual Memory of Protest. Amsterdam: Amsterdam University Press, 133–156. https://doi.org/10.2307/jj.5610579.

Mihelj, S. and C. Jiménez-Martínez, 2021. "Digital nationalism: Understanding the role of digital media in the rise of 'new' nationalism". *Nations and Nationalism*, 27 (2), 331–346. https://doi. org/10.1111/nana.12685

Mosse, G. L., 1999. "Aesthetics and society: Some considerations". *Journal of Contemporary History*, 31 (2), 245–252.

Perelman, C., 1979. "The new rhetoric: A theory of practical reasoning". In: C. Perelman (ed.), *The New Rhetoric and the Humanities*. Berlin: Springer, 1–42.

Ranta, M., 2016. "The (pictorial) construction of collective identities in the Third Reich". *Language and Semiotic Studies*, 2 (3), 107–124.

—, 2017. "Master narratives and the pictorial construction of Otherness: Anti-Semitic images in the Third Reich and beyond". *Contemporary Aesthetics*, 15 (1), Article 25.

Ravndal, J. A., 2020. "The Emergence of Transnational Street Militancy: A Comparative Case Study of the Nordic Resistance Movement and Generation Identity". *Journal for Deradicalization*, 25, 1–34.

Rose, G., 2016. *Visual methodologies: An introduction to researching with visual materials*. California: Sage.

Sakki, Inari and E. Hakoköngäs, 2022. "Dialogical construction of hate speech in established media and online discussions". In: K. Pettersson and E. Nortio (eds), *The Far-Right Discourse of Multiculturalism in Intergroup Interactions: A Critical Discursive Perspective*. London: Palgrave Macmillan, 85–111. http://doi. org/10.1007/978-3-030-89066-7_4.

—, E. Hakoköngäs, and K. Pettersson, 2018. "Past and Present Nationalist Political Rhetoric in Finland: Changes and Continuities". *Journal of Language and Social Psychology*, 37, 160–180. https://doi.org/10.1177% 2F0261927X17706945.

Shifman, Limor, 2014. *Memes in digital culture*. Cambridge: MIT Press.

—, 2013. "Memes in a digital world: Reconciling with a conceptual troublemaker". *Journal of Computer-Mediated Communication*, 18 (3), 362–377.

Thorleifsson, C., 2021. "From cyberfascism to terrorism: On 4chan/pol/ culture and the transnational production of memetic violence". *Nations and Nationalism*, 28 (1), 286–301. https://doi.org/10.1111/nana.12780

Yoon, I., 2016. "Why is it not just a joke? Analysis of Internet memes associated with racism and hidden ideology of colorblindness". *Journal of Cultural Research in Art Education*, 33 (1), 92–123.

Young, J. E., 2009. "Nazi aesthetics in historical context". In: R. Clifton Spargo and Robert M. Ehrenreich (eds), *After Representation? The Holocaust, Literature, and Culture*. New Jersey: Rutgers University Press, 89–98.

5. Same tools, different target: Countering hate speech with memes

Carmen Aguilera-Carnerero, Matthias J. Becker, Marcus Scheiber

Abstract

While memes, as communication practices, are inherently pluralistic and designed to express diverse opinions, they can also be used to propagate hateful ideologies. This is largely due to their strategic dissemination within moderate milieus of the digital public sphere (Ebner 2023). As a result, memes can act as catalysts for harmful ideas, contributing to the normalisation of hate (Schulze et al. 2022: 42). However, the same mechanisms that enable the spread of hate speech can be repurposed by digital actors to promote counter-speech and resist this normalisation. This chapter explores the multimodal communication strategies used in counter-speech memes, with a particular focus on their role in combating Islamophobia.

Keywords: *counter speech, hate speech, humour, Islamophobia, memes, image analysis, qualitative analysis, social semiotics, digital culture, multimodality*

Introduction

Creating and, especially, sharing memes has become central to the online experience of netizens. Memes are frequently used to disseminate political arguments and ideologies, as shown by Knobel and Lankshear (2006) and Yoon (2016). Ideology is thus substantial not only to the content of memes but also to the stance they convey. As Wiggins (2019: 62) notes, "the ideological practice afforded by Internet memes gains meaning only through acceptance by and incorporation into a group or community." In line with Hall's (1993) assertion, the images of popular culture that permeate our daily lives are ideologically and politically charged, with significant persuasive potential. This tenet is well understood by extremist groups, which exploit digital subcultures to recruit followers and spread their propaganda. Memes have evolved to serve other communicative functions, some of which are closely tied to extreme speech and radicalisation (Fielitz and Thurston 2019), allowing "extreme message to masquerade as a medium specific parody" (Crawford 2020). The potential of memes to channel and spread hate speech, defined here as any discriminatory or pejorative language targeting individuals or groups based on identity factors, is undeniable. This chapter, however, explores whether memes might also possess the potential to serve as tools for countering hate speech.

In particular, we analysed a corpus of 25 memes compiled from 2019 to 2021 that mock stereotypes commonly found in Islamophobic memes, which are often used to convey negative images of Muslims and Islam (Aguilera-Carnerero and Tegal 2023).[1]

---

1   The authors of this article acknowledge that the term 'Islamophobia' is contested in some contexts. Given its historical origins and political usage—including by authoritarian regimes—it is at times subject to instrumentalisation. Moreover, the term's emphasis on the emotion of fear does not fully capture the phenomenon, which often entails hatred, denigration, and structural discrimination. Nonetheless, the authors consider the term functionally equivalent to expressions such as 'anti-Muslim racism' or 'anti-Muslim bigotry', insofar as it denotes a linguistic pattern that has become conventional and evokes precisely those conceptions of hate—rather than fear. Other terms, such as 'antisemitism', also have a complex and contested history—most notably the fact that the term was coined by the antisemitic journalist Wilhelm Marr, whose aim was

Our aim is twofold: firstly, to analyse the meaning of memes as a feature of communication deeply rooted in specific communities of "prosumers" (Toffler 1980), and secondly, to explore the semiotic representation of counter-hate speech in this form of digital communication. The chapter begins with an overview of the key characteristics of hate speech and counter speech, followed by a discussion of the discursive semiotic conditions of memes. Finally, we demonstrate how memes can be employed as effective tools in countering hate speech.

Hate speech and counter speech

Hate speech

Despite the pressing need for a clear and unambiguous definition— particularly in legal contexts, institutional efforts to regulate discriminatory discourse, and natural language processing (NLP) research—hate speech remains conceptually vague and lacks a universally accepted definition. This vagueness has led to varied interpretations in research. Today, hate speech is often used as a 'catch-all' term to describe a wide range of conflicts occurring online. However, unlike terms such as verbal violence, offensive language, harassment, or abusive, insulting, and extreme speech—terms that are typically situational and interactional— hate speech represents the articulation of concepts or building blocks of established hate ideologies, such as antisemitism, anti-Black racism, or anti-Muslim bigotry. Thus, while its literal meaning might suggest speech that expresses general hatred, in practice, it specifically targets groups defined by legally protected characteristics such as race, ethnicity, religion, sex, sexual orientation, and disability.

---

to create a pseudo-scientific, and thus ostensibly legitimate, label for hatred directed at Jews. This point was also emphasised in personal conversations with the late scholar of antisemitism, Robert Fine. We therefore advocate for prioritising the analysis of the associated patterns of demonisation, devaluation, and rhetorical strategies over debates about the terminology used to describe the broader phenomenon.

The discursive devaluation and exclusion of these groups are often associated with the emotion of hatred directed towards the targeted group, as emphasised in key definitions of hate speech. For instance, Matsuda's (1989) early work defines hate speech as "messages of racial inferiority, messages that are designed to inferiority, and messages that are hateful or hostile." Even decades later, this interpretation has been maintained in fields such as linguistics: "Hate speech [...] generally refers to the verbal expression of hatred toward individuals or groups, especially through the use of language intended to belittle and vilify specific populations" (Meibauer 2013: 1, translated by the authors). The aim of such speech often revolves around "belittling and vilifying," which is frequently the case with racist remarks. However, this characteristic does not fully encompass the aspect of demonisation of a group conceptualised as omnipotent and acting in secret, as seen in instances of antisemitism (for emotions of fear and the process of self-victimisation, see below).

The United Nations Committee on the Elimination of Racial Discrimination emphasises the role of group targeting and the correlation with violence or acts in general by describing hate speech as "any kind of communication that is intended to insult, intimidate, or incite violence or prejudicial action against a person or group of people on the basis of race, religion, ethnic origin, sexual orientation, disability, or gender" (CERD 2013).

In contrast, the Council of Europe adopts a more inclusive approach, defining hate speech as "all forms of expression which spread, incite, promote, or justify racial hatred, xenophobia, anti-Semitism, or other forms of hatred based on intolerance, including: intolerance expressed by aggressive nationalism and ethnocentrism, discrimination and hostility against minorities, migrants, and people of immigrant origin" (1997). Similarly, the European Commission Against Racism and Intolerance recognises in its definition of hate speech "the advocacy, promotion, or incitement, in any form, of the denigration, hatred, or vilification of a person or group of persons, as well as any harassment, insult, negative stereotyping, stigmatization, or threat" (ECRI 2016). It also acknowledges that the presence of hatred as an emotion is not the sole determining factor for identifying hate speech. Therefore, hate speech should not be simply equated with hateful speech, just as the aforementioned hate ideologies are not solely based on the characteristics of hate.

Hate speech can be driven by a range of emotions, as researchers emphasise by discussing it in the context of feelings other than hatred, including fear, disgust, and even neutral or emotionless reproduction of exclusionary stereotypes.[2] Wodak also highlights the presence of emotionless rhetoric that perpetuates stereotypes without overt affective content. This observation is supported by researchers of the Decoding Antisemitism team, who demonstrate that, in the realm of antisemitic hate speech, such rhetoric is often emotionally neutral. It reproduces exclusionary stereotypes without direct emotional engagement, instead reinforcing biases through detached language (Becker et al. 2024).

The International Network Against Cyber Hate also emphasises that even emotionless statements can qualify as hate speech—and further notes that such speech does not necessarily need to be characterised by intent: "Hate speech is intentional or unintentional public discriminatory and/or defamatory statements; intentional incitement to hatred and/or violence and/or segregation based on a person's or a group's real or perceived race, ethnicity, language, nationality, skin colour, religious beliefs or lack thereof, gender, gender identity, sex, sexual orientation, political beliefs, social status, birth, age, mental health, disability, disease" (INACH 2024).

Aside from the issues of emotional basis and intentionality, on a structural level, hate speech is inherently complex and somewhat elusive, making it a challenging subject for linguistic study. It is not a singular phenomenon (see Guillén-Nieto 2023, see also Brown

---

2   Schäfer and Kistner (2023) analyse the correlations between various emotions and hate speech using detailed annotations of English online datasets. Schwarz-Friesel (2021) investigates how antisemitic hate speech often employs disgust and dehumanisation, particularly in portraying certain groups as fundamentally repugnant or threatening. Wodak (2015) explores how hate speech in right-wing populism can involve not only expressions of hatred, but also manipulative emotions like fear, where language is used to incite panic or exclusion (for the term "fear speech," see Saha et al. 2023).

2017 and 2018). Hate speech lacks a unified purpose and can manifest in various enduring forms, such as racial epithets, insults, dehumanising metaphors, group defamation, negative stereotypes, and ironic speech acts (see also Baider and Constantinou 2020). It can also appear in transient forms.

Hate speech is not limited to verbal expressions; it can also be expressed through different mediums and modalities: written and spoken words, as well as visual materials like gestures, symbols, images, video games, films, and especially memes (for the term "hate discourse" see Özarslan 2014). It is not confined to any specific genre or rhetorical style, ranging from carefully considered remarks in parliamentary speeches to spontaneous sarcastic comments or images in online posts. Hate speech encompasses numerous negative illocutionary and perlocutionary acts, including insulting, degrading, humiliating, harassing, threatening, provoking, inciting hatred, hostility or violence, and denying, justifying, or glorifying acts of genocide. The interpretation of hate speech is highly context-dependent, as the same semiotic expressions might be perceived positively or neutrally in certain communicative settings, such as through linguistic reclamation in specific communities (Brontsema 2004, Warner and Hirschberg 2012, Davidson et al. 2017).

In digital communication, it is important to consider not only the producer (including their stance and intentions) and the recipient of hate speech (and its effect on the latter) but also the so-called bystanders. As Ermida (2023: 4) notes, "the targets [of prejudiced content online], who directly bear the full force of the attack, both individually and collectively, are humiliated, offended, dehumanised, 'othered,' and, through fear, silenced" (see also Erikson 1968, Benesch 2014). Forms of hate speech "isolate, marginalise, disparage, and demonise vulnerable individuals and the communities they represent." Bystanders "absorb, more or less distractedly, the biased social meanings fed to them and may be persuaded to replicate them" and can become "targets of incitement, and simultaneously the recipients, or decoders, of hatred aimed at third parties" (ibid.: 5; Assimakopoulos 2020, O'Driscoll 2020).

Hate speech remains conceptually vague, lacking a universally accepted definition despite its growing relevance in legal, social, and linguistic contexts. Unlike terms such as verbal violence or harassment, hate speech specifically targets groups based on protected characteristics, often tied to hate ideologies like antisemitism or racism. It can be driven by various emotions, including fear or neutral detachment, and is not limited to speech alone, appearing in various forms such as written text, images, and memes. The impact of hate speech extends beyond its targets to bystanders, who may internalise or replicate the prejudiced messages they encounter.

Counter speech

When examining the impact of hate speech on bystanders and in digital environments, the strategy of counter speech becomes more apparent. Counter speech does not always involve the victim engaging in the discourse; instead, other participants may take a stand against the harmful constructs of a given ideology. Counter speech has gained increasing attention as a proactive response to hate speech, focusing on the role of communication in mitigating and challenging harmful discourse (cf. Baider et al. 2020). Unlike reactive measures such as censorship or legal interventions, counter speech emphasises the use of dialogue and persuasive communication to counteract hate speech and foster positive discourse. This approach has become particularly relevant in the context of social media, where the rapid spread of hate speech necessitates equally swift and effective countermeasures.

Counter speech broadly refers to any form of communication that seeks to directly address, refute, or counteract hate speech. It encompasses a wide range of semiotic activities, including public statements, social media posts, educational campaigns, and grassroots activism.

The goal of counter speech is not only to challenge the harmful narratives propagated by hate speech but also to promote inclusive and respectful discourse. Benesch et al. (2016) define the success of counter speech as having a "favorable impact on the original (hateful) user, shifting his or her discourse if not also his or her beliefs," as well as "positively affecting the discourse norms of the 'audience' of a counterspeech conversation."

The theoretical underpinnings of counter speech are grounded in several communication and social psychological theories. One important framework is the theory of social influence, which posits that individuals' attitudes and behaviours can be changed through exposure to persuasive messages and counter-narratives (Kelman 1961). Another relevant theory is the contact hypothesis, which suggests that increased interaction between different social groups can reduce prejudice and improve intergroup relations (Allport 1954). Counter speech leverages these theories by providing alternative perspectives and encouraging constructive dialogue.

Several meta-communicative strategies are commonly employed in counter speech initiatives.

- Direct Rebuttal: Engaging directly with hate speech by providing factual corrections or challenging f a l s e claims. For instance, debunking misinformation about marginalised groups can counteract harmful stereotypes (Garland et al. 2022, see also van Eerten and Doosje 2019, Schäfer et al. 2024).

- Positive Messaging: Promoting inclusive and respectful messages that offer alternative narratives to those propagated by hate speech. This includes campaigns that celebrate diversity and highlight positive contributions made by different communities (Baider 2023, Silva 2023).

- Empowerment and Support: Providing support and amplification for those targeted by hate speech. This can involve sharing personal stories, creating supportive communities, and standing in solidarity with victims (Kunst et al. 2021, Zapata et al. 2024).

- Educational Initiatives: Implementing educational programmes that raise awareness about the impact of hate speech and teach skills for constructive dialogue. These programmes can be aimed at various audiences, including students, community leaders, and online users (UNESCO 2021 and 2023).

- The effectiveness of counter speech in reducing the impact of hate speech varies depending on several factors. Research indicates that counter speech can be effective in mitigating the spread of hate speech when it is timely, well-targeted, and resonates with the intended audience (Hangartner et al. 2021, Baider 2023, Schäfer et al. 2024). However, counter speech faces several challenges, including the risk of backlash from hate groups, the potential for counter-narratives to be drowned out by louder hate speech, and the difficulty of measuring long-term impacts (Garland et al. 2022, Sponholz 2023).

Memes

Memes emerge as a communicative outcome of the diverse semiotic and medial possibilities enabled by the technological and socio-cultural affordances of digital communication. The collaborative practices facilitated by these conditions allow memes to function as communicative templates for social interaction. They can be understood as multimodal sign patterns characterised by:

i. Collective semiosis (meaning is shaped by multiple sign users);

ii. Re-semiotisations (the transposition of meaning from one context to another) (Iedema 2003: 41);

iii. A functional matrix of production conditions and reception possibilities;

iv. A family resemblance among individual memes; and

v. Discourse-semantic network structures (Scheiber, Troschke, and Krasni 2024).

Based on these semiotic properties, (discourse-)semantic conditions, and pragmatic usage, the prototypical meme is a text-image structure. However, not every text-image structure within digital communication qualifies as a meme: the texts and images within each artefact must follow a recognisable pattern while exhibiting significant variation, and the number of times a specific artefact is disseminated must exceed a certain "tipping point" before web users perceive it as a trend (Breitenbach 2015: 36). Thus, memes arise via collective semiosis processes; they are collaborative constructions of meaning, generated as users transform a singular artefact into a recurring (multimodal) pattern via its re-semiotisations (reproduction, imitation, and variation) (Klug 2023: 206).

On the one hand, memes are simple. The (mutual) integration of sign modalities reduces informational complexity, relying on structural and content-related simplicity (Breitenbach 2015: 37). On the other hand, memes are sophisticated, as the combination of verbal and pictorial sign modalities generates emergent meaning. To ensure the intended significance is conveyed despite these semiotic challenges, memes employ interpretation patterns during reception on the semiotic surface: The image of a person, for example, allows different interpretations of its function (representation, warning, emotionalisation, etc.). Since the image in one and the same meme always fulfils the same function, the meme frames the image used in its function and suggests a certain interpretation to the recipient. These patterns regulate pragmatic usability and selectively determine the use of semiotic resources within the arrangement. Memes thus establish shared spheres of cultural knowledge, making them accessible to web users familiar with the (communication) format (Breitenbach 2015: 45). In other words, the production of a meme is guided by a functional matrix that structures both the semantic organisation and pragmatic usability of text-image combinations. However, this same matrix limits the cognitive processing of memes, as both their production and reception depend on web users' knowledge of the world and their familiarity with related text-image structures. Hence, the constitution of meaning in a meme is shaped by the family resemblance of the individual artefacts to others within the same pattern.

The knowledge that underpins a specific meme is negotiated within social practices and is subject to the norms of epistemic practices. These practices, however, are revealed as socially constructed goods, formed through ongoing negotiation, recognition, and rejection of knowledge within a discursive community (Spitzmüller and Warnke 2011: 41). Knowledge is thus relative, not an ontological fact: the perception, interpretation, and experience of reality—and the constitution of meaning—are always contextualised within shared knowledge, shaped by socially embedded interpretive patterns (ibid.: 8). Signs, after all, do not carry inherent meaning; they acquire meaning ascribed by sign users, who, in turn, participate in shaping meaning within social discourses.

However, since sign users always evaluate and interpret meanings in different ways, there is a continuous competition for interpretive dominance. Each sign user in a discourse attempts to influence it by making their interpretation discursively dominant. This manifests through the imposition of conceptual-perspectival fixations of knowledge, often taking the form of semantic struggles.[3] Here lies the explosive potential of the competition for interpretive authority: sign actions can lead to harm. Hate typically does not begin with physical violence but with semiotic actions that qualify events and/or people in a particular way.

Hence, memes are not just media that represent a certain reality by providing referential access to it; their use actively constitutes that reality.[4] Successfully embedding a particular meaning or ideology within a meme allows the user to control how that meaning is referenced and predicated in discursive practices. This way, the intended interpretation is reinforced through recurring co-texts and contexts. As a result, a meme "not only realises a communicatively selected section of the world, but the world in the [meme] is staged according to the communicative intentions" and discursive practices of the users, thus constituting reality in an epistemic sense (Meier 2014: 169, translated by the authors).

The realisation of a meme should also be viewed as an expression of discursive practices. The compositional organisation

---

3   Semantic struggles are defined as "the attempt to assert certain [semiotic] forms in a domain of knowledge as an expression of specific, interest-driven and action-guiding patterns of thought" (Felder 2006: 14, translated by the authors).

4   Regardless of whether the meaning conveyed by the meme is accepted or rejected by the discursive community, it becomes a part of discursive practice and must be addressed or negotiated by its recipients.

of semiotic elements in a text-image structure provides information about the discursive practice it stems from: "At all points, design realises and projects social organisation and is affected by social and technological change" (Kress 2010: 139). The placement of individual sign modalities activates communicative structures, creates social relations through composition patterns, and realises communicative functionalities by linking or separating communicative elements (Kress and van Leeuwen 2006: 177). As web users employ a range of memes to convey hate speech or counter speech, memes function as a discursive practice of knowledge generation, ideology dissemination, and self-positioning:

> First, memes may best be understood as pieces of cultural information that pass along from person to person, but gradually scale into a shared social phenomenon. Although they spread on a micro basis, their impact is on the macro level: memes shape the mindsets, forms of behaviour, and actions of social groups (Shifman 2014: 18).

Each meme can be characterised as the sedimentation of a discursive process, using conventionalised templates to meet the communicative (and ideological) needs of digital interaction at the moment of its execution. An analysis of counter speech in and through memes therefore aims to reveal the "action-guiding and socially stratifying collective knowledge" (Spitzmüller and Warnke 2011: 8, translated by the authors) embedded in memes, as they are both a product of and an influence on social discourses.

Methodology

Our research adopts an eclectic approach, drawing from various theoretical frameworks to analyse the corpus. We begin with Segev et al.'s (2015: 418) concept of a "meme family"—groups of content units bound by two main forces:

  i. General attributes derived from the meme culture.

  ii. Specific quiddities or "recurring features that are unique to each family and constitute its singular essence" (Segev et al. 2015: 419).

To analyse memes' general attributes, we utilised Shifman's (2014) model, which consists of three dimensions: content (the ideas and ideologies conveyed), form (the physical embodiment of the multimodal message), and discursive stance (how creators position themselves about the meme). These dimensions align with Kress and van Leeuwen's (2006 [1996]) three interrelated meta-semiotic tasks: representational (how experience is visually encoded), compositional ("the way in which representations and communicative acts cohere into the kind of meaningful whole we call 'text'", Kress and van Leeuwen 1996: 181), and interactive (the patterns of interaction between participants, both depicted and real).

Each meme family displays both uniqueness—negotiated across the entire memetic network level and related to the general attributes of the meme—and cohesiveness, defined by local connections among instances within the same family. A meme family's cohesiveness increases when its instances share more similarities (Segev et al. 2015). Hence, meaning in a meme emerges on two levels: one, the text-image structure must be decoded and two, the resulting interpretation must be contextualised within the meme family framework. The individual meme is realised as a punctual event, which—as a text-image structure with communicative function— carries meaning in itself but also reveals a discourse-semantic network structure during reception or identification within a meme family. Its meaning is contingent upon its relation to other memes in the same pattern within the family.

Users may either adopt a position within a meme that they find appealing or adopt the opposite discursive orientation, which Shifman (2014: 40) refers to as "the ways in which addressers position themselves in relation to the texts, its linguistic codes, the addressees, and other potential speakers". This can be linked to Kress and van Leeuwen's semiotic interpersonal metafunction, which Shifman (2014) divides into three subcategories:

i. Participation structures—who is entitled to participate, and why?

   ii. Keying—the tone and style of communication (e.g. humour).

  iii. Communicative functions within a discursive reality, following Jakobson's typology of the functions of human communication (1960): referential, emotive, conative, phatic, metalingual, and poetic.

The analysis was conducted in two phases: In the first phase, the 25 selected memes were subjected to visual content analysis. We described each meme according to Shifman's three dimensions (content, form, and stance) and classified the corpus into broader, general theme categories. In the second phase, we focused on a cluster of frequently occurring memes, paying special attention to form and stance.

Data

The corpus consisted of 25 memes, retrieved from some of the most popular meme sites (imgflip, memecrunch, memecenter, Icanhascheezeburger) in April 2024. Our search was based on the general query "Muslim memes", filtering out any memes with negative features (both textual, visual, or multimodal) related to Muslims or Islam. In this way, we retrieved 25 memes containing "Islamophiliac" features – those that support (or at least do not attack) Muslims or Islam in various ways.

Analysis

The primary ideology in the meme family within our corpus is "Islamophilia", understood as the opposite of Islamophobia, reflecting support for Islam and Muslims. This ideology is linked both to the recurring "Islamophilic" message (quiddities) and the discursive stance adopted by the meme creators. Memes were grouped into two main categories, addressing key topics: the contempt for Islam as a religion and for Muslims as its followers. Although related, these are differentiated as distinct objects of scorn. In terms of content, we propose a taxonomy of memes based on these broad categories, which can be seen in Table 5.1.

Table 5.1 Taxonomy of memes according to their content.

Type of memes based on the content		Number of occurrences
Muslim women		4
Islamic traditions	Muslim Families	1
	Love	2
	Religious life	11
Islam in the media		6
Miscelanea		1
Total		25

Meta-communicative strategy of Positive Messaging: Islamic traditions

Fig. 5.1 meme on dating problems for young Muslims

Fig. 5.2 meme on fasting during Ramadan

This group contains the largest number of memes, sharing distinct features tied to Islamic practices and/or Muslim identity. We identified three main subgroups of positive messaging: love (memes that humorously address dating or love issues faced by Muslims, Fig. 5.1), Muslim families (memes that focus on family life within the Muslim community), common religious practices like daily prayers, Fig. 5.3) or religious duties (memes portraying Muslim festivals, such as Ramadan (Fig. 5.2).

Fig. 5.3 meme on the practice of daily prayers

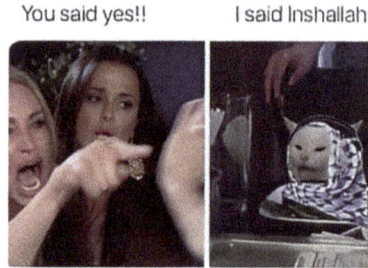

Fig. 5.4 meme on the use of religious phrases in daily discourse

Figure 5.1 portrays the challenges faced by a young Muslim whose religion prohibits dating, yet she still wants to attend the prom, so she goes alone. Figure 5.2 humorously describes Ramadan, the ninth month of the Islamic calendar, when Muslims fast, pray, reflect and spend time with their community. The meme compares Ramadan to *The Hunger Games*, a dystopian trilogy, using a scene featuring Donald Sutherland. In another example, Figure 5.3 plays on the phrase, "I didn't choose the rug life, rug life chose me", humorously referencing the five daily prayers observed by Muslims, adapted from rapper Tupac's famous line "I didn't choose the thug life, thug life chose me". Both memes in Figures 5.2 and 5.3 contain intertextual references to popular culture, offering a lighter, more humorous perspective on daily Muslim practices. Lastly, Figure 5.4 is an adaptation of the viral meme "Smudge Lord", where the popular cat meme faces a group of distressed women exclaiming "you said yes". The cat, donning a traditional keffiyeh (a semiotic symbol signifying the cat as Muslim), replies, "I said 'Inshallah'" (God willing), a common phrase Muslims use to emphasise that our lives are governed by God's will, not human decisions. All these memes attempt to counteract common negative stereotypes, prototypically expressed in hate speech, by reframing them positively through humorous engagement with memes.

Meta-communicative strategy of Direct Rebuttal: Muslim women

Islamophobic memes targeting Muslim women typically follow two patterns: either portraying them as passive victims of Muslim men or religion, or as active participants, depicted as terrorists or mothers of future terrorists (Aguilera-Carnerero and Tegal 2023). Oppression of Muslim women is often visually equated with the use of veils (hijab, niqab, or burqa), and in numerous cases, women are dehumanised by drawing visual analogies between them and inanimate objects such as garbage bags, umbrellas, egg crates, letterboxes, or saltshakers, based on their physical appearance.

Dehumanisation in Islamophobic memes frequently comes in the form of humour. The latter serves as a rhetorical device to denigrate 'the Other' (Muslim women) and to recruit like-minded supporters (recipients), reinforcing ingroup identity. As Hakoköngäs et al. (2020) argue, "when used by extreme groups, the humour seems to acquire a form of bitter irony, which actually brings a persuasive dimension to the joking". Similar rhetorical strategies have been observed in studies on the Ku Klux Klan (Billig 2001), racism (Yoon 2016), and the Palestine-Israel conflict (Gal 2019).

Fig. 5.5 meme that mocks the idea of Muslim women's oppression

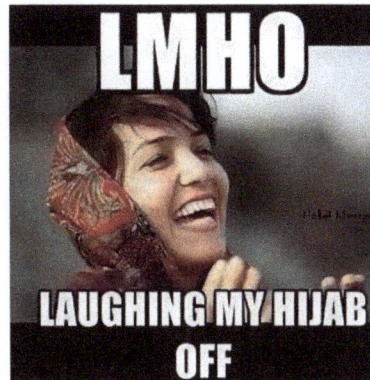

Fig. 5.6 meme subverting the idea that the veil implies submission

Memes in the corpus subvert these stereotypes and disprove them by mocking the idea of 'oppression'. For example, Figure 5.5 shows a young Muslim woman stylishly flipping up her coat collar while wearing trendy sunglasses, and Figure 5.6 specifically satirises the idea that wearing a hijab is a sign of submission by using a pun on the well-known Internet acronym LMAO (laughing my ass off), replacing the letter A in the acronym with the letter H (Hijab).

Figures 5.5 and 5.6 are examples of image macros. This type of meme combines a stock image with a superimposed text, usually distributed at the top and bottom of the image. The top text is a statement, while the bottom text delivers the punchline (or disjunctor), creating a humorous switch from the setup (Grundligh 2017).

Meta-communicative strategy of Empowerment: the media

A widely discussed contemporary issue related to hate speech is the treatment of Muslims in the media. This has often manifested as Islamophobia,[5] a neologism that refers to irrational hostility toward Muslims and Islam. This phenomenon is on the rise (Farokhi 2021), with Muslims increasingly cast as the global 'Other'. With the advent of the internet, cyber-Islamophobia has seen significant growth (Awan 2012; Larsson 2007), as digital spaces have become a platform for spreading such rhetoric. Islamophobic content primarily circulates through blogs, social media, and even traditional media outlets with an online presence. Henzell-Thomas from the Forum Against Islamophobia and Racism (FAIR) pointed out as early as 2001 that digital communication was becoming a rich source of Islamophobic utterances. The Online Hate Prevention Institute of Australia (2013) stated that online Islamophobia is not just an attack on the Muslim community, but on society at large.

---

5   The concept gained prominence in 1996 after the Runnymede Trust established the Commission on British Muslims. The usage of the term peaked in the aftermath of the 9/11 attacks and the subsequent War on Terror, becoming a central topic in many academic debates. The term is multifaceted and "groups together all kinds of different forms of discourse, speech and acts, by suggesting that they all emanate from an identical ideological core, which is an 'irrational fear' (a phobia) of Islam" (Maussen 2006).

One of the primary dangers of online Islamophobia and online hate speech in general is the normalisation of hate speech, making hostility toward Muslims appear acceptable. As such, Islamophobia is often intertwined with racism (Pintak et al. 2021: 4) which explains the frequently used alternative term, anti-Muslim racism. Islamophobic discourse on platforms like X/Twitter does not arise in isolation; it is the product of an interconnected ecosystem of influencers (Pintak et al. 2021: 4).

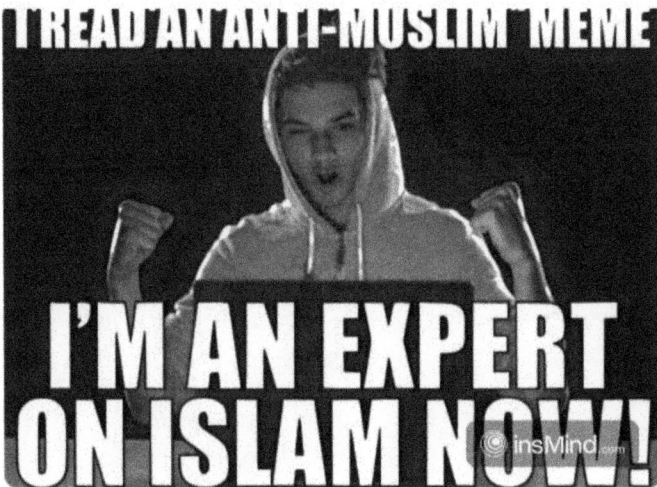

Fig. 5.7 satirical meme on Islam Internet experts

Memes play a key role in constructing identity and community cohesion, which is essential for defining the ingroup and outgroup—an aspect that is closely linked to humour. The audience must be familiar with racist tropes to understand the inside joke (Milner 2013). Topinka (2017) argues that humour creates distance from potentially offensive content while establishing a community of insiders able to grasp the political message beyond the joke. Memes are thus used to reinforce social bonds, rather than merely share information, solidifying the ingroup through the mockery of others (Zappavigna 2012). The satirical stance of the image macro in Figure 5.7, for example, depicts a young man in front of a computer celebrating the fact that reading an anti-Muslim meme makes him an "expert" on Islam. The meme parodies and critiques

Islamophobic media discourse through an ironic-satirical reversal, aiming to foster a sense of hope and cohesion among those targeted by such discourse.

As Gray et al. (2009: 11) point out, the main tenet of satire is "the ability to produce social scorn or damning indictments through playful means, and in the process, transform the aggressive act of ridicule into the more socially acceptable act of rendering something ridiculous". Greene (2019) further argues that satire has been a gateway for spreading hate and extremism from the margins to the mainstream. Humour and satire can push Islamophobic discourse while simultaneously strengthening the sense of community within Islamophiliac groups. Although memes spread on a micro level (person-to-person), their impact is felt on a macro scale (social groups): "like many Web 2.0 applications, memes diffuse from person to person, but shape and reflect general social mindsets" (Shifman 2014: 4). Thus, memes offer discursive potential for constituting certain realities, acting as tools for counter-speech strategies. They can influence social discourses and simultaneously serve as expressions of those discourses.

Conclusion

Previous studies have shown that Islamophobic memes largely echo the tropes previously identified in previous analyses of mainstream and new media (Whittaker 2002; Akbarzadeh and Smith 2005; Moore et al. 2008; Dahinden et al. 2011; Baker et al. 2013; Larsson 2007; Awan 2012; Aguilera-Carnerero and Azeez 2016). Islam is often portrayed as an ideology of destruction, and Muslims are stereotyped as extremely violent, constantly associated with acts of terrorism, driven by irrational beliefs, sexually unrestrained, and unable or resistant to integrating into Western societies. Muslim women are portrayed ambivalently: either as aggressive as their male counterparts or as victims of oppression, defined either by their faith or a dominant patriarchy, but always confined within their garments.

Although our corpus is limited, it seeks to challenge these tropes by using different meta-communicative strategies to counter hate speech, employing humour to share Muslim reality and allow citizens to encounter the Muslim world directly, without the filter of media bias. In this way, memes introduce new nuances to the dissemination of anti-Muslim rhetoric, and the spread of anti-Muslim racism via memes represents an innovative shift. This is not to say that ethnic and discriminatory humour is a new phenomenon (Billig 2001), but memes bring racist narratives to people in a supposedly easier, more accessible manner, so ingrained in everyday life that their ideological impact is sometimes overlooked (Boegerts and Fielitz 2019; May and Feldman 2019; Askanius 2021). As Askanius (2021: 15) argues, memes have enabled this type of discourse to shift from "the fringes of society to more mainstream spaces and actors in an informal, daily environment", highlighting their significance as ideological tools.

What is original is that the same tools used by Islamophobes to promote Islamophobic attitudes are being used to reverse this narrative and share the Muslim reality through ridicule. While the mass consumption of Islamophobic discourse risks desensitising and legitimising hatred and violence, there is potential for the reverse effect through the spread of counter-Islamophobic memes.

Since our conclusions are context-dependent and cannot be generalised, further research is necessary. On the one hand, more data is required to refine the taxonomy and to explore the role of the audience (e.g. through comments and reactions to the content); on the other, we must also analyse how platforms and social media contribute to the spread of cyber-Islamophilia. Our chapter serves a starting point for investigating such a complex and multifaceted phenomenon.

References

Aguilera-Carnerero, Carmen and Abdul-Halik Azeez, 2016. "'Islamonausea, not Islamophobia': the many faces of cyberhate speech". *Journal of Arab and Muslim Media Research*, 9 (1), 21–40. https://doi.org/10.1386/jammr.9.1.21_1.

—, and Megara Tegal, 2023. "Multimodal Islamophobia. Gendered Stereotypes in memes". *Journal of Muslim and Media Research*, 16 (2), 201–222. https://doi.org/10.1386/jammr_00063_1

Akbarzadeh, Shahram and Bianca J. Smith, 2005. *The Representation of Islam and Muslims in the Media (The Age and Herald Newspapers).* Melbourne: Monash University.

Allport, Gordon W., 1954. *The Nature of Prejudice.* Cambridge: Addison-Wesley.

Assimakopoulos, Stavros, 2020. "Incitement to discriminatory hatred, illocution and perlocution". *Pragmatics & Society*, 11 (2), 177–195. https://doi.org/10.1075/ps.18071.ass?locatt=mode:legacy.

Askanius, Tina, 2021. "On Frogs, Monkeys, and Execution Memes: Exploring the Humour-Hate Nexus at the Intersection of Neo-Nazi and Alt-Right Movements in Sweden". *Television & New Media*, 22, 1–19. https://doi.org/10.1177/1527476420982234.

Awan, Imran, 2012. "'I'm a Muslim not an Extremist': How the prevent strategy has constructed a 'Suspect Community'". *Politics & Policy*, 40 (6), 1158–1185.

Baider, Fabienne, 2023. "Accountability Issues, Online Covert Hate Speech, and the Efficacy of Counter-Speech". *Politics and Governance*, 11 (2), 249–260, https://doi.org/10.17645/pag.v11i2.6465.

—, and Maria Constantinou, 2020. "Covert hate speech: A contrastive study of Greek and Greek Cypriot online discussions with an emphasis on irony". *Journal of Language Aggression and Conflict*, 8 (2), 262–287, https://doi.org/10.1075/jlac.00040.bai.

—, Sarah Millar and Stavros Assimakopoulos, 2020. "Introduction: Defining, performing and countering hate speech". *Pragmatics & Society*, 11 (2), 171–176. https://doi.org/10.1075/ps.11.2.01bai.

Baker, Paul, Costas Gabrielatos and Tony McEnery, 2013. "Sketching Muslims: A corpus driven analysis of representations around the word 'Muslim' in the British press 1998–2009". *Applied Linguistics*, 34 (3), 1–25. https://doi.org/10.1093/applin/ams048.

Becker, Matthias J., Hagen Troschke, Matthew Bolton and Alexis Chapelan (eds), 2024. *Decoding Antisemitism: A Guide to Identifying Antisemitism Online.* Cham/London: Springer Nature/Palgrave Macmillan, https://link.springer.com/book/9783031492372.

Benesch, Susan, 2016. "Considerations for Successful Counterspeech". Dangerous Speech Project. https://dangerousspeech.org/wp-content/uploads/2016/10/Considerations-for-Successful-Counterspeech.pdf.

Billig, Michael, 2001. "Humour and hatred: The racist jokes of the Ku Klux Klan". *Discourse & Society*, 12, 267–289. https://doi.org/10.1177%2F0957926

Boegerts, Lisa and Maik Fielitz, 2019. "'Do you Want Meme War?' Understanding the Visual memes of the German Far Right". In:

Maik Fielitz and Nick Thurston (eds), *Post-Digital Cultures of the Far Right. Online Actions and Offline Consequences in Europe and the US*. Bielefeld: Transcript, 137–154.

Breitenbach, Patrick, 2015. "Memes. Das Web als kultureller Nährboden". In: Patrick Breitenbach, Christian Stiegler, and Thomas Zorbach (eds), *New Media Culture. Mediale Phänomene der Netzkultur*. Bielefeld: Transcript, 29–49.

Brontsema, Rhiannon, 2004. "A Queer Revolution: Reconceptualizing the Debate Over Linguistic Reclamation". *Colorado Research in Linguistics*, 17 (1), 1–15.

Brown, Andrew, 2017. "What Is Hate Speech? Part 1: The Myth of Hate". *Law and Philosophy*, 36 (4), 419–468.

—, 2018. "What Is So Special About Online (as Compared to Offline) Hate Speech?" *Ethnicities*, 18 (3), 297–326. https://doi.org/10.1177/14687968177098.

CERD (United Nations, International Convention on the Elimination of All Forms of Racial Discrimination), 2013. *General Recommendation No. 35: Combating Racist Hate Speech*. https://www.refworld.org/legal/general/cerd/2013/en/101142.

Council of Europe, 1997. *Council of Europe's Committee of Ministers' Recommendation No. R (97) 20, of the Committee of Ministers to Member States on "Hate Speech"*. https://rm.coe.int/1680505d5b.

Crawford, Blyth, 2020. "The Influence of Memes in Far-Right Radicalisation". *CARR webpage*. https://www.radicalrightanalysis.com/2020/06/09/the-influence-of-memes-on-far-right-radicalisation/.

Dahinden, Urs, Carmen Koch, Vinzenz Wyss and Guido Keek, 2011. "Representation of Islam and Christianity In the Swiss Media". *Journal of Empirical Theology*, 24 (2), 197–208. https:// doi.org/10.1163/157092511X603983.

Davidson, Thomas, Dan Warmsley, Michael Macy and Ingmar Weber, 2017. "Automated Hate Speech Detection and the Problem of Offensive Language". *Proceedings of the 11th International Conference on Web and Social Media*. Palo Alto: AAAI Press, 512–515. https://doi.org/10.1609/icwsm.v11i1.14955.

Ebner, Julia, 2023. *Going Mainstream: How Extremists Are Taking Over*. London: Bonnier Books.

ECRI (European Commission Against Racism and Intolerance), 2016. *General Policy Recommendation No. 15 on Combating Hate Speech*. https://www.coe.int/en/web/european-commission-against-racism-and-intolerance/recommendation-no.15.

Erikson, Erik H., 1968. *Identity: Youth and Crisis.* New York: Norton & Company.

Ermida, Isabel (ed.), 2023. *Hate Speech in Social Media: Linguistic Approaches.* London: Palgrave Macmillan. https://doi.org/10.1007/978-3-031-38248-2.

Farokhi, Zeinab, 2021. "Cyber Homo Sacer: A Critical Analysis of Cyber Islamophobiain the Wake of the Muslim Ban". *Islamophobia Studies Journal,* 6 (1), 14–32.

Felder, Ekkehard, 2006. „Semantische Kämpfe in Wissensdomänen. Eine Einführung in Benennungs- Bedeutungs- und Sachverhaltsfixierungs-Konkurrenzen". In: Ekkehard Felder (ed.), *Semantische Kämpfe. Macht und Sprache in den Wissenschaften.* Berlin: De Gruyter, 13–46.

Fielitz, Maik and Nick Thurston (eds), 2019. *Post-Digital Cultures of the Far Right. Online Actions and Offline Consequences in Europe and the US.* Bielefeld: Transcript. https://ec.europa.eu/home-affairs/system/files/2021-03/ran_ad hoc_pap_fre_humor_20210215_en.pdf.

Gal, Noam, 2019. "Ironic humour on social media as participatory boundary work". *New Media & Society*, 21, 729–749. https://doi.org/10.1177%2F1461444818805719.

Garland, Joshua, Keyan Ghazi-Zahedi, Jean-Gabriel Young, Laurent Hébert-Dufresne and Mirta Galesic, 2022. "Impact and dynamics of hate and counter speech online". *EPJ Data Science*, 11, Article 3. https://doi.org/10.1140/epjds/s13688-021-00314-6.

Guillén-Nieto, Victoria, 2023. *Hate Speech: Linguistic Perspectives.* Berlin: De Gruyter.

Gray, Jonathan, Jeffrey P. Jones, and Ethan Thompson, 2009. "The state of satire, the satire of state". In: Jonathan Gray, Jeffrey P. Jones and Ethan Thompson (eds), *Satire TV: Politics and Comedy in the Post-Network Era.* New York: New York University Press, 3–36.

Greene, Viveka S., 2019. "'Deplorable' satire: Alt-right memes, white genocide tweets, and redpilling normies". *Studies in American Humor*, 5 (1), 31–69. https://muse.jhu.edu/article/720967.

Grundlingh, Lezandra, 2017. "Memes as speech acts". *Social Semiotics*, 28 (2), 147–168.

Hakoköngäs, Eemeli, Otto Halmesvaara and Inari Sakki, 2020. "Persuasion through bitter humour: Multimodal Discourse Analysis of Rhetoric in Internet Memes of Two far-right groups in Finland". *Social Media & Society*, 6 (2), 1–11. https://doi.org/10.1177/2056305120921575.

Hangartner, Dominik, Gloria Gennaro, Sary Alasiri and Nicholas Bahrich, 2021. "Empathy-based counterspeech can reduce racist hate speech in a social media field experiment". *Proc Natl Acad Sci USA*, 14; 118 (50), e2116310118. https://doi.org/10.1073/pnas.2116310118.

Henzell-Thomas, Jeremy. 2001. *The Language of Islamophobia*. Paper presented at the "Exploring Islamophobia" Conference at The University of Westminster School of Law, London, 29 September. http://www.masud.co.uk/ISLAM/misc/phobia.htm.

Iedema, Rick, 2003. "Multimodality, resemiotization: extending the analysis of discourse as multi-semiotic practice". *Visual Communication*, 2 (1), 29–57.

INACH (International Network Against Cyber Hate), 2024. "What is cyber hate and why do we want to counter it". https://www.inach.net/cyber-hate-definitions

Jakobson, Roman, 1960. "Linguistics and Poetics". In: Thomas A. Sebeok (ed.), *Style in Language*. Cambridge: MIT Press, 350–377.

Kelman, Herbert C., 1961. "Processes of Opinion Change". *Public Opinion Quarterly*, 25 (1), 57–78. https://doi.org/10.1086/266996.

Klug, Nina-Maria, 2023. "Verstehen auf den ersten Blick – oder doch nicht? Zur (vermeintlichen) Einfachheit kleiner Texte am Beispiel von Internet-Memes". In: Angela Schrott, Johanna Wolf, and Christine Pflüger (eds), *Textkomplexität und Textverstehen*. Berlin: De Gruyter, 195–230.

Knobel, Michele and Colin Lankshear, 2006. "Online memes, affinities and cultural production". In: Michele Knobel and Colin Lankshear (eds), *A New Literacy Sampler*. New York: Peter Lang, 199–227.

Kress, Gunther, 2010. *Multimodality: A Social Semiotic Approach to Contemporary Communication*. London: Routledge.

—, and Theo van Leeuwen, 2006 [1996]. Reading Images. The grammar of visual design. New York: Routledge.

Kunst, Marlene, Pablo Porten-Cheé, Martin Emmer and Christiane Eilders, 2021. "Do 'Good Citizens' fight hate speech online? Effects of solidarity citizenship norms on user responses to hate comments". *Journal of Information Technology & Politics*, 18 (3), 258–273. https://doi.org/10.1080/19331681.2020.1871149.

Larsson, Göran, 2007. "Cyber-Islamophobia? The case of WikiIslam". *Contemporary Islam*, 1 (1), 53–67. http://doi.org/10.1007/s11562-007-0002-2.

Matsuda, Mari J., 1989. "Public Response to Racist Speech. Considering the Victim's Story". *Michigan Law Review*, 87 (8), 2320-2381.

May, Rob and Matthew Feldman, 2019. "Understanding the Alt-Right. Ideologues, 'Lulz' and Hiding in Plain Sight". In: Maik Fielitz and Nick

Thurston (eds), *Post-Digital Cultures of the Far Right. Online Actions and Offline Consequences in Europe and the US*. Bielefeld: Transcript, 25199–22736.

Meibauer, Jörg, 2013. Hassrede – von der Sprache zur Politik. In: Meibauer, Jörg (ed.), 2013. Hassrede/Hate Speech: Interdisziplinäre Beiträge zu einer aktuellen Diskussion. Gießen: Gießener Elektronische Bibliothek, 1–15. https://jlupub.ub.uni-giessen.de/items/daa10781-24f6-4cc9-978d-caf8ec8feee8.

Meier, Stefan, 2014. *(Bild-)Diskurs im Netz. Konzept und Methode für eine semiotische Diskursanalyse im World Wide Web*. Köln: Halem.

Milner, Ryan M., 2013. "Media Lingua Franca: Fixity, Novelty, and Vernacular Creativity in Internet Memes". *AoIR Selected Papers of Internet Research*, 14.0. https://journals.uic.edu/ojs/index.php/spir/article/view/8725.

Moore, Kerry, Paul Mason and Justin Lewis, 2008. *The Representation of British Muslims in the National Print News Media 2000–2008*. Cardiff: Cardiff School of Journalism, Media, and Cultural Studies.

O'Driscoll, Joan, 2020. *Offensive Language: Taboo, Offence and Social Control*. London: Bloomsbury Publishing.

Özarslan, Mehmet, 2014. "Introducing two new terms into the literature of hate speech, 'hate discourse' and 'hate speech act': Application of speech act theory to hate speech studies in the era of web 2.0". Galatasaray Üniversitesi İletişim Dergisi, 20, 53–75.

Pintak, Lawrence, Brian J. Bowe, and Jonathan Albright, 2021. "Influencers, Amplifiers, and Icons: A Systematic Approach to Understanding the Roles of Islamophobic Actors on Twitter". *Journalism & Mass Communication Quarterly*, 99, 1–25.

Saha, Punyajoy, Kiran Garimellab, Narla Komal Kalyana, Saurabh Kumar Pandeya, Pauras Mangesh Mehera, Binny Mathewa, and Animesh Mukherjee, 2023. "On the rise of fear speech in online social media". *arXiv*. https://arxiv.org/pdf/2303.10311.

Schäfer, Johannes and Elina Kistner, 2023. *HS-EMO: Analyzing emotions in hate speech. Proceedings of the 19th Conference on Natural Language Processing (KONVENS 2023)*. Association for Computational Linguistics, 165–173. https://aclanthology.org/2023.konvens-main.17.pdf.

Schäfer, Svenja, Isabella Rebasso, Ming M. Boyer and Anna M. Planitzer, 2024. "Can We Counteract Hate? Effects of Online Hate Speech and Counter Speech on the Perception of Social Groups". *Communication Research*, 51 (5), 553–579. https://doi.org/10.1177/00936502231201091.

Schulze, Heidi, Simon Greipl, Julian Hohner and Diana Rieger, 2022. "Zwischen Furcht und Feindseligkeit: Narrative Radikalisierungsangebote in Online-Gruppen". In: Uwe Kemmesies, Peter Wetzels, Beatrix Austin, Christian Buscher, Axel Dessecker, Sven Hutter and Diana Rieger (eds), *Motra-Monitor 2022*. Wiesbaden: MOTRA Bundeskriminalamt – Forschungsstelle Terrorismus/ Extremismus, 40–67.

Schwarz-Friesel, Monika, 2021. *Sprache und Emotion: Psycholinguistische Perspektiven*. 2nd updated and expanded edn. Stuttgart: UTB.

Segev, Elad, Asaf Nisenbaum, Solero Solero and Limor Shifman, 2015. "Families and Networks of Internet Memes: The Relationship between Cohesiveness, Uniqueness, and Quiddity Concreteness". *Journal of Computer-Mediated Communication*, 20 (4), 417–433.

Shifman, Limor, 2014. *Memes in Digital Culture*. Cambridge: MIT Press.

Silva, Cláudia, 2023. "Fighting Against Hate Speech: A Case for Harnessing Interactive Digital Counter-Narratives". In: Lissa Holloway-Attaway and John T. Murray (eds), *Interactive Storytelling*. ICIDS 2023. Lecture Notes in Computer Science, vol 14383. Cham: Springer. https://doi.org/10.1007/978-3-031-47655-6_10.

Spitzmüller, Jürgen and Ingo Warnke, 2011. *Diskurslinguistik. Eine Einführung in Theorien und Methoden der transtextuellen Sprachanalyse*. Berlin: De Gruyter.

Sponholz, Liriam, 2023. "Counter Speech: Practices of Contradiction on Hate Speech and their Effects". In: Gisel Febel, Kerstin Knopf, and Martin Nonhoff (eds), *Contradiction Studies – Exploring the Field. Contradiction Studies*. Wiesbaden: Springer, 163–181. https://doi. org/10.1007/978-3-658-37784-7_5.

Toffler, Alvin, 1980. *The Third Wave*. New York: Bantam.

Topinka, Robert J., 2017. "Politically incorrect participatory media: Racist Nationalism on r/Imgoingtohellforthis". *New Media & Society*, 20 (5), 2050–2069.

UNESCO, 2021. "Education as a tool for prevention: addressing and countering hate speech, Expert meeting: 13-18 May 2020". https:// unesdoc.unesco.org/ark:/48223/pf0000379146.

UNESCO, 2023. "Addressing hate speech through education: A guide for policy makers". https://www.unesco.org/en/articles/ addressing-hate-speech-through-education-guide-policy-makers.

Van Eerten, Jan-Jaap and Bertjan Doosje, 2019. *Challenging Extremist Views on Social Media: Developing a Counter-Messaging Response*. London: Routledge. https://doi.org/10.4324/9780429287145.

Warner, Michael and Julia Hirschberg, 2012. "Detecting Hate Speech on the World Wide Web". *Proceedings of the Second Workshop on Language in Social Media*. Montreal: Association for Computational Linguistics, 19–26. https://aclanthology.org/W12-2103.pdf.

Whittaker, Brian, 2002. "Islam and the British press after 9/11". https://al-bab.com/ (full link to article no longer available).

Wiggins, Bradley E., 2019. *The Discourse Power of Memes in Digital Culture. Ideology, Semiotics and Intertextuality*. London: Routledge.

Wodak, Ruth, 2015. *The Politics of Fear: What Right-Wing Populist Discourses Mean*. Los Angeles: Sage.

Yoon, Injeong, 2016. Why is it not a joke? Analysis of Internet memes associated with racism and hidden ideology of colourblindness. *Journal of Cultural Research in Art Education*, 33, 92–123.

Zapata, Jimena, Justin Sulik, Clemens von Wulffen and Ophelia Deroy, 2024. "Bystanders' collective responses set the norm against hate speech". *Humanit Soc Sci Commun*, 11 (335). https://doi.org/10.1057/s41599-024-02761-8.

Zappavigna, Michele, 2012. *Discourse of Twitter and Social Media. How We Use Language to Create Affiliation on the Web*. London/New York: Continuum.

6. Memefication of antisemitism: Antisemitic content on TikTok—a multimodal ethnographic analysis

Mohamed Salhi and Yasmine Goldhorn

Abstract

TikTok, currently the largest social media platform, is a breeding ground for various forms and types of hate speech, including antisemitism. This chapter addresses and analyses the concealment and survival of antisemitic content on TikTok through encoded semiotic, multimodal resources as a challenge to the existing regulations against hate speech on social media platforms. The article analyses the strategic concealment of antisemitic language as deployed in posts (i.e. memes and visual humour) and comments on TikTok, and suggests that antisemitic content is concealed using encrypted, multi-layered, and suggestive language (i.e. dog whistles) in both textual and symbolic forms. Moreover, this chapter surveys a significant array of semiotic modes, including textual, iconographic, visual, and auditory resources to examine the strategically, and seemingly 'humorous,' 'memetic,' and 'creative' ways of producing and maintaining antisemitic content. The memefication of antisemitic content, this chapter further argues, contributes to the concealment, banalisation, and normalisation of exclusion of and hatred against Jews. To systematically survey and analyse encoded antisemitism in TikTok memes and understand its primary trends, means of survival, and the banalisation of hate, this

https://doi.org/10.11647/OBP.0447.06

chapter employs mixed methods of Multimodal Discourse Analysis (MMDA) and Online Ethnography.[1]

Keywords: *Antisemitism, hate speech, TikTok, memes, humour, dog whistles, Memetic Vernacular*

Introduction

For many, the expressions "have a totally joyful day" and "a nice day" sound, *prima facie*, like friendly greetings. For a niche group of users, nonetheless, these are part of a large body of alternative semiotic resources deployed to express resentment and hatred against minorities in a rather joyful manner, without breaking laws and regulations regarding hate speech online (i.e. they are dog whistles). Such expressions, among many others, found their way to TikTok and social media platforms, and created an 'underground' hate-speech space that fosters violent and hate speech against Jews and other minorities.

TikTok defends itself against claims that it fosters and fuels antisemitism, and it argues that it is actively removing content that promotes exclusionary and hateful ideologies, including antisemitism (New York Times 2023). Despite such claims from the social media platform, antisemitism, among other forms of hate discourses and ideologies, has been a subject of multiple research projects over the past few years. Previous research on TikTok's accommodation of antisemitism indicates the deployment of, among other things, the denial of the Holocaust and conspiracy theories regarding Jewish control of the world (Weimann and Masri 2022: 173–5; see also Hauser and Janáčová 2020 for a detailed

---

1   During the course of conducting this research, many of the antisemitic expressions and resources have been banned from TikTok, particularly after the surge of antisemitic content following the attacks on 7 October 2023 and the following events. After receiving an open letter (https://www.deartiktok.com) asking TikTok to do more to protect Jewish users against rising antisemitism, TikTok declared that they made an additional effort to delete content violating their rules on hateful behaviour and therefore globally removed 730,000 videos between 7 October and 31 October 2023 (TikTok 2023).

analysis of visual antisemitism in Central Europe, and Hübscher and von Mering 2022 for a discussion on antisemitism on social media).

In this context, this chapter targets a niche, yet increasingly relevant communication mode on TikTok used to reinforce antisemitism online. Content makers of different ideological and/or political grounds (e.g. alt-right, hyper-nationalism) pursue similar approaches to share antisemitic discourse, largely through memetic, encoded language. In doing so, this content deploys and adapts its semiotic modes (i.e. textual, visual, iconographic, and auditory) to pursue a discursive strategy of concealment of what is generally considered illegal—both rhetorically, as memes convey political ideologies, and practically, as Nazi and antisemitic resources lead to possible censorship. As a result, antisemitic discourse on TikTok mutates to circumvent legal and organisational restrictions on social media apps (if any). The memefication of antisemitism, or the use of memes to express antisemitic sentiments, this chapter argues, renders hate and violence speech into a matter of humour, therefore normalises antisemitism online, and potentially offline.

To explore, survey, and analyse how antisemitism operates rhetorically on TikTok, a mixed-methods approach is pursued using digital ethnography to observe discursive trends and collect data, and multimodal discourse analysis to analyse the nature and functions of different semiotic modes. This methodological framework is suited for our research, since antisemitism is a phenomenon that has changed throughout history and always adapted to current political or societal realities (Messerschmidt 2010: 91). In regard to the adaptive nature of antisemitism, we use the relatively open working definition of the International Holocaust Remembrance Alliance, which states that "antisemitism is a certain perception of Jews, which may be expressed as hatred toward Jews. Rhetorical and physical manifestations of antisemitism are directed toward Jewish or non-Jewish individuals and/or their property, toward Jewish community institutions and religious facilities" (IHRA 2016). Using an inductive research method and an open definition of antisemitism, we try to understand the field-specific logic of the spread of antisemitism within digital culture on TikTok or how the alt-right scene uses new media to extend the spread of their ideologies.

Encrypted, multilayered language

Hate speech can take many shapes and forms, including "subtle as not to be obviously abusive or insulting" (Parekh 2012: 40). In this sense, the abusive, insulting, and angry form of hate speech does not necessarily need to be expressed explicitly, but rather shown through "ambiguous jokes, innuendoes, and images", rendering its form rather bland and subtle (ibid.: 41). In the context of antisemitism, for instance, the denial of the Holocaust, given the laws and regulations censoring this, has turned to expressions of an academic nature in order to "disguise" antisemitic propaganda such as questioning the extermination of Jews (Suk 2012: 159).

In the internet realm, the subtlety of hate speech fulfils multiple functions. Moreover, the mutual secrecy of encrypted language (e.g. dog whistles and cryptic messaging) arguably gives a sense of reality to movements such as the alt-right and to the "digital soldiers" that subscribe to it (Brandeis Magazine 2022); it also assists in these movements avoiding and surviving censorship (Donovan et al 2019: 54, Bhat and Klein 2020: 152); and signals the ideological, political, or cultural identifications of users (Bhat and Klein 2020: 162). Hence, although social media provides the opportunity to share hate ideologies more publicly than ever before (Strick 2021: 17), users have learned how to adapt to platform restrictions (when necessary) and use multi-layered language and symbols to evade the banning of their content.

The symbolic and iconographic resources of extremist movements (e.g. white supremacy, the alt-right, the radical right) have long been subject to scrutiny by academic and other entities including, among others, the Federal Office for the Protection of the Constitution, the Centre for Analysis of the Radical Right, the *Guardian*, and the *New York Times*.

To achieve the end of harming and hurting others, hate speech can be multifaceted—it can include harassment, humiliation, insults, and death wishes—and multilayered in the sense that it can be both overt and coated and coded (Guillén-Nieto 2023). Moreover, given its multilayered and multimodal character, hate speech requires expanding the linguistic analytical perspectives used to analyse it (ibid).

(Discriminatory) humour and hate speech

Jokes, above all, have always been "an important barometer of the attitude of a group" (Dundes and Hauschild 1983: 250). Humorous language has for too long been deployed to "mask and normalise hatred and bigotry" (Menon and Pratiksha 2023) and allows people to communicate contemptuous mockery against specific social actors "without fear of social sanctions" (Martin and Ford 2018: 36).

Based on readings of Sartre, Horkheimer, and Adorno, Billig (2021) points out the intrinsic connection between the world of jokes and that of political hatred (p. 268), a link approved also by, among others, Martin and Ford (2018: 217). In this respect, Weaver (2011) argued that racist jokes, given certain interpretation, uphold racist conceptions of truth, and convey and contribute to a sense of racist ambivalence (p. 416). Martin and Ford (2018), similarly, argue that discriminatory "disparagement humour" has calamitous social outcomes, including the delegitimisation of social groups subject to jokes by rendering them "acceptable targets for social denigration," enabling and normalising discriminatory attitudes against target groups within a given cultural context (p. 29).

The demonisation of Marie Antoinette in visual literature during the French Revolution, for instance, included a plethora of visual images grotesquely deforming the way she looked, including "pornographic aberrations" (Saint-Amand and Gage 1994: 393). The humorous, caricatured impersonation of Antoinette as a deformed freak led to the general conception of her as "pure disorder, as misfit, as a sexual monster, a divided individual, a figure of impropriety" (ibid), and as someone who rebelled against traditional norms and values (ibid). The aesthetics of the visual hatred expressed against Marie Antoinette were arguably repeated against Hillary Clinton during Bill Clinton's presidential campaign in 1993 (ibid.: 373). Pérez (2017) posits that racist or anti-ethnic humour and jokes also serve the social function of expressing racial or ethnic superiority. In this sense, racist or anti-ethnic humour reinforces racism through the perpetuation of societal racial or ethnic classifications, the presupposition of civic belonging (or lack thereof) based on such classifications, and the expression of superiority or inferiority based on racial or ethnic belonging (p. 963). In the context of antisemitism, too, jokes in Germany after World War II are argued to have dehumanised Jews and trivialised the Holocaust (Dundes and Hauschild 1983: 258). (For a literature review on exclusionary and discriminatory humour, see Pratiksha T. Menon, 2023a and 2023b). The mocking of accents, additionally, although generally overlooked by academic research (Bhatia 2018: 426) also offers a relevant theoretical background to this discussion. People who speak a language with a foreign accent rather than the dominant accent tend to be subjected to linguistic ridicule and insults (ibid). Discrimination against non-confirming accents is considered an "ego-cracking linguistic insult" (Kachru 1992 quoted in Bhatia 2018: 426).

Memes and memetic vernacular: Meanings, functions, and ideological practices

Memes can be defined in various, largely overlapping ways: as "user-generated media that share recognisable characteristics in content or form through which their creators seek to guide viewers' interactions and interpretations" and that are made to "go viral" (Greene 2019: 38), as "cultural information that pass[es] along from person to person, but gradually scale[s] into a shared social phenomenon" (Shifman 2014: 18), or as a "defined, iterated message that can be rapidly diffused by members of a participatory digital culture for the purpose of satire, parody, critique, or other discursive activity" (Wiggins 2019: 11). More importantly, memes represent a "short-hand tool for political communication online, as emblematic representation of world and images" (Önnerfors 2018), and 'bite-sized nuggets of political ideology' (DeCook 2018: 1). Their rhetorical expression of political ideology is rather "cunning", mainly due to memes being able to "conceal their status as persuasive texts" (Woods and Hahner 2019 quoted in Chevrette and Duerringer 2020: 256).

While memes agreeably refer to "artefacts" within a digital culture, this chapter deploys the notion of "memetic vernacular" to refer, rather loosely, to the way people talk and create knowledge with memes, or to the manner in which users express their ideas by adapting the logic, aesthetics, and humour of memes (Peck 2017: 7). In other words, memetic vernacular refers to the "casual" deployment (of parts of) memes in the phrasing of, among other things, comments, profiles, and captions.

In this respect, as a form of political dialogue, memes have the capacity to spark reactions and feelings in online users, generally laughter (Chevrette and Duerringer 2020: 256–7), and they have a foundational impact in shaping perceptions, behavioural patterns, and even group actions. This is particularly evident in the Web 2.0 era, where the rapid spread of memetic content across platforms such as Facebook and Instagram alter both media consumption patterns and social norms. Additionally, memes proliferate through imitation as easily remixable, mimicable, and shareable digital content, and through competition and selection as their degree of adaptiveness to their environment varies (Shifman 2013: 364–5/2014: 18).

Memes as an extension of a long tradition of political satire and humour foster solidarity within ingroups (as discursive communities and digital cultures) at the expense of an insulted, ridiculed, and distanced outgroup. Memes manipulate users, and discredit (political) opposition too (Greene 2019: 41–2). The 'Pepe the frog' meme, for instance, rose to fame before becoming a central emblematic symbol to alt-right, neo-Nazi groups for its representation of the condescending attitude of its users vis-à-vis political adversaries and social minorities (Miller-Idriss 2019: 127). Besides Pepe, many memes and memetic resources were appropriated by the far right, given new meanings, and circulated online (e.g. Finspång; see also Önnerfors 2018).

In this respect, the production of memes engages a process of understanding and interpretation, thus of "ideological formation"

(Wiggins 2019: 30). The analysis of the production of meaning through visual means, therefore, should be pursued through a semiotics lens, keeping in mind the intrinsic relationship between meaning-making processes and ideological practices (ibid: 31). To engage in this discussion, one must decipher memetic vernacular, requiring a degree of shared subcultural knowledge (ibid: 42) or literacy in the language accepted and used by individuals within a subculture (Milner 2012: 107).

Memes, humour, and the appropriation of youth culture have particularly been a success story for the alt right and its circulation and normalisation of racism and exclusion (Pérez 2022: 56; Strick 2021: 34). Being an almost exclusively digital and anonymous movement, the alt right "mastered the art of trolling" (Hawley 2017: 19). The use of humour, irony, and very specific jargon helps the alt-right trolls to shed the discourse of the older cohort of white nationalists, traditionally more bitter, aggressive, and offensive (ibid: 19–20). The attractiveness of memes to the younger online population lies in their capacity to co-opt and appropriate elements relevant to younger users (e.g. video games references), and in their ability to hide malicious and exclusionary slurs under a funny surface (Ebner 2019: 175).

Methodological considerations: Multimodal ethnographic analysis

The study of TikTok content is tricky, to say the least, primarily because of the absence of methodologies for systemic data collection and analysis. This chapter proposes an alternative route to explore and analyse antisemitism on TikTok, based on a mix of Multimodal Discourse Analyses (MMDA) and online ethnography. Such a mix provides the research approaches and tools to collect and analyse symbolic, multimodal resources that express, and make banal, hatred against Jews. In this respect, online ethnography, on the one hand, is deployed to explore antisemitic meme-making processes and outcomes on TikTok as digital culture, as a discursive community, and as a field of research. Multimodal Discourse Analysis, on the other hand, is deployed conceptually and methodologically to critically analyse the strategic concealment of antisemitic ideologies in perceivably harmless semiotic modes. In demystifying the concealment and reinforcement of antisemitism on TikTok, this chapter looks in depth into the subsequent banalisation of hatred against Jews through (visual) humour on social media.

Data collection: Online ethnography

The data collection for this chapter follows a digital ethnography approach. Digital ethnography is characterised as field observation with the online field as the object of analysis (Dellwing et al. 2021: 2). Following the shift from classical ethnography to online ethnography, the focus of analysis shifts from the physical to the online world, but the idea behind the method remains the same: The researcher tries to get as close to the lived reality as possible by engaging with the field to be studied, aiming to gain first-hand knowledge (Breidenstein et al. 2020: 38). Ethnographers study cultural practices that can be investigated, undertaking field observations of the everyday life within a culture; the term 'culture' does not have to refer to a population within national borders, but can refer to any subgroup of society with shared structures and meaning-making processes (Breidenstein et al. 2020: 36). The ethnographer dives into these cultural practices, becoming part of the culture during the period of study to understand its practices from within, but distancing one's self at the same time to theorise the observed textual and visual aspects from a scientist's perspective. For this purpose, the researcher must become familiar with the observed subject of research to analyse the logics of a field, especially when the ethnographer is investigating a subgroup of their own culture (Breidenstein et al. 2020: 109). Digital ethnography, which was initially criticised for its lack of face-to-face situations, has grown in popularity with the understanding that new technologies are now part of our everyday lives and the internet is now quite inseparable from the offline world—or as Christine Hine (2019: 19) describes it, "the E^3 internet [is an] embedded, embodied and everyday internet."

Because of the embeddedness of technology in our everyday lives, social scientists started using the term 'digital culture' to describe today's interaction between digital transformations and cultural conditions (Guy 2019: 56). At the same time, the term 'culture' highlights the widespread effects of digital technology that "involves a social dimension and therefore gets weaved into the functioning of social systems at all levels" (Guy 2019: 56), making ethnography the most suitable research method for investigating antisemitism on TikTok.

This approach allows us to navigate antisemitic trends and identify overt and concealed antisemitic statements and resources (i.e., auditory, visual, and textual). In other words, online ethnography grants the ability to observe the recurrent semiotic practices within a specific discourse community (or digital culture). In this case, online ethnography is used to locate the analyst within the broad antisemitic discourse community on TikTok. To get to this community, multiple keywords are used to access antisemitic content. Further content is found using the 'snowballing' method, mainly by accessing suggested search phrases.

Data analysis: Multimodal Discourse Analysis (MMDA)

Multimodality refers primarily to the deployment of multiple semiotic modes, such as aural, visual, and graphic components (Canale 2023: 9), in the production of a semiotic product, and the manner in which these modes are combined to form material forms or media (Kress and van Leeuwen 2001: 20). The combination of different semiotic modes can be a matter of mutual reinforcement, complementarity, or hierarchical organisation (ibid). Multimodal research, therefore, refers primarily to the pursuit of empirical research into data that involves multiple "modes" (Pflaeging et al. 2021: 10) and concerns itself generally with interpretive and explanatory approaches to the study of small-scale data (ibid.: 3). The need to study multimodal discourses stems from both the multimodal character of discourse and from the increasingly relevant "new" modes of communication and forms of discourse, enabled mainly by the internet (LeVine and Scollon 2004: 3). The distinction between modes and media is crucial to the analysis of memetic content on TikTok. Media is the set of observable elements in the digital research field (in this case, posts and memes) which mobilise a set of co-occurring meaning-making modes (Dicks et al. 2006: 82).

Multimodality departs from the idea that meaning is made once, at the moment of utterance. It stipulates that meaning is made through multimodal semiotic resources in multiple articulations— "in any and every sign, at every level, and in any mode" (Kress and Leeuwen 2001: 4). Moreover, the analysis of multimodal resources requires coverage of four main elements: firstly, discourse as a context-bound, socially constructed knowledge of reality or parts of it; secondly, design as the "conceptual side of expression," or the manner in which semiotic resources are used in different semiotic modes—in this sense, they are the (abstract) means through which discourse is realised in communication; thirdly, production as the "material articulation of the semiotic event"; and fourthly, distribution of semiotic artefacts to consumption (ibid.: 4–7; 21–22). MMDA, beyond its capacity to capture meaning-making processes beyond linguistic utterances, covers questions of power and ideology, which are important to the analysis of antisemitic content on TikTok. Signs carry ideological baggage, and realise the producer's cultural, social, and political positions (Kress 1993: 174). In this respect, language use is not solely a communication vehicle but constitutes "means of social construction and domination" (Machin and Mayr 2012: 23).

Moreover, this chapter, using participant-observation methods, attempts to identify antisemitic semiotic trends on TikTok, as well as their functions and roles in establishing exclusionary boundaries and maintaining hate speech. MMDA concerns itself with the strategic deployment of multimodal semiotic elements. This chapter unearths and explains humorous posts and memes on TikTok, with a particular focus on the following semiotic modes: the visual, including imagery, videos, and icons; textual, including explicit and implicit utterances (i.e. dog whistles), as well as typography (e.g. fonts, writing), which in itself constitutes a semiotic mode (Van Leeuwen 2004: 14); and the auditory, including sounds, speeches, and music meant to identify subjects of the multimodal resource, to provide context or feeling, or to enhance the meaning intended in the post. The auditory sources (mainly in terms of songs) also fulfil a "sound-surfing" purpose, defined as the deployment of (trendy) sounds as means to reach higher visibility on the platform (Bainotti et al. 2022: 3).

The relationship between ethnographic research and (critical) discourse analysis is an intricate one as each can fulfil different objectives. However, many common points can also be identified. These include, for instance, adopting an ethnographic perspective to meaning making, viewing discourse "as a situated practice which is shaped by—and at the same time shapes—situational, cultural, political, and historical conditions" (Canale 2023: 17–18). In other words, this chapter adopts tools from digital ethnography to analyse meaning-making processes as reflected in multiple 'novel' semiotic modes, and to analyse the discursive social, cultural, and ideological implications of such discourses. The mixing of the two, subject to academic debate (ibid.: 19), assists in analysing the 'antisemitic side of TikTok' as a digital culture and a discursive community, and how antisemitism is communicated on the platform, particularly using humour. (For previous research using this combination, see for instance Canale 2023, Gabrielli and Pàmies Rovira 2023).

In more practical terms, digital ethnography tools used in this chapter consist of participant observation of antisemitic memetic posts and the reactions they generate, particularly how they deploy various semiotic modes in their ideological humorous articulations (or in their use of media). Modes and media and their relationship in this process are central theoretical underpinnings offered by Multimodal Discourse Analysis. Moreover, this chapter examines antisemitic TikTok posts using ubiquitous expressions that reflect antisemitic sentiments (e.g. Now Yuo [sic] See, Every Single Time) as entry keywords to the research digital field, then follows the postings in different spaces under commonly used expressions, hashtags, and sounds. Once a field has become more or less visible, a process of data collection of posts and comments takes place. Data analysis follows by investigating TikTok memes and comments (i.e. media) and the most recurrent semiotic modes they use (i.e. visual, textual, auditory, and iconographic).

Findings: Memetic, humorous antisemitism on TikTok

The systemic analysis of the collected data posted on TikTok in the period between January 2022 and November 2023 reveals that antisemitic content thrives on the platform using largely, although not exclusively, memetic and humorous language, including a variety of multimodal semiotic resources (i.e. textual, visual, iconographic, and auditory). Within TikTok's antisemitic sphere, moreover, four consistent trends are found to be highly recurrent: stereotypical and essentialist representations of Jews (including the deployment and reinforcement of conspiracy theories), romanticisation of Nazi ideology and aesthetics, the trivialisation, relativisation, celebration, and denial of the Holocaust, and calls for violence against Jews. The deployment of memes, memetic vernacular, and multimodal semiotic resources, on the other hand, fulfils three major functions: concealment of blatant and brutal hate speech in humour and alternative semiotic modes, the banalisation of hate and violence, and the marking of identity and belonging.

In the next section, this chapter analyses the use of memes, memetic vernacular, and encoded language to produce and maintain antisemitic content, and surveys the most recurrent trends in memetic antisemitism on TikTok, then proceeds to analyse the functions and roles of such humorous and encoded language in the production and maintenance of hate speech on social media.

Trends in TikTok's antisemitic sphere

Upon a critical examination of the antisemitic content posted on TikTok in the period between January 2022 and November 2023, as expressed using the various semiotic resources, four recurrent and central themes are found. These themes are not always separate from each other in posts or comments but are also found simultaneously in the same content. They are the following:

1. Essentialist representations of Jews: Based on and reinforcing stereotypical representation of Jews, physically and morally. The representations of Jews also includes conspiracy theories, which revolve largely around the conception that Jews control the world or certain aspects of it (i.e. banks, media, forced migration towards Europe, and non-normative gender identities).

2. Romanticisation of Nazism, the Nazi regime, and Nazi individuals: Both as part of the antisemitic rhetoric or on its own, the romanticisation of the Nazi era, its ideologies, and aesthetics (e.g. weaponry, uniforms).

3. Trivialisation, celebration, relativisation, and denial of the Holocaust: Antisemitic content includes the celebration of the Holocaust (as an event), relativisation of its scale, and denial of its occurrence. Closely related, calls for violence against and extermination of Jews take place, largely using Holocaust-related ideas.

Essentialist representations of Jews, conspiracy theories, and calls for violence

Essentialist representations of Jews form a recurrent trend in antisemitic memetic posts and comments on TikTok. In surveying and analysing the representation of Jews, several semiotic resources appear to be used in antisemitic memes and posts. The semiotic resources (presented in the table below) are complementary as they contribute to the global meaning of the posts.

The auditory resources in videos and memes generally have the function of determining or emphasising the theme of, and/or add up to the humour in the post or the meme. The most recurrent auditory resource is *Hava Nagila* (sometimes edited), and it is deployed as a direct soundtrack of the theme of the post or meme, mainly antisemitic jokes. Other auditory resources used regularly by posters include condescending elements such as mocking imitations of a Jewish accent, pronunciation, pitch, and phonetics (e.g. "Hello Goyim, my name is Schlomo Sheckelbergstein" in a high pitch and with a Yiddish accent); extracts with seemingly extreme statements by Jewish people (e.g. "How can I not be happy, when I see millions of Goyim bowing down to one Jew (Jesus)" by Rabbi Mizrachi, "Shame on the Goyim" by an unknown Jewish person); or soundbites remixed into music (e.g. "well well well"). It is also worth noting that these resources, which function generally as a soundtrack for antisemitic content, are also present in other trends such as the trivialisation of the Holocaust, racial discrimination, and Islamophobia, and are also appropriated by Jewish content makers or used for unrelated content.

Secondly, the textual resources are abundant, including recurrent expressions and wordplay from popular and alt-right culture. These expressions, although used collectively, are effectively dog whistles used to communicate specific ideas based on a certain degree of shared knowledge, and to avoid expressing antisemitic ideas more directly (in order to avoid censorship). In both cases, the ubiquitous expressions tend to express a sense of predictability of Jewish character or behavior (e.g., essentialist representations such as greed) and enlightenment (i.e., finding out hidden actions and motives of Jews, including conspiracy theories). Similarly, posts by Jewish content makers attract a cascade of comments using the same expressions (or frequently a modified version of them). In this case, commenters foreground Jewishness of the post and poster as a central target to denigration, linking it to conspiracy theories and essentialist representations.

On the one hand, both the sarcastic epizeuxis "well well well" and "like a moth to the flames" originate as appropriations of Uncle Ruckus' racist outbursts in the animated show *The Boondocks*. The two expressions are very clear instances of how the internet expresses the correlation between a certain people and their stereotypes, and, to a certain extent, the conspiracy theories about them (for instance Jews and, among other supposed characteristics, being money-grabbing or controlling the world). On the other hand, the expressions "Now yuo see" and "every single time" are expressions rooted in the online culture of the alt-right movement, and express a sense of enlightenment, largely when a post or meme presents conspiracy theories involving Jews (e.g. that they control banks and the media). Similar examples of such wordplay include, for instance, "As jewsual".

These expressions are not only used in their original forms, but are often remixed for comedic purposes, and/or to conceal antisemitic ideas even further (essentially to avoid possible bans by the platform). The modification on the epizeuxis "Well Well Well" for instance occur in a variety of ways: homonyms (e.g. whale, we'll, will), including emojis (whale or a well emoji) or special characters (e.g. w€ll, w3ll); translations (e.g. bien, bene); remixing (e.g., attaching suffixes of typically Jewish names to memetic references, e.g., Wellstein Wellmann Wellberg); and replacing the words entirely with other relevant ones (emphasis on the epizeuxis form, e.g., heil, heil, heil). The concealment of references to Jews also includes a comical alteration of some words such as Joos, Jooz, Jooish, Jude (in English sentences), J's, and J**s, analogies or metaphors such as Goblins, and playful remixing of multiple memetic resources (e.g. [never lose your smile]+[now yuo [sic] see]+[money] > never lose yuor money).

The iconographic resources deployed in antisemitic posts or comments tend to be deployed as alternatives to words or expressions for comedic and/or concealment purposes. In this respect, emojis are used to refer to Jews (i.e. Juice emoji, Star of David, or Israeli flag), or to essentialist representations of Jews (e.g. Pinocchio emoji as a big nose/lying reference). On the other hand, there is a plethora of visual references. Two general categories can be identified: visual references to the Jews themselves (or to their physical appearance) and explanatory resources to prove conspiracy theories (as slide presentation, frequently includes other visual and iconographic references). The visual references to the physical appearance of Jews tends to be comical. For instance, the Happy Merchant and Jewish Wojak or Goblins revolve around foregrounding and emphasising essentialist conceptions of the physical and moral outlook of Jews, while goblins reflect a process of dehumanisation. The table below summarises our findings:

Table 6.1 Semiotic resources used in the essentialist representations
of Jews on TikTok (01/2022–11/2023)

Type	Genre	Modal Resources	Function
Auditory	Edits/Music	Songs (e.g. *Hava Nagila*), including edited versions. Speeches (edited) e.g. Rabbi Yosef Mizrachi, "Shame on the Goyim" and comedic imitation of Jews ("my name is Shlomo Sheckelbergstein")	Provides auditory structure to the post/meme or assists in emphasising the theme or meaning of the post/meme.
Textual	Popular Culture References	Well well well, Like a moth to the flames	In response to posts that address or present essentialist representations of Jews. Used to express inevitability of stereotypical behaviors (and sometimes conspiracy theories).
	Conspiracy Theories / Alt-Right Catchphrases	Enlightenment conspiracy theories: Now yuo see, Every single time, 109, (Oy vey) Shut it down, The goyim knows Destructive actions: spreading corruption, encouraging the decline of white people by importing immigrants, supporting wokeness, control over Hollywood, media, and banks	(Alt-right) expressions as response to posts claiming aspects of conspiracy theories. Refer to sense of enlightenment (i.e. finding the truth). The 109 number references the theory that Jews were expelled from 109 countries throughout history and is often used without any additional explanations. E.g. @CulturaEuropa: Do you think Germany just woke up one day and hated J's? They have a historical record of doing this, no other race gets kicked out of 109 countries.

	Hebrew/ Yiddish Terminology	Oy vey, Goy, Goyim, Shalom, Scheckel	Words/expressions in Hebrew are used (sometimes out of context) as an allusion to the Jews, either to highlight the subject of the meme, or as an implicit confirmation of someone else's essentialist utterance. E.g. BearOfRussia: oi vey goyim you aren't meant to point it out now give me shekels 🙏
	Names/ Expressions	Joos, Jooish, J's, J**s, Goblins	Replaced references to Jews with comically written homonyms or metaphorical references to avoid detection by the algorithm. E.g. @steakydrip: if theres one thing that unites everyone, its hating the goblins.
		((())) / Triple brackets	(Alt-right) encoded expression used briefly to automatically detect and encircle Jewish names in triple brackets to signify the effect of Jews. In this case, empty triple brackets are generally used as reference to Jewish people instead. Other references include: (((them))), (((They))), (((nose emoji))), (((Capitalists)))
	Additional Nominations	Cancer, evil, paedophile, Satan, Satanic, corrupt	Additional nominations, predications, and metaphors include, among others "cancer" and "mafia". E.g. @qbix365: Now you know why the moustache man did what he did. The cancer and the evil is real. 😏😏😏 Goodluck humanity E.g. @chad95941: the divide and conquer agenda in full effect. the corrupt satanic pedophiles that run the world thank you for not thinking for yourselves

Visual	Representation	Facial characteristics (The Happy Merchant, Phenotype Human Meme), visual metaphors (Goblins)	Visual representations are used to 1) portray Jews in a comedic, banal light, 2) enforce social Darwinist perspectives to justify a social order (i.e. Aryan/European people as superior).
		Behavioural characteristics (Money-grabbing, controlling the world)	Visual representation of 'Jewish behaviour' as money-loving or money-grabbing, malevolent...etc.
		Conspiracy theories (e.g. infographics, historical evidence)	Posts tend to be made as presentation slides, including infographics, quotes, historical evidence.
	Iconography	Emojis that refer to Jews (e.g. Star of David, Pinocchio emoji, Juicebox emoji)	To avoid direct use of the word Jews, alternative iconographic resources are deployed. For instance, the Juicebox emoji draws on the homonym (Jews and Juice), while the Pinocchio emojis draws on the 'long nose' and lying tropes. Other emojis include worms, roaches, and snakes.

Examples: Antisemitic memetic references and concealment

This examples section presents three selected cases as representative of how semiosis is produced in memetic (trolling, shitposting) environments, particularly using different semiotic modes. The first example is an antisemitic post by @trol1080alt (19.09.23) that expresses the conspiracy theory that Jews purposefully facilitate immigration to Europe and the United States. The post generated several comments (37 comments as of 12.12.23), all of which are flagrantly antisemitic. As expected, given that the post reinforces conspiracy theories, comments include references to the "well well well" phrase expressed collectively. In this example, the first "well" could be considered an ellipsis (i.e. the rest is understood from its contextual settings). The following replies contribute to expressing the full sound bite. If we consider the epizeuxis to be automatically signalled as hate speech, the collective approach avoids it.

Fig. 6.1 Collectively produced dog whistle under an antisemitic post (22.09.2023, https://www.tiktok.com/@trol1080alt/video/7280595155529370888).

The following comment section reflects some of the most recurrent references to Jews. These include deployment of the triple brackets, within which the pronoun they (in reference to Jews) is used; the juice emoji, drawing on the fact that the two words (juice and Jews) are a homonym; physical descriptions of Jews ("long hooked noses to smell Money"); and conspiracy theories (that they are responsible for immigration). These comments are, to a certain extent, representative of discursive references to Jews through humorous and memetic methods, without a direct use of the nomination "Jews".

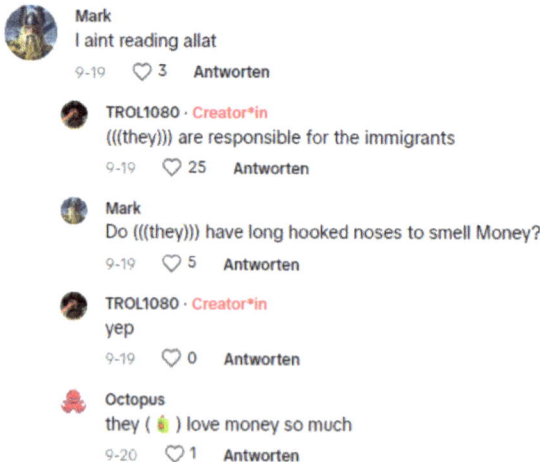

Fig. 6.2 Memetic references to Jews under an antisemitic post (19.09.2023, https://www.tiktok.com/@trol1080alt/video/7280595155529370888).

The comment below, for instance, remixes different textual resources known within online antisemitic spaces: "oy vey" (from Oy Vey! The Goyim Know/Shut it Down) and "yuo" (from Now Yuo See). The remixed expression still expresses a sense of enlightenment and finding out, and it acts as an implicature related to conspiracy theories regarding Jewish control. The supporting iconographic semiosis includes the Pinocchio emoji (as allusion to big noses and lying), Money-Face emoji (an allusion to a supposed money-loving/money-grabbing character), and the Star of David emoji, as a direct reference to Judaism. In a memetic, humorous manner, the semiotic outcome reflects the knowledge and dissemination of conspiracy theories of the original poster, and at the same time it perpetuates essentialist visual and moral representations of Jews.

BG 🏴
oy vey! 🥴 yuo caught me 🤮 🔯 🧑‍🦳 !
10-1   ♡ 7   **Antworten**

Fig. 6.3 Memetic references to Jews under an antisemitic post (01.10.2023, https://www.tiktok.com/@trol1080alt/video/7280595155529370888).

Secondly, the following meme posted by the user @Bayayanka (04.09.23) is an instance of a recurrent memetic trend where users post Jewish versions of objects from daily life (e.g. pizza, gum, etc.). The post, which gathered over 137,000 likes and over 5600 comments since its posting, reflects a meme trend that reinforces the essentialist, malicious representation of Jews as money-loving/money-grabbing. While the meme itself is self-explanatory, the theme is reinforced through auditory resources, in this case the Jewish song *Hava Nagila*.

Figs. 6.4a and 6.4b Instances of the "Jewish things"
meme trend (04.09.2023, https://www.tiktok.com/@
bayayanka/video/7274971819445144834?lang=de-DE).

The comments underneath the memetic post follow the same
general trend of 'figuring out' or referring to the inevitability of
Jewish malice. Interestingly, the preset patterns (e.g. 'well well
well') are also frequently remixed (distorted or translated), for
comedic and/or concealment purposes. For instance:

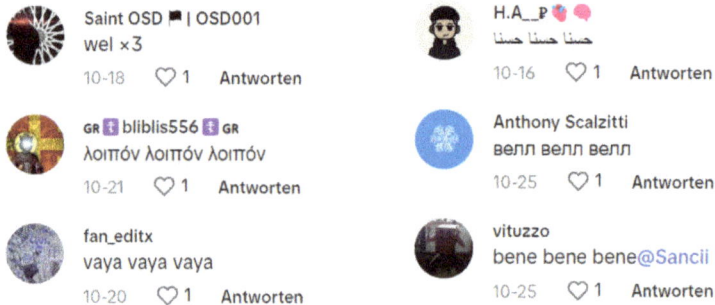

Figs. 6.5a and 6.5b Comments under the post in Figure 6.4 containing
remixed versions of the "well well well" sound bite, both translated (into
Greek, Russian, Spanish, Italian, and Arabic) and distorted ("wel x3")

The third example is a fascist series of unrelated memes (in a slide
show format) that includes, among others, racist, transphobic,
and antisemitic memes, including neo-Nazi and alt-right symbols.
In expressing and reinforcing malice and world dominance as
inherent characteristics of Jews, various semiotic resources are

deployed. The auditory resource is a techno edit that begins with the quote: "my name is Schlomo Shekelsbergstein" in a supposedly Jewish accent and voice. In setting the theme, this auditory resource already reflects an essentialist representation of Jews. Secondly, the two visibly antisemitic slides (memes) in this post allude to the same conspiracy theory of malice and control, as well as the trope of finding out/enlightenment (expressed in the first image with the implication that the Happy Merchant is responsible for, and benefits from, social divides and polarities, and in the second image as the clear pill, which, as opposed to the red pill for example, provides clarity and knowledge).

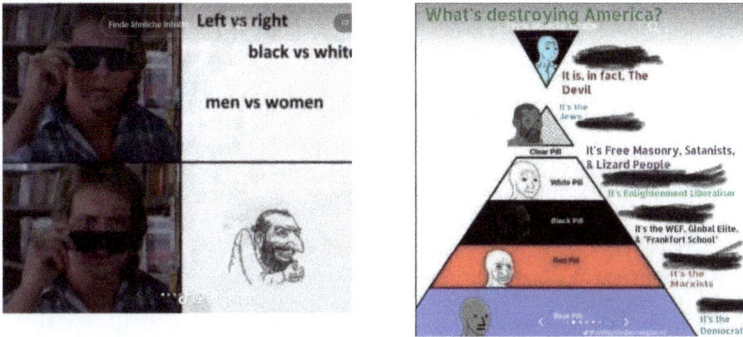

Figs. 6.6a and 6.6b Selected antisemitic slides in a multi-slide memetic post on TikTok (03.09.2023, https://www.tiktok.com/@girahym/video/7274677364355861792?lang=de-DE).

Romanticisation of Nazism

TikTok hosts a plethora of discourses and meme genres that romanticise and to a certain degree glorify Nazism. The process of concealment is pursued to avoid being censored through hate speech regulations. In doing so, codified antisemitic content exceeds usual codifications such as 88 or HH, but involves a plethora of codes and symbolic references. In relation to antisemitic content, memetic content and comments tend to deploy and remix generally similar semiotic resources. Textually, the encoding of fully-fledged Nazi terminology (which would be likely to result in a ban) in memetic posts and comments occurs in at least three ways: using aliases, cryptographic references, and special characters. References to Adolf Hitler as a heroic historical figure, or as someone who was correct in his views about the world, occur through aliases. Aliases in this respect are used as proxies to avoid algorithmic detection. Some of the most recurrent examples include the expression the Austrian Painter, as reference to Adolf Hitler's early profession, and the Moustache Man, in reference to his iconic moustache. Further aliases and metaphorical accounts include nominations such as Adolfo and Uncle Adolf. Secondly, cryptographic references are used to refer to Adolf Hitler, either through abbreviations (e.g. A.H.) or through alternative alphabets and numbers (i.e., leetspeak, e.g. H!tler, H1tl3r). Finally, special characters, unavailable in conventional keyboards are also deployed as direct references to Nazism, including, among others, the SS bolts (⚡⚡) and the swastika (卐, 卍). While such strategies are deployed primarily for concealment purposes, the references to Nazi ideology and figures using these occur generally in contexts of the glorification and/or romanticisation of Nazism.

In an argumentative sense, the glorification of Nazism within the bounds of antisemitism is pervasive. Users tends to treat Nazism (or Hitler) as either doing the right thing or as needed again. This is expressed in different ways, ranging from clear statements (e.g. "Hitler was right," @basswaffen), coded references ("A.H saved us 🫠," @wisetree_; "millions wear the hats[2] and the Austrian painter should come back," @i_mog_), and subtle implicatures or presuppositions ("Epstein, Ukraine War, the Federal Reserve, inflation, this woke ideology, Hollywood....all proves he was right on any things as was," @cody.1877).

Visually, a plethora of visual resources are used in memetic posts on TikTok in the context of antisemitic Nazi glorification. Posters tend to conceal the Nazi outlook of such figures or aesthetics by partially hiding/blurring parts of them (e.g. the swastika, Hitler's

---

2   This mimics the sentence structure of "Billions Must Die", an
     alt-right meme intended to express anger at immigration and
     overpopulation, and is often linked to the Great Replacement conspiracy
     theories. See also https://knowyourmeme.com/editorials/guides/
     what-does-millions-wear-the-hats-mean-is-gnome-hunting-a-dog-whistle.

face), remixing such figures in different meme genres (e.g. the squint-eye meme, Kitler, Chat Hitler), or using an element of Nazi iconography as a visual allusion to Nazism. Further visual incorporation of Nazi aesthetics appears in minimalist designs (e.g. Hitler's hair and moustache), as well as in surreally edited memes. Comments, on the other hand, tend to create visual representations of Nazi aesthetics by using emojis as an alternative to the written form. In doing so, collections of emojis are used to refer generally to Adolf Hitler as an anthropomorphic representation of Nazism. For instance, to refer to the "Austrian painter" alias, users deploy a combination of the Austrian flag and a drawing palette and/ or painter emoji. References to Nazi aesthetics are reflected in the use of, among other things, thunder emojis (SS bolts), salute emojis (face+hand, salute emoji), and colour emojis (red, black, and white). Additionally, emoji art (picture made with emojis) and text art (letters made using pictures and special characters) are deployed to create images of, among other things, Adolf Hitler or the swastika. More camouflaged references to Nazism also include the ubiquitous nomination "Ryan Gosling" (or other variations, e.g. "Aryan Gosling") in usernames and comments, as well as the picture of the American actor. The use of Ryan Gosling as an antisemitic, Nazi-glorification token derives from the similar appearance of the actor and the former Mufti of Jerusalem, Amine Al-Husseini, who is conceivably and debatably antisemitic in the real world, but is certainly an antisemitic, Nazi icon in the imagination of some internet users, mainly neo-Nazis. Perhaps the most concealed acceptance of Nazi ideology lies in some accounts with the name and picture of the actor (looking rather like an unofficial fan page). This also extends to clearer cases, e.g. the profile named *⚡Ryan gosling⚡* (using a Never Lose Your Smile profile picture).

Auditory resources, finally, are used for multiple purposes, mainly to establish the theme, foreground Nazism as the ideological brand, and connect it to the antisemitic aspect of the post. In doing so, memetic posts use and remix several auditory resources including, among others, remixed Nazi speeches into techno, house, or opera music tracks. Appropriated German or Nazi music (e.g. the song *Erika*) has also become co-opted as an auditory symbol for Nazism online. Other music resources used alongside posts that glorify Nazism include opera and epic music. The table below summarises the findings of this section:

Table 6.2 Semiotic resources for the use and romanticisation of Nazism under antisemitic/Jewish posts on TikTok (01/2022–11/2023).

Auditory	Edits/music	Remiixes including Adolf Hitler's speeches; recordings of Adolf Hitler's speeches (modified tone, e.g. reverb), songs (e.g. *Erika* or *Auf Der Heide*).
Textual	Aliases	Austrian painter, Moustache man, Adolfo, Uncle, Uncle A, Ryan Gosling.
	Leetspeak/cryptographic references and codes	H1tle4, H1tl3r, H!tler, H*tler,, A.H, 88, 18, 1488.
	Special characters	⚡⚡, ᛋ, 卍, as well as typing with Fraktur font (used in the Nazi era) in comments, usernames, and bios.
Visual	Nazi symbolism and aesthetics	Swastika, Hitler photos, Reichsadler (Nazi eagle), Moustache memes, Nazi salute, Hitler in Paris, Baby Hitler, Child Hitler, Joachim Peiper, Oswald Mosley, Other fascist/white supremacist icons.
	Iconographic resources	Austrian Flag + painting emojis; raised hand emoji; color emojis (red, white, black).
	Emoji art/emojigrams and text art	Swastika or Adolf Hitler art.
	Genres of memes	Tilt-to-read memes, Squint-your-eyes memes, Hidden imagery in AI, AI-generated, Photoshopped, Face-morphing, Historical pictures, Cartoons, Human phenotype.

Example: Antisemitism and Nazi glorification

This section presents two selected cases as representative cases of how the romanticisation of Nazi ideology and aesthetics occurs and is concealed in memetic posts and comments. The first memetic post creates a typical happy/sad template with Joseph Goebbels. The meme posted by the user @girahym (18.06.23) expresses an anti-Jewish sentiment using Goebbels' seemingly irritated facial expressions in response to the hypothetical presence of Jews, referred to as "coin eating, big nose people".

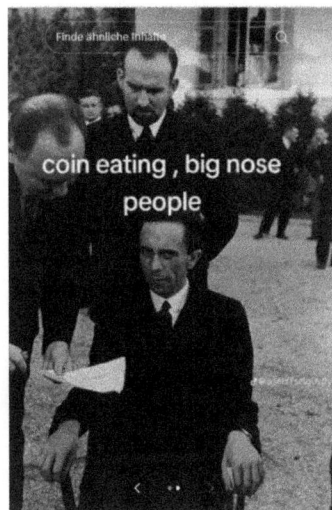

Figs. 6.7a and 6.7b Meme deploying a Nazi figure (Joseph Goebbels) to express anti-Jewish contempt (18.06.2023, https://www.tiktok.com/@girahym/video/7245993948399914267?lang=de-DE).

The second post (@belgian_nationalist._, 29.10.23) involves a variety of semiotic resources connecting antisemitism to Nazi ideology. The post consists of slides highlighting the Jewish presence in the American media landscape (e.g. at CNN, NYT, NBC), and one slide with the Happy Merchant. While the post is undeniably antisemitic, additional semiotic resources connect it to (romanticised) Nazism. On the one hand, the auditory resource used as the "sound" of the meme (i.e., the sound played when viewing the meme/post) is a musical remix of the song *Silhouette* by Pastel Ghost, which includes a speech by Adolf Hitler given at Krupp Factory in 1935. On the other hand, textual and iconographic resources allude to, among others, Nazism, neo-Nazism, fascism, white supremacy, and hyper nationalism. The caption of the post includes the following tags:

Fig. 6.8 Caption of an antisemitic post containing Nazi symbolism.

Nazi glorification comments often occur under antisemitic and Jewish content makers' posts. In the examples below, emojis are used to glorify Nazism. In the first extract, SS bolts and the Nazi salute are used. In the second, a picture of Hitler is drawn using emoji art.

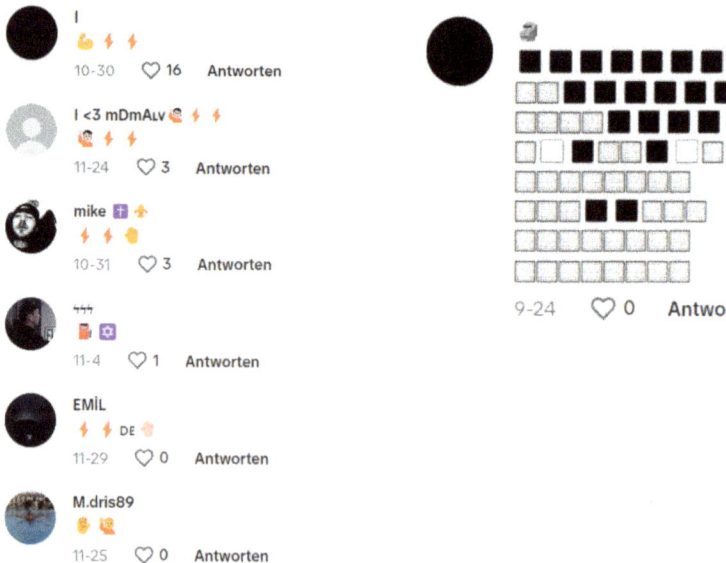

Figs. 6.9a and 6.9b Nazi glorification using emojis and emoji art under an antisemitic post and a Jewish content maker's post.

Trivialisation, relativisation, and denial of the Holocaust and calls for violence

The celebration of the Holocaust and calls for violence towards Jewish people are recurrent on the antisemitic side of TikTok. Content makers and commenters bury their celebration and banalisation of the Holocaust under different layers that require a certain degree of knowledge to decipher, or they represents social actors (e.g. Holocaust victims) through symbolic or memetic references (i.e. a visual synecdoche).

While the auditory resources tend to be the same as in the previous two examples, the visual and textual resources are various. Textually, the relativisation of the Holocaust uses plethora of sound bites and expressions, including the number 271k. This term (often used without additional explanations) refers to the neo-Nazi conspiracy theory that only 271,000 Jewish victims were subject of extermination at the Nazi camps. For instance, "how can i get 6million kills if there Is only 271k players?" @xrfgh__. Similarly, the theory of wooden doors (as being insufficient to seal the gas chambers, therefore used to deny them) is also recurrent. The denial of the Holocaust also takes the shape of ubiquitous statements such as (the Holocaust) "never happened".

Holocaust celebration and calls for violence, on the other hand, tend to be reflected in three general discursive strategies: firstly, the dog whistle "TJD" (sometimes given as "Totally Joyful Day") is a neo-Nazi, white supremacist replacement of the expression Total Jewish Death. Secondly, the metaphor "six million cookies" (and other metaphors, e.g. pizza) mocks the victims of the Holocaust (and tends also to be used to deny the occurrence of the Holocaust). Thirdly, calls for violence are expressed in sound bites and ubiquitous comments such as "round two" or "six million wasn't enough" (generally written as the abbreviations "6MWE" or "6M+1").

Trivialisation of the Holocaust is often more subtle than the increasingly recognisable codes and soundbites that this chapter presents. For instance, the username @cclxxmccci is the romanisation of the number 271,301, a common number used in Holocaust relativisation and denial. The user's biography, as with many white supremacist and/or neo-Nazi accounts, includes a link to *Europa: The Last Battle,* an antisemitic revisionist film from 2017.

Visually, references to the victims of the Holocaust are generally metaphorical when using emojis in support of the textual resources. Through emojis, users tend to refer to the victims of the Holocaust as soap (in reference to the alleged use of human remains to make soap), cookies and pizza (as things that bake in an oven), and the concentration camps as gas pumps, ovens, and fire emojis. On TikTok, the following characteristics have been identified in antisemitic memes:

Table 6.3 Semiotic resources in the celebration, denial, and relativisation of the Holocaust and celebrations of violence under antisemitic/Jewish posts on TikTok (01/2022–11/2023).

Auditory	Edits/music	Similar to the previous two trends.
Textual	Holocaust relativisation and denial	Relativisation: 271k, 271.301, 271.
		Denial: Now yuo see, Never Happened, Holohoax, Fakehaust, wooden doors.
		Six million: Often associated with different words such as banks, cookies, or pizzas (as reference to Nazi ovens).
		Remixing: 6m XP (experience point, a gaming reference), six million followers in four years, six million reps (a gym reference).
		Comedic wordplay between different antisemitic dog whistles: 6 Million Not Enough, 6 Million Gassed, 6 Gazillion (gaz+million), 6 goybillion (goy+billion), 6 million Gorillion (alt-right expression).
		Also includes the use of Auschwitz as the location of posts as a joke.
	Calls for violence and Holocaust celebration	Dog whistles: Totally Joyful Day (or TJD*).
		Metaphors: Six Million Cookies (or other varieties).
		Calls for violence: Round Two/2, 6MWE, 6M+1.[3]
Visual	Iconography	Victims: soap, 6m (cookie emoji), pizza.
		Camps: fire, gas pump, oven.
	Imagery	Holocaust visuals: Concentration camps.
		Visual metaphors of Holocaust victims: Coal, soap, ash.

---

3   Some of these expressions were banned during the course of this research.

Example: Calls for violence and Holocaust denial/celebration/relativisation

This section presents two selected cases as representative in order to demonstrate the construction and concealment of both Holocaust trivialisation/denial and the celebration of violence. The first example is a comment under an antisemitic post which celebrates, among others, Joseph Goebbels. Despite being a clear call in support of violence, the comment survives the regulations on hate speech simply by switching the first letters of the two key words of the violent soundbite, "Gas the Jews". In conjunction with it are the SS bolts, functioning as a visual identity marker or a Nazi glorification trope (see also the discussion of identity markers earlier in this chapter).

user14882711161
jas the gews⚡⚡   ♡
10-10   Antworten   29
6 Antworten anzeigen ⌄

Fig. 6.10 Call for violence under an antisemitic post. To avoid explicit language, which would lead to the post being censored, the commenter exchanges the first letters of the main words ("gas" and "Jews") (10.10.23, https://www.tiktok.com/@gtarsss/video/7288375886255033632).

In turning Holocaust scepticism into jokes and/or memetic references, users deploy sound bites to express denial or relativisation of the Holocaust. The following extracts reflects the different approaches to the trivialisation of the Holocaust (in terms of relativisation, celebration, and denial) using, among other things, conspiracy theories.

One of the most recurrent discursive tropes used in relativisation is the expression of the theory that, instead of six million Jews exterminated in the German concentration camps, 271,301 victims is the accurate number. Therefore, such references (271k, 271,301) are recurrent in the antisemitic sphere and under Jewish content makers' comments, and they are ubiquitously remixed in posts and comments, mainly in analogical or metaphorical terms. These moetaphors or analogues tend to emphasise the impossibility of reaching six million (reps, money, experience points), with 271k given instead as the best one can reach. For instance:

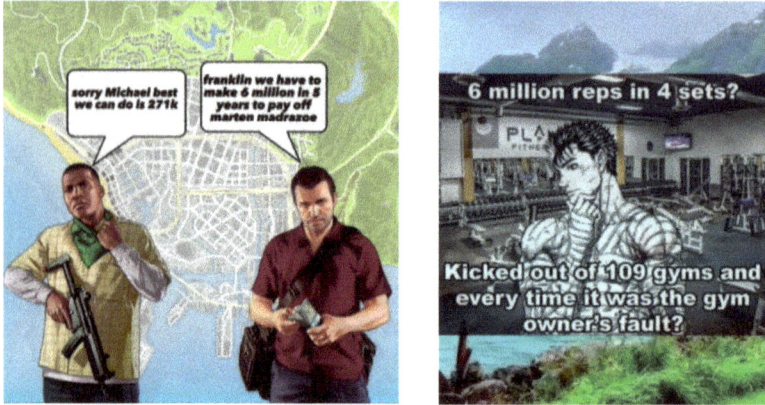

Figs. 6.11a and 6.11b Relativisation of the Holocaust through metaphorical posts (@le.crusader, 25.10.2023, https://www.tiktok.com/@le.crusader/video/7294001710576487723; 2. trol1080alt, post deleted).

Comments also pervasively deploy this trope, for instance:

he only played 271k matches but somehow died 6 million times

8-4   ♡ 469   Antworten

how can i get 6million kills if there Is only 271k players?

10-23   ♡ 0   Antworten

1 Antwort anzeigen ⌄

Figs. 6.12a and 6.12b Antisemitic comments using the 271k trope under an antisemitic post (@le.crusader, 29.07, https://www.tiktok.com/@le.crusader/video/7261277224362429739).

Functions of multimodal resources in antisemitic memes: Concealment, banalisation, and identification

Antisemitic content is prevalent on TikTok and thrives largely through memetic and humorous genres, deploying various (alternative) multimodal semiotic resources (i.e. textual, visual, iconographic, and auditory). Given their discursive power and the ideologies they underpin, memes and memetic vernacular tend to fulfil three foundational functions on TikTok: concealment of blatant hate speech and ideology by using humour to bypass censorship, the banalisation of hate and violence, and the marking and reinforcement of (collective) identities. Given these functions, the role of antisemitic discourse on TikTok goes past the confirmation and re-enactment of pre-existing patterns and discourses of antisemitism, and the associated social relationships with and behaviour toward Jews. It "also renegotiates social relationships and introduces new meanings and new behaviours" (Lemke 1995: 16).

Concealment and survival of censorship

Through the multimodal character of memes and memetic vernacular, firstly, a process of concealment of blatant and visible antisemitism takes place, largely by relegating clearly articulated expressions (e.g. Jews control the world, or the Holocaust never happened) to alternative semiotic resources (i.e. dog whistles and encrypted language; visual and iconographic resources), relying in this process on a degree of shared knowledge to decrypt and understand what is happening. This occurs generally within a memetic or humorous mode. Therefore, memetic and humorous content conceals antisemitic ideology under the guise of humour and through coded semiotic modes.

Arguably, concealment through multilayered, encrypted, and multimodal language helps content makers circumvent regulations against hate speech on social media platforms, and to plant malicious ideologies in apparently harmless content. The ability to conceal blatant and banal antisemitism reflects the ability of hate speech to mutate and survive censorship. This, therefore, poses many questions about the survivability of hate speech on social media platforms, and the capacity of the platforms themselves to live up to their community guidelines and regulatory requirements.

Circumventing the censorship of antisemitic hate speech on TikTok led to the development of a large body of go-to semiotic elements to resort to when making (largely humorous) posts and memes, or when commenting. Concealment through coded language takes different shapes and forms, mainly using and remixing ubiquitous (or trendy) sound bites, jokes and puns, meme templates, and more importantly, coded placeholders (i.e. dog whistles, encrypted codes). Textually, users deploy a variety of linguistic and discursive tropes and strategies to conceal blatant antisemitism under a playful, humorous memetic outlook. The following devices have been identified in the textual form of antisemitic posts and comments on TikTok. This list is nonetheless non-exhaustive:

1. Spoonerism: users purposefully transpose the initial letters or sounds of two or more words, both for humorous and for concealment purposes. For instance, "Jas the Gews" instead of "Gas the Jews", or "Kate Hikes" instead of "Hate Kikes".

2. Phonetic spelling: users write words as they are pronounced (with an accent), resulting generally in distorted spelling of the words (e.g. "Shejm on d gojim" instead of "Shame on the Goyim").

3. Homoglyph: users avoid the clear use of specific words by replacing some of their letters that appear identical (e.g. capital I and lower-case l in "WeII", é and e in "Jéwish").

4. Homonym: users replace words with others that sound the same or similar. Some of the words might be deliberately misspelled as well (e.g. Joo instead of Jew).

5. Loanwords/borrowing: users tend to deliberately borrow terms in German as an indirect reference to Nazi Germany and the Holocaust (e.g. "Juden", "Guten Tag").

6. Metaphors, metonymies, synecdoche, and analogies: users tend to replace words with, among others, metaphorical references from the Holocaust or Nazism (e.g. soap

instead of Jew; "Austrian painter" instead of Adolf Hitler), descriptions (e.g. "big nose people").

7. Puns, wordplay, and portmanteau: users tend to create new words or mix others and encode them with antisemitic meaning.

8. Sarcasm and irony: users tend to use words or expressions ironically and paradoxically as, among others, captions to antisemitic posts (e.g. "I am Jewish and proud!! Have a totally joyful day"; "#proudtransnonbinary #Jewtok #Jewish") or as usernames (e.g. "Transgender black gay jew").

9. Allusions, presuppositions, and implicature: users, in a more general sense and through the devices mentioned in this list, refer to antisemitic ideas and representations indirectly by creating connections between them and based on shared knowledge.

Secondly, users deploy two sorts of visual resource: on the one hand, iconographic resources are used in the form of emojis to replace words (e.g. soap metaphor, gas, fire, oven) or ideas (e.g. saluting, raised arm, SS bolts). On the other hand, a more complicated deployment of videos and photos takes place in the form of, among others, memes, slides, and infographics. Visually, users tend to remix different meme templates and genres (e.g. shitposting, maxxing). Some of the most recurrent types of meme in the antisemitic sphere of TikTok make fun of the Holocaust as a lie, and of Jews and their stereotypical representations. In either case, antisemitism is understood using a certain degree of contextual knowledge, particularly when social actors are replaced by other placeholders (e.g. coal or soap for Jews).

Concealment in antisemitic (visual) memes relies on (i) accentuating Jewish stereotypical physical appearances in a cartoonish manner (e.g. Jewish Wojak, The Happy Merchant, Goblin), and (ii) on converting ideological beliefs regarding Jews and the Holocaust into comedic situations and/or dialogues. These tend to be hypothetical and take place in other universes. For instance, characters from *Grand Theft Auto* talk about how unattainable six million steps are, and that 271k is the maximum one can achieve, or others allude to the idea that Jews were expelled from 109 different countries by framing it as being expelled from 109 gyms (see Fig. 6.11). At a surface level, this does not express any visible forms of Holocaust relativisation, but it can only be understood through a shared knowledge of the deployed codes (e.g. 271k, 109) and the underpinning ideological convictions they represent. This is intrinsically connected to the banalisation of hate and violence, as the ideological utterances become something to take lightly.

Banalisation of hate and violence

The memetic, humorous antisemitic language on TikTok, secondly, drives the banalisation of hatred and violence against and dehumanisation of Jews. Such content trivialises exclusion, violence, and hate against Jews by turning it into a matter of recognisable humour. Simultaneously, as it dehumanises a group of people, the humorous language also reinforces such discursive practices, as would a direct utterance using literal vocabulary (Billig 2001: 278). Perhaps one of the most eye-catching explanations for the alt-right's use of humour is captured in the following quote: "Humor is one of the more effective tools we have at our disposal. Properly executed, it can be utilised to disarm our opposition, unravel their narratives, and pierce their arguments with elements of taboo truths we use to tactically nuke their agenda" (Hawley 2017: 76)

The impact of memes and memetic vernacular, among other discursive and communication styles, surpasses the boundaries of groups such as the far and alt-right, but it also reaches the mainstream, consequently desensitising the latter to exclusionary and violent ideologies (e.g. antisemitism) and discourses (e.g. dehumanisation of victims) (Miller-Idriss 2017: 25). Such an approach to meaning-making is intended to expand the limits of public tolerance of the trivialisation and banalisation of hate, violence (Tuters 2019: 39), and hostility against political opponents and minorities (Miller-Idriss 2019: 127), as well as to encourage the normalisation of hate-driven ideologies (May and Feldman 2019: 28). The naturalisation of hate and violence also occurs in the context of national belonging fantasies as reflected in, for instance, Nordic mythology linked to modern nationalist ideologies. The deployment of allusions to violence in this context render inseparable the justifiable violence, racial supremacy and purity, and national belonging and restoration in right-wing, hypernationalist discourses (Miller-Idriss, 2017: 125). The analysis by Askanius and Keller (2021) of the symbolic and iconographic resources in the use of memes in the case of the Swedish Nordic Resistance Movement also alludes to similar ideas. Moreover, the logic behind such normalisation and trivialisation of, among other things, hate and violence lies in the function of memes and memetic vernacular in detaching taboo symbols (e.g. Nazi iconography) from their general historical meaning and converting them into mere "floating signifiers" to fit the culture of memes (Tuters 2019: 42).

The findings of this chapter are consistent with these theoretical underpinnings, particularly considering the trivialisation of the Holocaust, Jewish hate, and Nazism. The most basic example of turning these things into jokes is the conversion of "6 million Holocaust victims" into a memetic reference, implying in the process the celebration or the denial of the Holocaust. Beyond alt-right and neo-Nazi references (e.g. "6 Gorillion"), users find entertainment in creatively remixing "6 million" and in creating context-bound jokes implying an attitude towards the Holocaust while apparently expressing something else (e.g. "i listen to this 6 million times a day," @immeg06cz; "I expect 6 million views," @ipersborra; "6 trillion of cookiews"[4]), or coming up with creative wordplay (e.g. "gazillion", "goyillion"). The same applies to jokes that include death wishes and calls for violence (e.g. "Back to the chambers," @yonnyyyyyy, and "Strawberry juice[5] Millions of strawberries must be liquidated," @user37588479768 under a post of a strawberry that looks like a nose; or "Soon we will warm the oven for you," @100_s0rrow_100 as a response to a Jewish user).

---

4   Portmanteau word: cookies and Jews
5   Homonym of Jews.

In some respects, Nazism too turns into jokes and comestible sound bites, normalising its appeal beyond its historical horrors into—at a minimum—appealing aesthetics and humorous moments, and at most the survival and continuity of extreme ideologies, including antisemitism. In other, less humorous respects, Nazism remains alive due to ideologically loaded, coded semiotic resources.

In this sense, in the process of banalisation through humour, the act of exterminating six million Jews loses its horror and historical relevance, dimming the urgent response that this must never happen again. It is rather greeted with laughter and scepticism.

Identity markers

The semiotic resources function, to a lesser extent, as an identity marker to foreground the posters/commenters' political and ideological affiliations and/or objectives. As identity markers, encoded resources on TikTok (visual, auditory, and textual) are deployed to identify the boundaries of a discursive community and/or subculture. In analysing biographies, comments, and profile pictures, community boundaries and the purpose of posting antisemitic content can be identified. Expressions of race, national, religious, or civilisational supremacy were recurrent in the accounts with antisemitic content. Three major discursive communities were identified: Christian Fundamentalism or Christian Nationalism, Western Civilisationism, and Nazi/Neo-Nazi/Alt-Right Ideologies.

By investigating the semiotic resources used in captions and comments, as well as in biographies and profile pictures of posters/commenters, five recurrent (often overlapping) discursive communities have been identified: Alt-right/far-right/neo-Nazi (including Nazi glorification); anti-communism; hyper-nationalism; racial supremacy; and religious supremacy. Additional categories can also be identified, including that of trolling. In this case, no specific political or ideological orientations appear to be the ground for hate speech, as these accounts simply post, in a comedic, light manner, hateful content against, among other groups, Jews,

Muslims, and immigrants. Each of the five discursive communities can be identified through the recurrent use of specific semiotic resources.

Ideology	Semiotic resources in usernames, biographies, posts, and comments
Alt-Right/ Neo-Nazi Ideology or Nazi Glorification/ Fascism	Emojis: Thunder, Raising Hand; Man Saluting; Emoji Face with Moustache; Painter, Painter/Paint Palette+Austrian flag; red, white, black circles/cubes/hearts as Nazi colours.
	Special Characters: 卐, 卍, ⚡.
	Codes/Leetspeak: 18 (Adolf Hitler), 88 (Heil Hitler), HH.
	Profile Pictures/Visual Resources: Swastikas and Adolf Hitler (e.g. Eye Squint Photos, AI Generated, Emoji Art); Edited/Blurred or Artwork of Nazi/Fascist Leaders (including Face Morphing, e.g. Hitler/Swastika as a Cat, Chad Hitler).
	Ubiquitous Expressions: Never Lose Your Smile (or other humorous alternatives, e.g. Never Lose Yuor [sic] Skeleton).
	Bios: References to conspiracy theories, documents, and shows (e.g. *The Last Battle*).
Anti-Communist Action; Anti-Woke, Anti-Feminism	Emojis: Crossed-out flags of, among others, EU and LGBTQA+.
	Codes/Leetspeak: 131 (Anti-Communist Action), 1161 (Anti-Antifa Action).
	Profile Pictures/Visual Resources: Anti-Communist Action Logo.
Hyper-Nationalism	Emojis: National Flags, Flags and Crosses, Crossed-out EU flag.
	Profile Pictures/Visual Resources: Edited pictures of statement/leaders from different countries, National Flags with Weapons, National Flag with Cross, Totenkopf with embedded flag.
	Usernames: Country+Nationalist, Nationality+Fighter/ Warrior/Patriot.

Racial Supremacy/ White Supremacy/ Civilisationism	Ubiquitous Expressions: Save Europa, Aryan Supremacy, Never Lose Your Smile, TJD/TND/TMD, Übermensch.
	Codes/Leetspeak: 18, 88, 1488.
	Profile Pictures/Visual Resources: Never Lose Your Smile + Totenkopf; Arno Breker's Rammstein (a.k.a. Aryan Stare) as a part of Aryan TikTok Aesthetics; Schwarze Sonne.
	Other Resources: Germanic and Nordic Mythological References.
Religious Fundamentalism/ Supremacy	Emojis: Cross, Orthodox Cross, Crossed-out LGBT/EU flags.
	Textual Resources (e.g., Usernames or Bios): Deus Volt, Orthodox, Christian, Christ is Lord; Crusader; Defender.
	Profile Pictures/Visual Resources: Religious Emblems and Aesthetics (crosses, orthodox cross, knights); Iconic Religious leaders and Figures (e.g. Jesus, Baldwin IV of Jerusalem).
	Crusaders/Crusade iconography, Photos of religious characters tend to be modified into a muscular Chad meme to emphasise arrogance and rightness.

The consistent deployment of such symbols arguably reinforces feelings of belonging to specific groups (e.g. hyper-nationalism or civilisationism), and, beyond that, it supports the construction of "aspirational nationhood" as the ideal (Miller-Idriss 2017: 125). This is consistent with posts (not necessarily memetic, nor outright antisemitic) that glorify Nazism as a 'what-could-have-been' ideal world (morally and aesthetically). The romanticisation of Nazi aesthetics (e.g. symbols, outfits, weaponry, and architecture) is, however, a separate issue.

Conclusion: Hate speech on social media

It is worth noting that the antisemitic discourse on TikTok occurs as a part of a larger body of exclusionary discourses—Islamophobic, anti-migrant, anti-LGBT, as well as anti-communist, and anti-woke perspectives. In particular, analysis has identified anti-trans, anti-Black, anti-Roma, and misogynistic sentiments, including—just as this chapter identifies in the case of antisemitism—calls for violence and the annihilation of specific groups. A distinction can also be made between social-Darwinist perspectives that allude to a sense of the genetic superiority of the white race vis-à-vis the parasitic 'other', and an ethno- or religio-supremacist perspective that celebrates the ethnic and religious superiority of specific groups and fosters a desire for the exclusion of their 'typical enemies'.

The supply of antisemitic and other hateful memes on social media platforms conceivably fulfills a demand from actual bigots and also feeds the unaware and uncritical public, including teenagers and children. Previous research indicates that the internet is not only equipped to assist in disseminating hate speech, but in customising it (including using subtle messaging) to cater to the needs of, and to appeal to different online communities, including children (McNamee et al. 2010: 261; Bliuc et al. 2018: 38). Existing literature also emphasises the link between the likelihood of teenagers being exposed to hate speech and several predictors, including the amount of their time spent on social media and the level of their communication with strangers (Harriman et al. 2020: 1).

To deal with the propagation of hate speech of all types online, this chapter proposes two routes: academically, on the one hand, this chapter emphasises the inseparability of critical media education from education about democracy (Schnabel and Berendsen 2024: 34). The exposure of teenagers and young adults to hate speech using manipulative language (including antisemitic documentaries and conspiracy theories) requires us, not necessarily to ban the use of such language, but to learn to deal with it healthily and critically, initially by recognizing it. Practically, on the other hand, there is an urgent need to enforce moderation over illegal and harmful content on social media. Previous research indicates that social media platforms, including TikTok, tend to overlook the repercussions of unmoderated content, particularly on the mental health of users. The algorithm on such platforms, more importantly, creates echo chambers, in which users are exposed to similar or more extreme content, leading to deeper exposure and encouraging 'rabbit hole' behaviour among users. In so doing, the algorithm tends to offer more of the harmful content that users spend time watching, in order to encourage greater use of such platforms, thus increasing revenues (WSJ 2021). We therefore need to moderate algorithms in a more transparent manner.

References

Askanius, Tina and Nadine Keller, 2021. "Murder fantasies in memes: fascist aesthetics of death threats and the banalization of white supremacist violence". *Information, Communication & Society,* 24 (16), 2522–2539, https://doi.org/10.1080/1369118X.2021.1974517.

Bainotti, Lucia, Sarah Burkhardt, Yan Cong, Jingyi Zhu, Jesper Lust, Kate Babin, Salma Esserghini, Iliass Ayaou, Amine Kerboute, Micky L. Mocombe, Frédéric Lecat, Amina Mohamed, Simran Tamber, Devin Mitter, Sama K. Ooryad, Jasmin Leech, Tommaso Elli and Kristen Zheng, 2022. *Tracing the Genealogy and Change of TikTok Audio Memes.* Digital Methods Winter School, University of Amsterdam.

Bhat, Prashanth and Ofra Klein, 2020. "Covert hate speech: white nationalists and dog whistle communication on Twitter". In: Gwen Bouvier and Judith E. Rosenbaum (eds), *Twitter, the Public Sphere, and the Chaos of Online Deliberation.* Cham: Palgrave Macmillan, 151–172.

Bhatia, Tej K., 2018. "Accent, intelligibility, mental health, and trauma". *World Englishes, 37* (3), 421–431. https://10.1111/weng.12329.

Billig, Michael, 2001. "Humour and hatred: the racist jokes of the Ku Klux Klan". *Discourse & Society,* 12 (3), 276–289. https://www.jstor.org/stable/42888362

Bliuc, Ana-Maria, Nicholas Faulkner, Andrew Jakubowicz and Craig McGarty, 2018. "Online networks of racial hate: A systematic review of 10 years of research on cyber-racism". *Computers in Human Behavior,* 87, 75–86. https://doi.org/10.1016/j.chb.2018.05.026.

Brandeis Magazine, 2022. "Code Words and Crumbs: Deciphering QAnon Messaging". *Brandeis Magazine.* https://www.brandeis.edu/magazine/2022/summer/inquiry/qanon.html

Breidenstein, Georg, Stefan Hirschauer, Herbert Kalthoff and Boris Nieswand, 2020. *Ethnographie. Die Praxis der Feldforschung.* München: UVK Verlag.

Canale, Germán, 2023. *A Multimodal and Ethnographic Approach to Textbook Discourse.* London: Routledge.

Chevrette, Roberta and Christopher M. Duerringer, 2020. "Bros Before Donald Trump: Resisting and Replicating Hegemonic Ideologies in the #BROTUS Memes After the 2016 Election". In: Gwen Bouvier and Judith E. Rosenbaum (eds), *Twitter, The Public Sphere, and the Chaos of Online Deliberation.* Cham: Springer, 235–266.

DeCook, Julia R., 2018. "Memes and symbolic violence: #proudboys and the use of memes for propaganda and the construction of collective identity". *Learning, Media and Technology*, 1–20. https://doi.org/10.108 0/17439884.2018.1544149.

Dellwing, Michael, Alessandro Tietz and Marc A. Vreca, 2021. *Digitaler Naturalismus: Grundlagen der Ethnografie in der Onlineforschung.* Wiesbaden: Springer.

Dicks, Bella, Bambo Soyinka and Aamanda Coffey, 2006. "Multimodal ethnography". *Qualitative Research, 6* (1), 77–96. https://doi. org/10.1177/1468794106058876.

Donovan, Joan, Becca Lewis and Brian Friedberg, 2019. "Parallel Ports. Sociotechnical Change from the Alt-Right to Alt-Tech". In: Maik Fielitz and Nick Thurston (eds), *Post-Digital Cultures of the Far Right. Online Actions and Offline Consequences in Europe and the US.* Bielefeld: Transcript, 49–66.

Dundes, Alan and Thomas Hauschild, 1983. "Auschwitz Jokes". *Western Folklore, 42* (4), 249–260. https://www.jstor.org/stable/1499500

Ebner, Julia, 2019. "Counter-Creativity: Innovative Ways to Counter Far-Right Communication Tactics". In: Maik Fielitz and Nick Thurston (eds), *Post-Digital Cultures of the Far Right. Online Actions and Offline Consequences in Europe and the US.* Bielefeld: Transcript, 169–182.

Greene, Viveca S., 2019. "'Deplorable' Satire: Alt-Right Memes, White Genocide Tweets, and Redpilling Normies". *Studies in American Humor, 5* (1), 31–69. https://muse.jhu.edu/article/720967.

Guillén-Nieto, V., 2023. "DISMANTLING HATE SPEECH: TIME FOR LINGUISTS TO STEP UP". *Degruyter*, 14 April. https://blog.degruyter. com/dismantling-hate-speech-time-for-linguists-to-step-up/

Guy, Jean S., 2019. "Digital Technology, Digital Culture and Metric/ Nonmetric Distinction". *Technological Forecasting and Social Change*, 145, 55–61.

Harriman, Nigel, Neil Shortland, Ma Su, Tyler Cote, Marcia. A. Testa and Elena Savoia, 2020. "Youth Exposure to Hate in the Online Space: An Exploratory Analysis". *International Journal of Environmental Research and Public Health*, 17 (22), 1–14. https://doi.org/10.3390/ ijerph17228531.

Hübscher, Monika and Sabine von Mering, 2022. *Antisemitism on Social Media.* London: Routledge Publications.

Hawley, George, 2017. *Making Sense of the Alt-Right.* New York: Columbia University Press.

Hine, Christine, 2015. *Ethnography for the Internet: Embedded, Embodied, and Everyday.* New York: Routledge.

IHRA, 2016. "Working definition of antisemitism". *International Holocaust Remembrance Alliance.* https://holocaustremembrance.com/resources/working-definition-antisemitism

Kress, Gunther, 1993. "Against arbitrariness: the social production of the sign as a foundational issue in critical discourse analysis". *Discourse & Society,* 4 (2, Special Issue: Critical Discourse Analysis), 169–191.

—, and Theo van Leeuwen, 2001. *Multimodal Discourse: The Modes and Media of Contemporary Communication.* London: Arnold.

Lemke, Jay L., 1995. *Textual Politics: Discourse and Social Dynamics.* London: Taylor and Francis.

LeVine, Philip and Ron Scollon, 2004. "Multimodal Discourse Analysis as the Confluence of Discourse and Technology". In: Philip LeVine and Ron Scollon (eds), *Discourse and Technology: Multimodal Discourse Analysis.* Georgetown: Georgetown University Press, 1–6.

Machin, David and Andrea Mayr, 2012. *How to Do Critical Discourse Analysis: A Multimodal Introduction.* London: Sage.

Martin, Rod A. and Thomas E. Ford, 2018. *The Psychology of Humor: An Integrative Approach.* Oxford: Academic Press.

May, Rob and Matthew Feldman, 2019. "Understanding the Alt-Right: Ideologues, 'Lulz' and Hiding in Plain Sight". In: Maik Fielitz and Nick Thurston (eds), *Post-Digital Cultures of the Far Right. Online Actions and Offline Consequences in Europe and the US.* Bielefeld: Transcript, 25–36.

McKerrell, Simon and Lyndon C. Way, 2017. "Understanding Music as Multimodal Discourse". In: Lyndon C. Way and Simon McKerrell (eds), *Music as Multimodal Discourse: Semiotics, Power and Protest.* London: Bloomsbury Academic, 1–20.

McNamee, Lacy. G., Britanny L. Peterson, and Jorge Peña, 2010. "A Call to Educate, Participate, Invoke and Indict: Understanding the Communication of Online Hate Groups". *Communication Monographs,* 77 (2), 257–280. https://doi.org/10.1080/03637751003758227

Meddaugh, Priscilla M. and Jack Kay, 2009. "Hate Speech or 'Reasonable Racism?' The Other in Stormfront". *Journal of Mass Media Ethics: Exploring Questions of Media Morality,* 24 (4), 251–268. https://doi.org/10.1080/08900520903320936.

Menon, Pratiksha T., 2023a, "Racist Humor: Explanatory Readings". *Jstor Daily,* 18 August. https://daily.jstor.org/racist-humor-exploratory-readings/

Menon, Pratiksha T., 2023b, "No Joke: Using humor to mask and normalize hatred and bigotry has a long, ugly history". *Jstor Daily,* 30 August. https://daily.jstor.org/no-joke/

Messerschmidt, Astrid, 2010. "Flexible Feindbilder -Antisemitismus und der Umgang mit Minderheiten in der deutschen Einwanderungsgesellschaft". In: Wolfram Stender, Guido Follert and Mihri Özdogan (eds), *Konstellationen des Antisemitismus*. Wiesbaden: VS Verlag für Sozialwissenschaften, 9–108.

Miller-Idriss, Cynthia, 2017. *The Extreme Gone Mainstream: Commercialization and Far Right Youth Culture in Germany*. Princeton: Princeton University Press.

—, 2019. "What Makes a Symbol Far Right? Co-opted and Missed Meanings in Far-Right Iconography". In: Maik Fielitz and Nick Thurston (eds), *Post-Digital Cultures of the Far Right. Online Actions and Offline Consequences in Europe and the US*. Bielefeld: Transcript, 123–137.

Milner, Ryan M., 2012. *The World Made Meme: Discourse and Identity in Participatory Media* [PhD Dissertation]. University of Kansas.

New York Times, 2023. "TikTok Pushes Back Against Claims It Fuels Antisemitism". *New York Times*, 2 November. https://www.nytimes.com/2023/11/02/business/tiktok-antisemitism-claims-israel-palestinians.html

Önnerfors, Andreas, 2018. '*Finspång*' *– An Execution Meme of the Swedish Radical Right Ignites the Political Discourse*. Center for Analysis of the Radical Right, 6 July. https://www.radicalrightanalysis.com/2018/07/06/fins

Parekh, Bhikhu, 2012. "Is There a Case for Banning Hate Speech?" In: Michael Herz and Peter Molnar (eds), *The Content and Context of Hate Speech: Rethinking Regulation and Responses*. Cambridge: Cambridge University Press, 37–56.

Peck, Andrew, 2017. "The Memetic Vernacular: Everyday Arguments in the Digital Age". [Dissertation] *University of Wisconsin-Madison Digital Library*. https://search.library.wisc.edu/digital/AJ4NABMHUJVLXF9B.

Pérez, Raúl, 2017. "Racism without Hatred? Racist Humor and the Myth of 'Color-blindness'". *Sociological Perspectives*, 60 (5, Special Issue: New Frontiers in the Study of Colorblind Racism), 956–974. https://doi.org/10.1177/0731121417719699.

—, 2022. *The Souls of White Jokes: How Racist Humor Fuels White Supremacy*. Stanford: Stanford University Press.

Pflaeging, Jana, John A. Bateman and Janina Wildfeuer, 2021. "Empirical Multimodality Research: The State of Play". In: Jana Pflaeging, John A. Bateman and Janina Wildfeuer (eds), *Empirical Multimodality Research: Methods, Evaluations, Implications*. Berlin: De Gruyter, 3–34.

Saint-Amand, Pierre and Jennifer C. Gage, 1994. "Terrorizing Marie Antoinette". *Critical Inquiry,* 20 (3), 379–400. https://www.jstor.org/stable/1343862.

Schnabel, Deborah and Eva Berendsen, 2024. Report #Nahostkonflikt. Die TikTok-Intifada - Der 7. Oktober und die Folgen im Netz. Analysen und Empfehlungen der Bildungsstätte Anne Frank.

Shifman, Limor, 2013. "Memes in a Digital World: Reconciling with a Conceptual Troublemaker". *Journal of Computer Mediated Communication,* 18 (3), 362–377. https://doi.org/10.1111/jcc4.12013.

—, 2014. *Memes in Digital Culture.* Cambridge: MIT Press.

Strick, Simon, 2021. *Rechte Gefühle.* Bielefeld: Transcript.

Suk, Julie C., 2012. "Denying Experience: Holocaust Denial and the Free-Speech Theory of the State". In: Michael Herz and Peter Molnar (eds), *The Content and Context of Hate Speech: Rethinking Regulation and Responses.* Cambridge: Cambridge University Press, 144–163.

TikTok, 2023. "The Truth About TikTok Hashtags and Content During the Israel-Hamas War". https://newsroom.tiktok.com/en-us/the-truth-about-tiktok-hashtags-and-content-during-the-israel-hamas-war

Torices, José R., 2021. "Understanding Dogwhistles Politics". *Theoria,* 36 (3), 231–339. https://doi.org/10.1387/theoria.22510.

Tuters, Marc, 2019. "LARPing & Liberal Tears: Irony, Belief and Idiocy in the Deep Web Vernacular". In: Maik Fielitz and Nick Thurston (eds), *Post-Digital Cultures of the Far Right. Online Actions and Offline Consequences in Europe and the US.* Bielefeld: Transcript, 37–48.

Van Leeuwen, Theo, 2004. "Ten Reasons Why Linguists Should Pay Attention to Visual Communication". In: Philip LeVine and Ron Scollon (eds), *Discourse and Technology: Multimodal Discourse Analysis.* Georgetown: Georgetown University Press, 7–19.

WSJ, 2021. "Investigation: How TikTok's Algorithm Figures Out Your Deepest Desires". *The Wall Street Journal.* https://www.wsj.com/video/series/inside-tiktoks-highly-secretive-algorithm/investigation-how-tiktok-algorithm-figures-out-your-deepest-desires/6C0C2040-FF25-4827-8528-2BD6612E3796

Weaver, Simon, 2011. "Jokes, rhetoric and embodied racism: a rhetorical discourse analysis of the logics of racist jokes on the internet". *Ethnicities,* 11 (4), 413–435. https://www.jstor.org/stable/23890708.

Weimann, Gabriel and Natalie Masri, 2022. "New Antisemitism on TikTok". In: Monika Hübscher and Sabine von Mering (eds), *Antisemitism on Social Media.* Milton Park: Taylor and Francis, 167–180.

Wiggins, Bradley E., 2019. *The Discursive Power of Memes in Digital Culture: Ideology, Semiotics, and Intertextuality.* London: Routledge.

7. Unveiling populist tactics on TikTok: A multimodal critical discursive psychology approach

Inari Sakki

Abstract

This chapter investigates the use of multimodal communication by Riikka Purra, leader of the Finnish populist radical right-wing Finns Party (FP), on TikTok. It aims to uncover how Purra uses multimodal tactics to deliver her populist messages, especially during the 2023 Finnish parliamentary elections. The study employs a multimodal critical discursive psychology (MCDP) approach to analyze 59 TikTok videos posted by Purra preceding the 2023 elections. This methodology integrates critical discursive psychology with multimodal discourse analysis to scrutinize the content, form, and function of Purra's political communication. The analysis focuses on identifying patterns of multimodal functions in her TikTok posts, emphasizing verbal, visual, and sonic components.

The research identifies four primary multimodal functions in Purra's TikTok communication: othering, colloquialization, mocking, and victimization. These are accomplished through various multimodal resources, including emojis, casual attire, direct camera engagement, and intertextual references. The study shows how these elements simplify complex political messages, foster intimacy with viewers, and strategically obscure derogatory rhetoric. The findings indicate that TikTok's multimodal affordances allow populist politicians to modernize their image

https://doi.org/10.11647/OBP.0447.07

and connect with younger audiences. This research contributes to the limited understanding of TikTok as a tool for populist political communication.

Keywords: *populist discourse, multimodal critical discursive psychology, TikTok, the Finns Party*

Introduction

Riikka Purra, the current leader of the Finnish populist radical right-wing Finns Party (FP), found herself at the centre of a racism controversy in the summer of 2023, shortly after being elected as Finland's financial minister. Her old racist blog posts and social media comments were unearthed and brought into the public discourse. Like many other right-wing politicians, Riikka Purra is an active user of social media and has successfully built her support base using these new communication channels.

The success of populist radical right parties (PRRPs) can at least partly be explained by their focused and skilled use of social media channels to communicate their messages and mobilise electoral support for their anti-elite and anti-immigration agendas (Atton 2006, Sakki and Pettersson 2016, Pettersson 2017). This is also the case in Finland, the focus of this chapter, where the success of the Finnish PRRP, the FP, has been closely connected to its skillful use of new media, which has enabled politicians to mobilise support for their political agendas and then claim space in traditional media (Pettersson 2017). The effective spread of nationalist and anti-immigration ideologies has contributed to the mainstreaming of their rhetoric among the political 'elite' (Sakki and Pettersson 2018, Pettersson and Augostinous 2021) and led to the normalisation of nationalist and xenophobic discourse in society (Horsti and Nikunen 2013).

One such influential but understudied social media platform is TikTok. Since 2020, TikTok's presence in Finland has seen significant growth, with the platform, owned by a Chinese company, now boasting approximately a 1,6 million active adult users within the nation (Statista 2024). This user base is predominantly comprised of young individuals, with the majority falling under the age of 24. The FP has been at the forefront of embracing TikTok as the first political party to do so, and among Finnish political parties, it boasts the largest following on the platform. A comprehensive analysis has revealed that TikTok played a significant role in shaping Finland's 2023 elections, with a considerable number of young voters aligning themselves with the FP. Many of them acknowledged the influence of TikTok on their voting. TikTok offers a diverse range of multimodal communication tools, including visuals, audio, text, emojis, and special effects, allowing users to create expressive, interactive, and visually captivating content that engages audiences in multiple ways. This underscores the need to adopt a multimodal approach to investigating political communication on TikTok.

In this chapter, we focus on Riikka Purra's TikTok posts leading up to the 2023 parliamentary elections. Inspired by recent media controversies surrounding Purra and her past social media usage (Pettersson and Sakki 2020, 2023, 2024) and previous studies showing how the FP uses multimodal communication and humour to mask hatred (Sakki and Martikainen 2021, Pettersson et al. 2022), we seek to study the ways in which the right-wing populist party leader mobilises an audience through TikTok. More specifically, the purpose of this chapter is to illuminate the ways in which Purra, in her position as an FP leader, employs multimodality to convey her populist message.

Populist communication, multimodality and TikTok

Populist communication can be defined as a type of political discourse that frames political issues in terms of a dichotomy between 'us' and 'them,' emphasising a moral division between the 'ordinary people' and the 'corrupted elite' (e.g. Laclau 2005, Sakki 2025). Populist actors identify public sentiments and cultivate shared grievances to create a sense of shared victimhood, uniting followers under a common identity transcending economic and cultural divides (Mols and Jetten 2020). Previous research has outlined some common characteristics of populist rhetoric.

These include, among other things, simplifying complex issues, appealing to common sense, using colloquial and emotive language, and attributing blame to elites and 'dangerous others' (Bos and Brants 2014, Engesser et al. 2017, Hameleers et al. 2017, Rovamo et al. 2023).

Populist movements have been particularly skillful at leveraging online communication for mobilisation (e.g. Moffitt, 2016). Online platforms provide fertile ground for constructing antagonistic divisions between 'us' and 'them,' spreading hate speech, conspiracy theories, and fake news (Sakki and Pettersson 2016, Sakki and Castrén 2022, Pyrhönen and Bauvois, 2020). Forceful language, along with the masking of derogatory messages behind visual images, hyperlinks, humour, and sarcasm, contributes to this phenomenon (Forchtner and Kølvraa 2017, Sakki and Martikainen 2021).

Online communication inherently encompasses multiple modes, including verbal, sonic, digital, and audiovisual elements. Kress and van Leeuwen (2021) define multimodality as the utilisation of multiple semiotic codes, such as images, sound, and text, to convey meaning. This multimodality is significant because images, sounds, and music often wield more influence than mere words in eliciting emotional responses from audiences (van Leeuwen 2012).

Multimodality is also gaining increased attention in research on populist communication. Recent studies have explored multimodal discourse across various digital platforms, revealing how visual and digital affordances enhance the persuasive power of populist messages (Kilby and Lennon, 2021, Martikainen and Sakki 2021, Pettersson and Sakki, 2020, 2024, Salojärvi et al. 2023). Previous research has shown, among other things, how racist messages can be mobilised in a subtle and delicate way through a combination of verbal, visual, and auditory tools. Even if there is no verbal message, multimodal semiotic resources—images, rapid cuts in a video, and violent sounds—enable the representation of the outgroup as dangerous (Sakki and Martikainen 2021). In the multimodal construction of meaning, co-contextualization serves as a powerful tool to either amplify or depict contrast (Liu and O'Halloran 2009, O'Halloran 2008). In the study by Pettersson et al.

(2022), various resources, including verbal, visual, and sonic, were used to create an antagonistic 'us' and 'them' between the 'sensible' male common people and the 'stupid and irrational' female politicians in the FP's campaign video. Another study focusing on the multimodal communication of FP's political memes published during Russia's war in Ukraine in the spring of 2022 shows how specific features of internet memes—humour, entertainment, open-endedness, and interactivity—can be creatively utilised in populist persuasion (Pettersson, Martikainen and Sakki 2024).

While research on TikTok is thriving in general (Abidin et al. 2022), very little is still known of the ways in which TikTok is used by PRRP politicians. However, some recent studies suggest that since TikTok encourages creating short, multimodal, and entertaining content, it provides an ideal platform for PRRP politicians to engage young audiences (Albertazzi and Bonansinga 2023). A study conducted in Spain (Cervi and Marín-Lladó 2021) revealed that populist parties like Vox and Podemos have harnessed TikTok to foster interaction and connect with their followers. Their posts tend to be successful when they incorporate elements of engagement and entertainment, such as political leaders twerking or interacting with young tiktokers. In a similar way, other studies suggest that humour and entertainment encourage engagement from followers, compared to posts that include hate speech elements (González-Aguilar et al. 2023). Indeed, based on their analysis of the TikTok communication of PRRP leaders, such as Marine Le Pen and Matteo Salvini, Albertazzi and Bonansinga (2023) challenge the notion that PRR parties solely use negative content to radicalise audiences on TikTok, but instead demonstrate that positive messages, celebrating national virtues, and offering optimistic visions are also prevalent. While fear and anger were occasionally utilised, established PRR party leaders often opt for less negative content, aiming to connect with audiences by being entertaining, approachable, and relaxed. Another study conducted in Canada explored how Jagmeet Singh, the leader of the federal New Democratic Party, has become a TikTok sensation among young people. Moir (2023) showed how Singh deploys TikTok's features, such as the formulation of slogans, critique of the political establishment, and the use of memes, to establish his distinct brand of left-wing populism. This chapter aims to contribute to this emerging avenue of research, shedding light on how TikTok can be harnessed in the political communication of PRRP.

Method

Our materials consist of TikTok videos of the leader of the FP, Riikka Purra. In order to investigate the role played by multimodality in her political communication, after TikTok provided the Research API, we selected and downloaded all her TikTok videos prior to the Finnish parliamentary elections of 2023. There were 59 videos in total. The length of the postings varied from 10 seconds to five minutes 57 seconds, with the average length being two minutes.

We call our methodological approach to studying multimodal political communication: multimodal critical discursive psychology (MCDP). This approach allows for a more nuanced understanding of how different discursive and multimodal components can come together to coproduce meanings (Pettersson and Sakki 2017, 2020, Kilby and Lennon 2021). Our approach is informed by work in critical discursive psychology (CDP) (Wetherell 1998, Edley 2001) that combines conversation-analytical and post-structuralist perspectives (Wetherell 1998) and enables the researcher both to examine the detailed rhetorical construction of discourse (micro level) and consider its broader social and political implications, for instance, for societal power relations (macro level). This characteristic makes it particularly well-suited for studying political communication in social media as embedded in its surrounding social and political environment (Pettersson and Sakki 2020).

Our application of MCDP follows the three-phase analytic procedure that we proposed elsewhere (Sakki and Pettersson 2016, Pettersson, Payotte and Sakki 2023), which examines the content (what was said), form (how it was said), and function (the potential social and political functions of what was said) of political discourse. Although CDP was originally developed for the study of verbal discourse, it is well-suited to the analysis of multimodal communication, as we have demonstrated in several studies (e.g. Pettersson and Sakki 2017, 2020, 2023, Hakoköngäs and Sakki 2023, see also Kilby and Lennon 2021). In practice, we extended our three-phase CDP analysis with principles of multimodal discourse analysis (MDA) (Kress 2011). MDA research focuses on different modalities (e.g. verbal, visual, and sonic) and how they co-construct a persuasive argument that becomes more than the sum of its parts. Important to this approach are the ways in which the convergent and divergent semantic orientations of verbal, textual, visual, and sonic communication are identified and interpreted by employing the concepts of co-contextualization (elements conveying congruous meanings and reinforcing each other's semantic potential) and recontextualization (elements communicating controversial meanings, resulting in the expansion of semantic potential) (Liu and O'Halloran 2009). MDA has its roots in social semiotics (Kress and van Leeuwen 2021), which considers how (political) communication draws from the socially shared reservoir of meanings (Kress 2011) and provides tools to study multimodal grammar by paying attention to the meaning (content) and the compositional and interpersonal (form and function) characteristics of online political communication. In combination, the traditions of CDP and MDA complete each other in a methodological approach that we call MCDP.

We first watched through all the videos several times to familiarise ourselves with them, and started coding the videos into different content categories based on the topics of discussion, such as immigration, financial politics, energy, climate, elections, etc. We then made multimodal transcriptions of all 59 TikTok postings. This meant transcribing the videos scene by scene across different modes that allowed us to pay attention, not just to different content, but also to forms of communication: verbal narration (rhetorical devices, see Potter 1996, Sakki and Pettersson 2016), textual elements (e.g. colours, font), visual elements (e.g. emojis, clothes), interpersonal elements (e.g. distance, gaze), habits and actions (e.g. walking, pointing finger), and sound (e.g. tone of voice, music). These multimodal transcriptions of the 59 TikTok postings served as the basis for searching for patterns of multimodal functions in Purra's TikTok postings. As the outcome of the analysis, we were able to identify four ways Purra used multimodality in the service of her populist communication.

Multimodality as a tool of populist communication

Our analytic approach aimed to identify the content, forms, and functions of Purra's TikTok communications. Regarding the content of Purra's TikTok, her posts cover various themes such as immigration, climate change, monetary policy, energy policy, and Finnish identity. The locations of the videos vary. Many videos are recordings of parliamentary plenary sessions, while others are shot in home settings, offices, or outdoors, such as during campaign events in marketplaces or streets.

In this section, we focus on the forms and functions of multimodal rhetoric. In analysing Purra's TikTok posts, four functions of multimodal rhetoric were identified: othering, colloquialization, mocking, and victimisation. Different verbal, visual, and sonic resources are utilised to serve these multimodal functions. In what follows below, the four multimodal functions are briefly described in terms of their form and function. Two illustrative examples of the material are discussed in more depth.

Othering through multimodality revolves around subjects like immigration, international development aid, street begging, and street criminality. The multimodal communication utilised in these posts often employs a simplified rhetoric frequently found in populist discourse (Bos and Brants 2014, Engesser, Fawzi and Larsson 2017). This rhetoric employs straightforward and explicit language, establishes stark verbal and visual dichotomies, and offers simple solutions. Textual elements added to the videos are often used to simplify the key message and to juxtapose two alternatives. Bigger fonts and highlighting of the added textual elements are used to juxtapose and emphasise the urgency of the political message (Martikainen and Sakki 2021). In these videos, Purra often speaks to the camera up close, from the viewer's perspective, and addresses the viewer directly (sometimes with a pointing finger), emphasising both a close and equal relationship with the audience and direct contact with the viewer (Kress and van Leeuwen 2006).

Colloquialization through multimodality is deployed in informal settings, such as Purra's home or an office. Many TikTok posts are also filmed outside in public places, such as marketplaces or streets, where Purra is campaigning and engaging with ordinary people. Her relatability is emphasised through elements like casual attire and being featured in group photos with individuals of varying ages and appearances. Purra also frequently uses colloquial language and addresses the camera directly. Instead of formal clothing, she opts for a sweater and frequently wears a beanie. All this aims to create a more approachable impression of her.

Fig. 7.1 Screenshot of Purra's TikTok video (18 November 2022).

Mocking the elite through multimodality often takes place during parliament sessions. These videos differ from Purra's other types of postings as they usually start with a video recording from the plenary sessions of the Parliament of Finland. Unlike the two previous multimodal strategies, othering and colloquialization, these videos do not include any other added verbal narration by Purra. These postings often begin with Purra delivering a speech in the parliament and posing a question to the parliament's ministers. The ministers' responses are occasionally presented, but they are recontextualized with the incorporation of multimodal resources like textual elements and emojis aimed to mock, as Figure 7.1 below demonstrates.

Figure 7.1 is a screenshot of a TikTok video that uses multimodality to question and mock the government's climate policies. The visual and verbal communication displays a clip of video recordings from a parliamentary session. The multimodal communication based on this authentic session recording is spiced with simple textual and visual elements (emojis).

In Figure 7.1, the textual element placed at the top ("agriculture is suffering") simplifies the message that farmers are facing difficulties and underscores its emotionally distressing nature by employing red highlighting (Kress and van Leeuwen 2021). The textual element in the lower section gives more information, suggesting that the suffering of farmers is due to inflexible climate goals (Kress and van Leeuwen 2021). The critique of climate politics expressed through textual elements is co-contextualized by verbal communication of Purra's speech in the parliament ("The legislation coming from the EU and the excessively ambitious national climate goals pile up into a massive bureaucratic jungle for farmers") that deploys various rhetorically compelling techniques such as consensus warranting and metaphoric and hyperbolic expressions (Sakki and Pettersson 2016) to accentuate Purra's point about overly ambitious climate policies. Following this, Purra addresses Prime Minister Marin and asks, "Could you consider more flexible climate goals?"

In response, Marin asserts in the parliamentary session that "Finland is committed to more ambitious climate objectives than the EU." As she gives her response, a simple multimodal halo emoji appears above her head, suggesting hypocrisy in relation to climate politics. Multimodal resources are used to recontextualize her statement with a new, less favourable interpretation. The same technique reappears later in the video when Marin is paired with another emoji, a gold medal this time, implying that instead of prioritising the nation's well-being and defending Finnish interests, she is actually trying to enhance her personal reputation and is motivated by self-interest (Sakki and Martikainen 2022, Pettersson et al. 2022). This strategic use of basic multimodal resources like emojis is used to challenge and redefine the meaning conveyed by the other resources (in this case, Marin's verbal response to Purra's question) and to ridicule the government and its ministers. This form of mockery achieved through straightforward and simple multimodal resources, often emojis, appears to serve as a key multimodal strategy for Purra to mock and ridicule her political opponents.

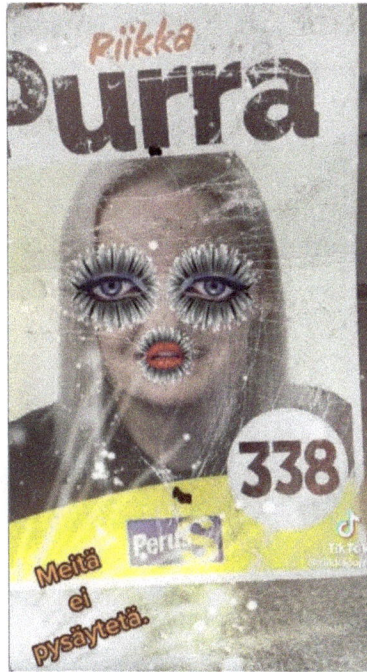

Fig. 7.2 Screenshot of Purra's TikTok video (19 March 2022).

Victimisation through multimodality used multimodal affordances to portray the FP as innocent victims of the mainstream media and the other political parties. Previous studies have demonstrated how populist leaders, globally and in Finland, create a sense of shared victimhood that enables them to differentiate virtuous people from perceived 'others', typically the malicious leftist urban elite, immigrants, and other minorities (e.g. Moffitt 2016, Sakki and Pettersson 2016, Bos et al. 2020, Mols and Jetten 2020).

Figure 7.2 is a screenshot of one of Purra's TikTok posts that utilizes multimodality to construct and mobilize the victimhood narrative. The visual focus of the TikTok post is Purra's election campaign poster, which has been defaced by an unknown attacker. The multimodal rhetoric is composed of visual, textual, and musical elements. A verbal narrative is not included in this TikTok video.

The video starts with an eye-catching textual element with large font asking, "Who is afraid of the FP?" that shows up in the middle of the visual illustration (Kress and van Leeuwen 2021). This works as an intertextual reference to an outdoor children's play from 20 years ago called "Who is Afraid of a Black Man?" Although the "Black man" in the play's title is nowadays replaced by "octobus" ("Who's Afraid of Octobus?"), on the level of interpersonal metafunction (Kress and van Leeuwen 2021), the textual element implies an implicit racist cue to Purra's audience, which is likely to be familiar with the former racist name of the children's play. Thus, it serves a kind of dog-whistling purpose meant to be noticed by those who understand the rhetoric, while remaining unnoticed by those who don't.

The visual communication showing Purra's election poster being attacked is combined with a textual element in orange reading "we will not be stopped." This works to co-contextualize the meaning that portrays not just Purra herself but the FP ("we") as victims of attacks from others. Later in the video, other multimodal elements are added to change the meaning. As Figure 7.2 illustrates, the torn and defaced parts of the poster around the areas of the eyes and mouth are replaced with multimodal eye and mouth emojis, which offer a playful reaction to the act of vandalism and a hint of moral self-satisfaction that provides a morally superior stance for the FP (Sakki and Martikainen 2021). Accompanied by the textual element in orange ("we will not be stopped"), it conveys to the viewer that the FP cannot be defeated.

As often in TikTok posts, there is also background music to this video, which serves as another powerful multimodal resource that together with the visual and textual semiotic modes works to co-contextualize the victimisation and empowerment of the FP. The video plays a catchy pop song that was released by the youth section of the FP before the elections and gained popularity on social media. The lyrics of the music reiterate the core political agenda of the FP by evoking a strong sense of injustice in the listener. The lyrics criticise modern society and the government, along with their political decisions. Concerns such as mass immigration, the imposition of climate worries on youth, and issues in the healthcare sector are mentioned. The proposed solutions to these concerns are aligned with the policies of the FP. The song encourages voting for the FP as an expression of hope for change. This further co-contextualizes the meaning and depicts the mobilisation of victimhood as appealing: despite being treated unfairly by other parties, the FP will "keep on rocking". The format of a pop song, with an engaging rhythm, energy, and easily memorable lyrics, has interpersonal and emotive power (Machin 2010) that enables the creator to recontextualize the serious political message in an appealing format that resonates with popular culture, and for this reason, it may be particularly powerful in attracting younger audiences (cf. Forchtner and Kølvraa 2017).

Conclusion

The era of new media has introduced a fresh array of instruments for PRRP politicians employing multimodal persuasive techniques (Pettersson and Sakki 2017, 2020). This chapter has examined the multimodal political communication of the current leader of the Finnish PRRP and the Minister of Finance Riikka Purra on TikTok.

As demonstrated in our analyses and consistent with previous work (e.g. Pettersson et al. 2022, Sakki and Martikainen 2021), multimodality was used to veil and soften overtly hostile and derogatory rhetoric. Deploying emojis, which can be considered as simple multimodal intersemiotic additives (Liu and O'Halloran 2009), the authentic talk of the FP's political opponents were redefined as ridiculous and hilarious. This use of satirical and ironic humour in social media communication can be understood as a strategic adjustment of rhetorical tactics aimed at engaging and appealing to fresh audiences (Forchtner and Kølvraa 2017). This humour (Billig 2005) serves the rhetorical purpose of evoking emotional responses, particularly anger directed at minority groups (othering through multimodality), while also questioning the credibility of those currently in power (mocking through multimodality).

Research on the use of TikTok as a tool for political communication is still limited. In relation to what is known about the style of populist rhetoric, the format of TikTok as a platform of social communication supports simplification, directness, emotionalisation, and negativity rather than complex political messages (Bos et al. 2020, Engesser, Fawzi and Larsson 2017). The multimodal affordances of TikTok communication supports creativity that political actors can deploy to modernise their image and reach diverse audiences, especially the younger voter base. Moving images and narration in TikTok videos, accompanied by music, serve as powerful communication tools. Through TikTok videos, political messages can be presented as trendy, relatable, and inspiring (Albertazzi and Bonansinga 2023), as our analysis of Purra's TikTok communication clearly demonstrates. Colloquialization through multimodality took place through elements like casual clothing (e.g. a beanie was worn in many videos), colloquial (youth) language, direct eye contact, and close-up framing that served to create intimacy with the viewer (Kress and van Leeuwen 2021). Additionally, intertextuality drawing from popular culture and shared reservoirs of meanings, such as old racist children's plays or a pop song, operated in tandem with other multimodal resources to mask the hatred towards the 'other' in this new medium (Pettersson et al. 2022). In this case, multimodality enabled dog-whistling and flirting with like-minded audiences without risking accusations of racism (Sakki and Martikainen 2021).

Methodologically, combining MDA (Kress 2011 and CDP (Wetherell 1998, Edley 2001) into MCDP provides a useful tool for approaching the contents, forms, and functions of multimodal TikTok communication. As both approaches take seriously the micro and macro levels of communication as well as social and political functions of meaning, this combination enabled us to better identify and unpack the complexity of political rhetoric at the same time as discursive, visual, and sonic acts that constructs social reality. The combined use of MDA and CDP into MCDP emerges as a valuable methodological approach for unravelling the intricate layers of meaning in multimodal political communication. Indeed, we suggest that the MCDP approach has the potential to unveil the complex interplay through which prejudice and hatred, although verbally silenced, can be subtly implied through the interaction of multiple modes (Sakki 2025).

In conclusion, our analysis of Riikka Purra's TikTok rhetoric reveals the diverse ways in which multimodal communication is utilised in contemporary political discourse. Using the framework of MCDP, we uncover Purra's strategic use of humour, colloquial language, and intertextuality to mobilise her audience. This research contributes to the limited understanding of TikTok as a tool of populist communication while recognizing that much more remains to be explored in this emerging field.

References

Abidin, C., 2021. "Mapping Internet Celebrity on TikTok: Exploring Attention Economies and Visibility Labours". *Cultural Science Journal*, 12, 77–103. https://doi.org/10.5334/csci.140

Albertazzi, D. and D. Bonansinga, 2023. "Beyond Anger: The Populist Radical Right on TikTok". *Journal of Contemporary European Studies*, 1–17. https://doi.org/10.1080/14782804.2022.2163380

Atton, C., 2006. "Far-Right Media on the Internet: Culture, Discourse and Power". *New Media & Society*, 8 (4), 573–587. https://doi.org/10.1177/1461444806065653.

Billig, M., 2005. *Laughter and Ridicule: Towards a Social Critique of Humor*. London: Sage. https://doi.org/10.4135/9781446211779.

Bos, Linda and K. Brants, 2014. "Populist Rhetoric in Politics and Media: A Longitudinal Study of the Netherlands". *European Journal of Communication*, 29, 703–719. https://doi.org/10.1177/0267323114545709.

—, Christian Schemer, Nicoleta Corbu, Michael Hameleers, Ioannis Andreadis, Anne Schulz, Desirée Schmuck, Carsten Reinemann and Nayla Fawzi, 2020. "The Effects of Populism as a Social Identity Frame on Persuasion and Mobilization: Evidence from a 15-Country Experiment". *European Journal of Political Research*, 59 (1), 3–24.

Cervi, L. and C. Marín-Lladó, 2021. "What Are Political Parties Doing on TikTok? The Spanish Case". *Profesional de la Información/Information Professional*, 30 (4), e300403. https://doi.org/10.3145/epi.2021.jul.03.

Edley, N., 2001. "Analysing Masculinity: Interpretative Repertoires, Ideological Dilemmas and Subject Positions". In: M. Wetherell, S. Taylor and S. J. Yates (eds), *Discourse as Data: A Guide for Analysis*. London: Sage, 189–228.

Engesser, S., N. Fawzi and A. O. Larsson, 2017. "Populist Online Communication: Introduction to the Special Issue". *Information, Communication and Society*, 20, 1279–1292.

Forchtner, B. and C. Kølvraa, 2017. "Extreme Right Images of Radical Authenticity: Multimodal Aesthetics of History, Nature, and Gender Roles in Social Media". *European Journal of Cultural and Political Sociology*, 4 (3), 252–281.

González-Aguilar, J. M., F. Segado-Boj and M. Makhortykh, 2023. "Populist Right Parties on TikTok: Spectacularization, Personalization, and Hate Speech". *Media and Communication*, 11 (2), 232–240. https://doi.org/10.17645/mac.v11i2.6358.

Hakoköngäs, E. and Inari Sakki, 2023. "Multimodal Nationalist Rhetoric in Finland". In: W. Wei and J. Schnell (eds), *Routledge Handbook of Descriptive Rhetorical Studies and World Languages*. London: Routledge, 234–248.

Hameleers, M., L. Bos and C. H. de Vreese, 2017. "'They Did It': The Effects of Emotionalized Blame Attribution in Populist Communication". *Communication Research*, 44 (6), 870–900. https://doi.org/10.1177/0093650216644026.

Horsti, K. and K. Nikunen, 2013. "The Ethics of Hospitality in Changing Journalism: The Response to the Rise of the Anti-Immigrant Movement in Finnish Media Publicity". *European Journal of Cultural Studies*, 16 (4), 489–504.

Kilby, L. and H. Lennon, 2021. "When Words Are Not Enough: Combined Textual and Visual Multimodal Analysis as a Critical Discursive Psychology Undertaking". *Methods in Psychology*, 5. https://doi.org/10.1016/j.metip.2021.100071.

Kress, G., 2011. "Multimodal Discourse Analysis". In: J. P. Gee and M. Handford (eds), *The Routledge Handbook of Discourse Analysis*. London: Routledge, 35–50.

—, and Theo van Leeuwen, 2021. *Reading Images: The Grammar of Visual Design*. 3rd edn. London: Routledge.

Laclau, E., 2005. *On Populist Reason*. London/New York: Verso.

Liu, Y. and K. O'Halloran, 2009. "Intersemiotic Texture: Analyzing Cohesive Devices between Language and Images". *Social Semiotics*, 19 (4), 367–388.

Machin, D., 2010. *Analysing Popular Music: Image, Sound, Text*. London: Sage.

Martikainen, J. and Inari Sakki, 2021. "Boosting Nationalism through COVID-19 Images: Multimodal Construction of the Failure of the 'Dear Enemy' with COVID-19 in the National Press". *Discourse and Communication*, 15 (4), 388–414.

Moffitt, B., 2016. "The Global Rise of Populism: Performance, Political Style, and Representation". Stanford: Stanford University Press.

Moir, A. 2023. "The Use of TikTok for Political Campaigning in Canada: The Case of Jagmeet Singh". *Social Media + Society*, 9 (1). https://doi.org/10.1177/20563051231157604.

Mols, F. and J. Jetten, 2020. "Understanding Support for Populist Radical Right Parties: Toward a Model That Captures Both Demand- and Supply-Side Factors". *Frontiers in Communication*, 5, 1–13.

O'Halloran, K. L., 2008. "Systemic Functional-Multimodal Discourse Analysis: Constructing Ideational Meaning Using Language and Visual Imagery". *Visual Communication*, 7 (4), 443–475. https://doi.org/10.1177/1470357208096210.

Pettersson, K., 2017. *Save the Nation: A Social Psychological Study of Political Blogs as a Medium for Nationalist Communication and Persuasion*. Helsinki: Unigrafia.

—, and M. Augoustinos, 2021. "Elite Political Discourse on Refugees and Asylum Seekers: The Language of Social Exclusion". In: C. Tileagă, M. Augoustinos and K. Durrheim (eds), *The Routledge International Handbook of Discrimination, Prejudice and Stereotyping*. Abingdon: Routledge, 261–272.

—, J. Martikainen, E., Hakoköngäs and Inari Sakki, 2022. "Female Politicians as Climate Fools: Intertextual and Multimodal Constructions of Misogyny Disguised as Humor in Political Communication". *Political Psychology*, 44 (1), 3–20.

—, J. Martikainen and Inari Sakki, 2024. "Flexible Populist Ideology During Russia's War in Ukraine: A Multimodal Analysis of Internet Memes". *Journal of Visual Political Communication*, 10 (2), 173–197. https://doi.org/10.1386/jvpc_00032_1.

—, S. Payotte and Inari Sakki, 2023. "Harsh Punisher or Loving Mother? A Critical Discursive Psychological Analysis of Marine Le Pen's Presidential Twitter Campaign". *Ethnicities*, 23 (6), 905–930.

—, and Inari Sakki, 2017. "'Pray for the Fatherland!' Discursive and Digital Strategies at Play in Nationalist Political Blogging". *Qualitative Research in Psychology*, 14 (3), 315–349.

—, and Inari Sakki, 2020. "Analysing Multimodal Communication and Persuasion in Populist Radical Right Political Blogs". In: M. Demasi, S. Burke and C. Tileagă (eds), *Political Communication*. London: Palgrave MacMillan, 175–203.

—, and Inari Sakki, 2023. "'You Truly Are the Worst Kind of Racist!': Argumentation and Polarization in Online Discussions around Gender and Radical-Right Populism". *British Journal of Social Psychology*, 62, 119–135.

—, and Inari Sakki., 2024. *Double Bind or Political Advantage? The Negotiation of Womanhood in the Online Discourse of Female Right-Wing Populist Politicians*. London: Palgrave Macmillan.

Potter, J., 1996. *Representing Reality: Discourse, Rhetoric and Social Construction*. London: Sage.

Pyrhönen, N. and G. Bauvois, 2020. "Conspiracies Beyond Fake News. Produsing Reinformation on Presidential Elections in the Transnational Hybrid Media System". *Sociological Inquiry*, 90 (4), 705–731. https://doi.org/10.1111/soin.12339.

Rovamo, H., K. Pettersson, K. and Inari Sakki, 2023. "Who's to Blame for Failed Integration of Immigrants? Blame Attributions as an Affectively Polarizing Force in Lay Discussions of Immigration in Finland". *Political Psychology*, 45, 235–258. https://doi.org/10.1111/pops.12917.

—, and Inari Sakki, 2024. "Mobilization of Shared Victimhood in the Radical Right Populist Finns Party Supporters' Identity Work: A Narrative-Discursive Approach to Populist Support". *European Journal of Social Psychology*, 54, 495–512. https://doi.org/10.1002/ejsp.3021. Sakki, I. (2025). Qualitative Approaches to the Social Psychology of Populism: Unmasking Populist Appeal. Abingdon: Routledge. https://doi.org/10.4324/9781003492276

and L. Castrén, 2022. "Dehumanization through Humour and Conspiracies in Online Hate towards Chinese People during the COVID-19 Pandemic". *British Journal of Social Psychology*, 61 (4), 1418–1438.

—, and J. Martikainen, 2021. "Mobilizing Collective Hatred through Humour: Affective-Discursive Production and Reception of Populist Rhetoric". *British Journal of Social Psychology*, 60 (2), 610–634.

—, and J. Martikainen, 2022. "'Sanna, Aren't You Ashamed?': Affective-Discursive Practices in Online Misogynist Discourse of Finnish Prime

Minister Sanna Marin". *European Journal of Social Psychology*, 52 (3), 435–447.

—, and K. Pettersson, 2016. "Discursive Constructions of Otherness in Populist Radical Right Political Blogs". *European Journal of Social Psychology*, 46 (2), 156–170.

—, and K. Pettersson, 2018. "Managing Stake and Accountability in Prime Ministers' Accounts of the 'Refugee Crisis': A Longitudinal Analysis". *Journal of Community and Applied Social Psychology*, 28 (6), 406–429.

Salojärvi, V., E. Palonen, L. Horsmanheimo and R.-M. Kylli, 2023. "Protecting the Future 'Us': A Rhetoric-Performative Multimodal Analysis of the Polarising Far-Right YouTube Campaign Videos in Finland". *Visual Studies*, 38 (5), 851–866. https://doi.org/10.1080/14725 86X.2023.2249430.

Van Leeuwen, Theo, 2012. "The Critical Analysis of Musical Discourse". *Critical Discourse Studies*, 9 (4), 219–328. https://doi.org/10.1080/17405 904.2012.713204.

Wetherell, M., 1998. "Positioning and Interpretative Repertoires: Conversation Analysis and Post-Structuralism in Dialogue". *Discourse and Society*, 9, 387–412.

8. Pictured hate: A visual discourse analysis of derogatory memes on Telegram

Lisa Bogerts, Wyn Brodersen, Maik Fielitz, and Pablo Jost

Abstract

Memes have become a propaganda weapon of far-right groups. While several studies highlight the strategic use of memes in far-right contexts, there is little empirical research on which groups these memes target, and how. As the visual stigmatisation of outgroups is a central means of communicating far-right worldviews, this study examines the visual propaganda of far-right and conspiratorial actors from a quantitative and qualitative perspective. To do this, we analysed memetic communication using computational and interpretive tools selected according to the visual discourse methodology. We collected our material from 1,675 alternative right-wing German-speaking channels of the messenger service Telegram, which we categorised into different sub-milieus and monitored continuously. Our findings suggest that there are significant differences in the way certain groups are targeted and a tendency to highlight the trigger points of current polarised public debates.

Keywords: *Memes, Germany, Telegram, far-right, conspiracy theories*

https://doi.org/10.11647/OBP.0447.08

Introduction

Digitalisation has led to the emergence of new formats and dissemination strategies for far-right politics, particularly aimed at younger generations. With the advent of social media and the potential for building a large online audience, far-right actors have adopted communication tactics that have the potential to go viral in online contexts. These include a shift towards visual and audio-visual propaganda, as well as the targeting of online-savvy milieus that congregate to attack individuals and marginalised groups (Askanius 2021a, Thorleifsson 2021). From these converging online milieus, far-right terrorists have been recruited. Before, during and after their killing spree, several far-right terrorists publicly referred to meme cultures and encouraged their audience to produce memes glorifying the violence of perpetrators.

Memes have become an effective tool of far-right online propaganda, as well as a common way of expressing emotions and political ideas. In fact, politics, social relations, and public entertainment are today hardly imaginable without the use of memes (Mortensen and Neumayer 2021). As a pervasive digital phenomenon, they combine political messages with (moving) images from pop or everyday culture. In extremist contexts, memes have the potential both to radicalise and to make far-right ideas mainstream. On the one hand, they make extremist ideas mainstream by appealing to popular communication habits (Schmid 2023). On the other hand, they may have a radicalising effect on consumers as the massive spread of hatred may contribute to turn towards the conduct of political violence (Crawford and Keen 2020).

Because they are semiotically more open than pure text, image-based memes circumvent analogue and algorithmic content moderation. In fact, memes disseminated by notorious actors often only imply extremist messages, while refraining from clearly expressed extremism (Bogerts and Fielitz 2019). In light of this, research has examined cross-platform circulation (Zannettou et al. 2018), strategic mainstreaming (Greene 2019) especially through the use of humour and irony (Mc Swiney et al. 2023), as well as the aesthetic features of far-right memes (Bogerts and Fielitz 2023).

However, even though we know a lot about the strategic use of memes, few studies show empirically how groups such as women, queer persons, or Jews are attacked by derogatory memes—even less over a longer period. As the (visual) stigmatisation of outgroups is a central vehicle for communicating far-right worldviews (Winter 2019), this study scrutinises the visual propaganda of far-right and conspiracist actors using computational methods and interprets selected images according to visual discourse analysis (Bogerts 2022). We gathered our material from 1,675 far-right and conspiracist German-speaking channels on the messenger service Telegram.

Our findings indicate that there are significant differences in the ways certain groups are caricatured by diverging visual elements, aesthetic styles and rhetorical means. Furthermore, we found a tendency to emphasise the trigger points of current polarised public debates. To explain how we reached these conclusions, we begin by delving into the state of research on far-right memes in digital communication. Next, we present our methodology and the quantitative results. We then dive deeper into the narratives, elements, and persuasion strategies of misogynistic, trans-hostile and antisemitic memes and, finally, examine which group of derogatory memes are disseminated most widely. By comparing different forms of visual discrimination, we can better understand how different memes contribute to spreading ideologies of inequality—a central element of far-right politics—from below.

Far-right (and) hate memes in digital communication

With the proliferation of audiovisual platforms, memetic content has become a central element of everyday communication. Originally, the phenomenon was broadly defined and stems from evolutionary biology. The term "meme" goes back to Richard Dawkins (2006) and is etymologically composed of two parts: Mimesis for imitation, and Gene for genetics. Similar to the gene, the meme spreads in the "meme pool" (Dawkins 2006: 192), but, unlike genetics, memes do not reproduce and rather infect, like a virus. When a meme goes viral, it is constantly being imitated, but through mutation it adapts to new contexts and constantly forms new variants (Dawkins 2006). Dawkin's general understanding of a meme as a spreading idea—or, as Richard Brodie (2009) describes it, as a virus of the mind—therefore cannot be limited to material or digital entities.

In digital communication, a meme is usually understood as an image-text combination in which a text is layered on top of an existing image (macro). Since both the text and the macro contain references to other memes or cultural phenomena, memes are characterised by "complex reference structures" (Nowotny and Reidy 2022: 33) and fall into two categories. On the one hand, there are those memes that are shared as a trend, such as a successful video, without change; on the other hand, there are those types of memes that become known only through changes in form and content (Marwick 2013). As this research is interested in the latter and based on large datasets prepared for automated analysis, we chose a minimal definition of memes as image-text combinations shared for the purpose of broad diffusion (see also Schmid et al. 2023). Screenshots of text messages, thumbnails, statistics, charts, stock photos, and product advertisements and photographs without text were excluded from the analysis.

Understood as the "intentional production and dissemination of 'a group of digital objects' [...] transformed by the transmission of many users through the Internet" (Shifman 2014: 41), the online memes encompasses a variety of content and format types. Memes are used to convey the idiosyncrasies of everyday life, which often defy verbal expression (von Gehlen 2020). They reflect the prevailing zeitgeist of simplifying the complexities of the world into a format that can be quickly consumed. And they are an effective means of attracting attention. It is therefore not surprising that memes are also used strategically to achieve political goals. The so-called 'meme wars' of the US alt-right, which erupted around the first election of Donald Trump in 2016, are a case in point (Dafaure 2020, Donovan et al. 2022).

Since then, memes have served as a means of disseminating extremist ideas to the masses, often in ways that are both timely and pop-cultural. In this context, memes convey far-right messages in a seemingly innocuous way, creating their own unique viewing habits and dynamics. The use of humour and irony allows extreme ideas to be expressed in a deliberately ambiguous way (Askanius 2021, McSwiney et al. 2021). They are semiotically open as they communicate on different levels and address different audiences. This means that the messages conveyed in a meme may never be fully understood by recipients, as the true origin of memes is often unclear. Elements of far-right ideology can thus circulate freely, even if they are shared by organisations with different agendas.

Unlike text, image-based memes can be grasped in a matter of seconds. Through their repetitive consumption, they appeal to both affect and cognition (Huntington 2015). To be created and understood, they require subcultural knowledge of codes and aesthetic composition, as well as an understanding of the factors that contribute to the virality of online materials (Grundlingh 2018). These skills are disseminated and acquired in specific online forums, such as 4chan, which are notorious for generating some of the most popular internet trends while also facilitating extremist communication (Philipps 2015). Consequently, despite the anonymity that memes offer their creators, they have the potential to rely on shared symbols, aesthetics, and modes of communication (Beyer 2014).

Many memes, not only in extremist contexts, refer to a rough net-cultural atmosphere and use humor at the expense of minority groups (Beran 2019). Stereotypical characters are combined with depictions of ingroup superiority to convey derogatory messages. We also find multiple discriminatory messages against different groups combined in one meme. Concerningly, research on intergroup conflict suggests that group degradation like this can be effective. According to the concept of group-focused enmity, diverse groups are cumulatively degraded on the basis of allegedly immutable characteristics in order to justify ideologies of inequality (Zick et al. 2009). However, the persuasive power of memes does not necessarily derive from ideological indoctrination, but also from sophisticated aesthetics, creative in-jokes and the potential for virality (Miller-Idriss 2020).

Methodology

To investigate the cross-phenomenal patterns of hate memes, we used a combination of computational and qualitative methods. We selected a dataset of 4,584 public German-speaking channels and groups on Telegram, which have shared around 8.5 million images since 2021.[1] These channels and groups are constitute a network of monitored Telegram channels by forwarding messages via public channels. Due to the diversity of their orientation, we further classified these channels in order to better analyse and categorise their ideological orientation and their shifts in discourse positioning.

We were interested in text-image combinations that potentially discriminate against one or more of the following groups: women, the LGBTQ community, Muslims, Jews, and people of colour in general. To generate a diverse dataset while minimising pandemic-related content, the time period was limited to 1 January 2022 to 30 June 2023. From the 2,787,282 remaining images a random sample of 25,000 images were selected that were equally distributed along diverse sub-milieus identified by the in-house monitoring of the Federal Association for Countering Online Hate.[2]

To increase the likelihood of selecting files containing both text and images, the 327,266 remaining images were filtered using the image embeddings from OpenAI's CLIP model (version clip-ViT-B-32), which is trained to understand both text and images. This automated process reduced the dataset by 82.8%, minimising the risk of excluding potentially interesting memes. Next, a random sample of 2,000 images per subset was selected and deduplication

---

1   For more information on the methodology of the Telegram monitoring, see: https://machine-vs-rage.bag-gegen-hass.net/methodischer-annex-01/.

2   This typology encompasses the following German-specific sub groups: Neo-Nazis, Sovereign Citizens (Reichsbürger), Populist Right, New Right, Extreme Right, Conspiracy Ideologues, Esotericists, QAnon, Anti-Vax activists and the Querdenken movement.

was applied using CLIP embeddings, cosine similarity and a high threshold to eliminate nearly identical images. This resulted in a final corpus of 40,728 images, which were used for manual annotation.

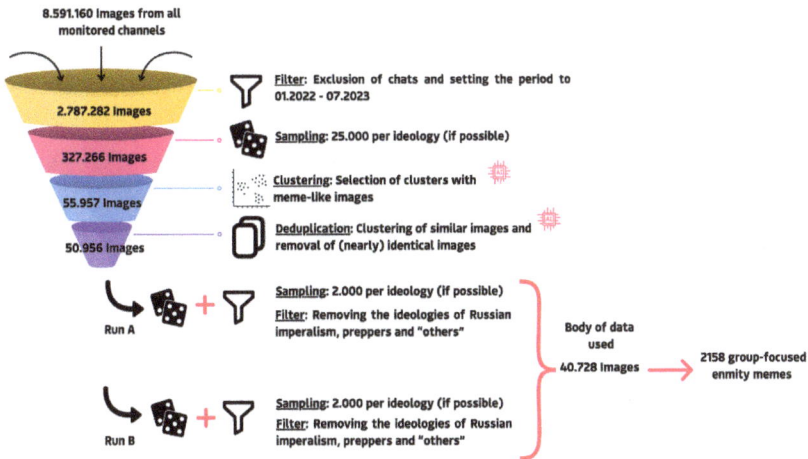

Fig. 8.1 Visualisation of the multi-stage sampling process.

In the first step (see description below), the images were annotated by a group of students who underwent a three-stage training programme to sensitise them to the content. The annotation process involved the research team in complex and nuanced steps to ensure thorough and accurate classification.

The material was analysed using a visual discourse analysis approach. Following Gillian Rose (2016: 187), we understand "visual discourse to be a set of visual statements or narratives that structures the way we think about the world and how we act accordingly" (Bogerts 2022: 40). For our analysis it is particularly important what social groups are made visible, how often they are depicted and how they are represented. Therefore, we combined a quantitative content analysis—i.e. counting of the visual elements (Bell 2004)—with the qualitative identification of narrative structures and strategies of persuasion, which also takes into account the image-text relationship that is characteristic of memes as we define them in this chapter. In order to delve deeper into the visual terrain of far-right memes, we proceeded according to five steps.

In the first step, the material was sorted according to the five pre-defined group-related hate categories [1] (antisemitism, misogyny, LGBTQ hostility, hostility towards Muslims, racism) and one category for other affected groups. Each image was annotated three times and only those with at least two concurring annotations, e.g. as conveying "racism," were selected for the category "racism". To achieve consistent annotation among the research team, we agreed on definitions about what each form of group-related degradation entails, which were informed by research literature e.g. on forms of antisemitism and misogyny. Multiple classifications within one image were possible and received special attention due to the intersectionality of the phenomena.

Secondly, the narratives [2] of the memes were annotated to understand the degrading arguments made by the images in the respective categories. These narratives were derived inductively from the material and specified with the help of research literature on group-related hate. In other words, the research team went through numerous memes from each group-related category and identified recurring themes, 'arguments', and stories. For instance, it became obvious that many memes conveying racism portrayed racialized people as being "criminal", a "threat to public health" or a threat to the alleged "purity of an imaginary German *völkisch* community". After deriving several such key narratives, we tested whether they were exhaustive and as unambiguous as possible, and revised them when necessary (Bell 2004: 15-16). In this step, memes that had previously been incorrectly annotated as one category in the first step were now reassigned to the correct category.

To go beyond the tendency to interpret memes according to their text elements and gain insights into visual communication, the visual elements [3] of the memes were annotated according to classic content analysis (Bell 2004). Several types of visual elements were distinguished (people in general, specific celebrities, objects, nature, and symbols), each containing 5–11 different elements (Bogerts 2022: 42). To do so, as in the previous step, the research team went through the material with "fresh eyes" (Rose 2016: 205) in order to see what is usually overlooked when superficially and subconsciously interpreting images. For instance, the category "symbols" contained annotations like "German flag" or "other flags", the category "objects" included "weapons" or "money".

Persuasive meme strategies also work with different rhetorical means [4]. Depending on which feeling the meme producer aims to evoke in the consumer to make the message convincing, they might choose a certain form of "argumentation". As humour is ubiquitous in memes, we went through the material to test which memes were intended to be humorous and which ones use other means of persuasion. As a result, in this final step, we annotated the rhetorical means of humour, outrage (about an alleged behaviour of the targeted group), open threat of violence against the marginalised group, ingroup victimhood/reverse victim and offender, and ingroup superiority or pride. We were already familiar with the latter categories from a previous study (Bogerts and Fielitz 2019), where we had observed ingroup "victimhood" e.g. of white Germans who feel disadvantaged by refugees who receive social security benefits in Germany, and ingroup superiority e.g. by white Germans who expressed feeling (racially) superior to racialized (non-white) people.[3]

Following this, the aesthetic styles [5] of the images were annotated. In doing so, the researchers paid further attention

---

3   The choice of reliability coefficients was based on scientific recommendations (Holsti reliability coefficient, Krippendorff's alpha) and popularity in the field (Cohen's kappa). According to the literature on intercoder reliability, a classification of "excellent" (greater than 0.8), "good" (0.6 to 0.8), and "moderate" (0.4 to 0.6) is considered acceptable (Cicchetti and Sparrow 1981, Landis and Koch 1977, Regier, et al. 2013). For the purposes of this research, a conservative mixed approach was used. Significant differences in reliability scores were observed in the annotation of hate categories [1], partly due to the fact that more than 95% of the data were not assigned to any category in this step. Disagreements in annotation were resolved by at least two researchers. A notable trend across all hate categories is that narratives [2] that require literacy (e.g. knowledge of conspiracy theories) were also particularly difficult for researchers to annotate, resulting in lower reliability scores. In all subsequent analysis steps [3–5], reliability scores ranged from moderate to excellent agreement. Notably, items requiring background knowledge were significantly more difficult to consistently annotate than descriptive items such as objects.

to the visual characteristics of memes that might influence our interpretation and classification subconsciously. We inductively derived from the material several aesthetic styles that meme producers employed to communicate their messages. This procedure builds on our previous study on far-right memes (Bogerts and Fielitz 2019) where we had identified a limited set of typical aesthetics that seem to make a meme attractive or persuasive in the eye of its producer, depending on the content of the message. Recognizing some of these aesthetics and identifying new ones, we categorised all memes as modern photography, historical imagery (photography, painting), comic/cartoon, advertisement/fake advertisement, pop culture reference, statistics/diagrams, screenshots, chat aesthetics (emojis, etc.), or collage.

Lastly, a regression analysis [6] was conducted to examine which group of memes went viral in the Telegram sphere. Virality, in this context, was measured by the number of times a message was forwarded. The analysis is based on 2,158 messages. For comparison, a random sample of 6,474 messages from 322 channels where memes were also shared was used as a reference dataset, resulting in a combined total of 8,632 messages. Two models were developed for this analysis. The first model used the distinction between messages containing hate memes and those without as the independent variable, with the analysis conducted on the entire dataset. The second model focused on the meme-specific dataset to assess the influence of hate categories on virality. These categories were treated as independent variables. In both models, the number of subscribers to the channels was included as a control variable to mitigate potential bias from channels with disproportionately high reach.

Results

In examining our data, we focus on four dimensions. Firstly, we present the statistical frequencies of memes in different sub-milieus, breaking down the data to quantify which of the pre-defined groups were most targeted. We then move to a more fine-grained qualitative examination, looking at the narrative composition of misogynistic memes to better understand the versatility of memes within a single category of group-focused enmity (whereas misogyny is also the most prevalent). In a third step, we illustrate our approach of element coding and visual rhetorical strategies in the cases of LGBTQ hostility and antisemitism. Finally, we measure the virality of the memes in our dataset using regression analysis methods. Our aim was to find out whether hate memes are more widespread than other formats, and whether there are different rates of spread between the categories of group-focused enmity studied.

Quantitative analysis

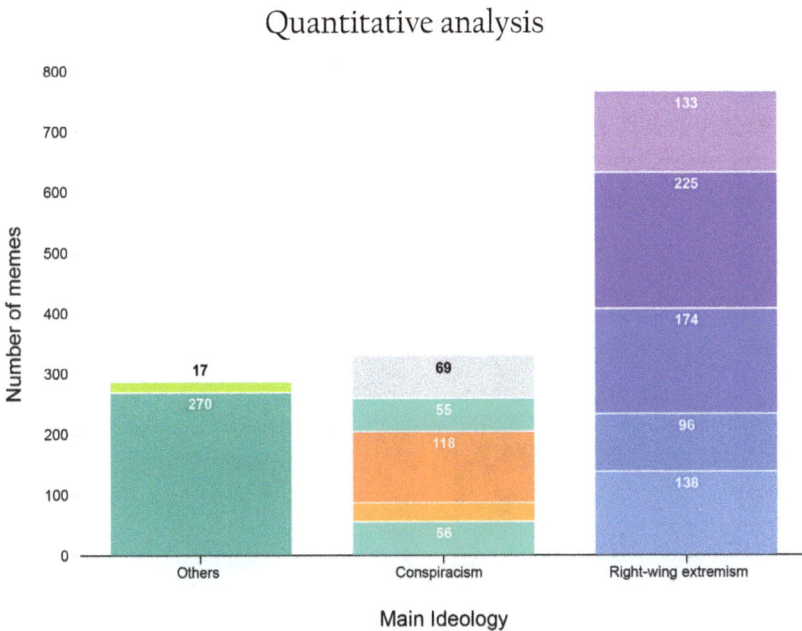

Fig. 8.2 Meme prevalence divided into ideological sub milieus (n=2.158).

In the quantitative part of the analysis we find significant differences in the use of memes by different anti-democratic sub-milieus and targeted groups. From a global perspective, a total of 5.3% (2,158) of the memes in our sample were annotated and interpreted as derogatory memes at the expense of our predefined groups. At first glance, this seems like a small number, as the Telegram platform has been described as a hotbed of extremist communication, especially in Germany (Buehling and Heft 2023, Jost and Dogruel 2023). There are profound differences in the use of such memes. In particular, far-right actors (766) were found to share hate memes more often than those in the conspiratorial milieu (287) or other channels (287). This is not necessarily surprising, as we see a strategic use of memes in far-right contexts.

This is also reflected in the results of the annotation process in general. When analysing a representative sample, most hate memes can be categorised as misogynistic. In total, 31% of the derogatory memes fall into this category and can be read or interpreted as misogynistic. There were also significant levels of racist references and LGBTQ hostility, each present in 28% of the images. Antisemitic content made up 18% of the hate memes analysed, while hostility towards Muslims was the smallest category at 6%. Notably, 9% of the memes showed intersections of several hate categories. Our findings highlight the frequent overlap between misogyny and LGBTQ hostility, as well as between racism and hostility towards Muslims.

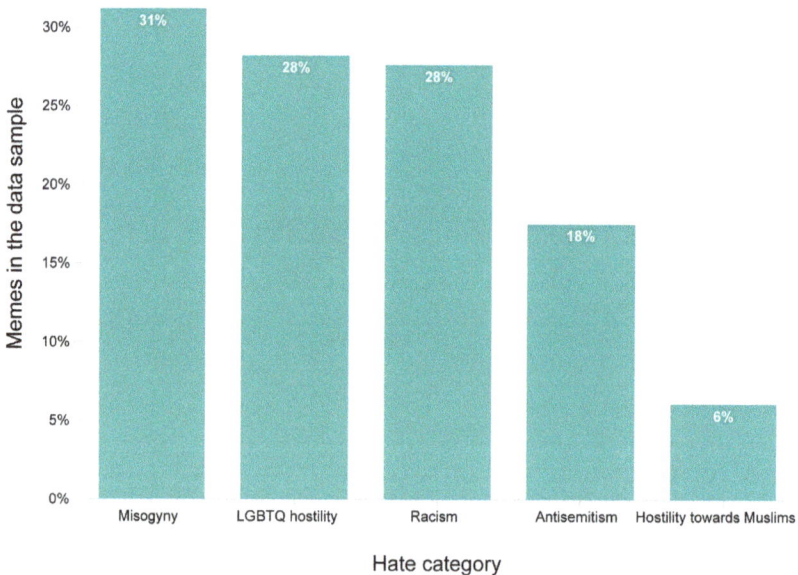

Fig. 8.3 Relative frequency of hate categories.

A more detailed picture emerges when looking at which ideological actors discriminate against which marginalised social groups. The channels used by QAnon supporters are particularly noteworthy. Within these channels, almost one in three (32%) hate memes can be interpreted as antisemitic. Hate memes from these channels account for 19% of all antisemitic memes in the dataset. Similarly, in esoteric channels, 39% of hate memes can be interpreted as racist, accounting for 18% of all racist memes in the dataset. The far-right populist channels are striking. Channels from this ideological spectrum degrade women the most. Almost half (49%) of the hate memes used here can be classified as misogynistic. This accounts for more than a quarter (28%) of all misogynistic memes in the entire dataset.

The narrative composition of misogynistic memes

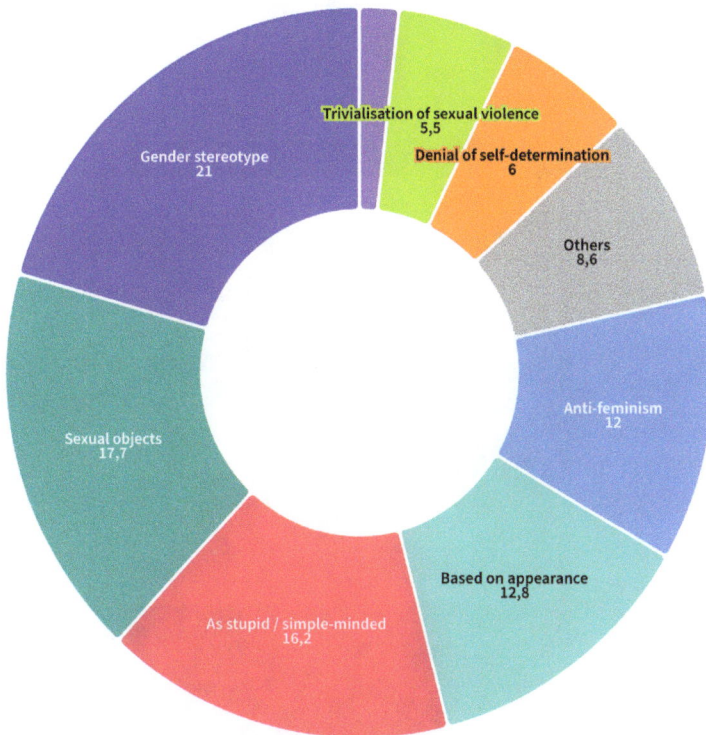

Fig. 8.4 Pie chart of narratives identified as misogynistic, segmented by percentage.

Deeper insights into the form of hate were gained by annotating the underlying narrative structures. In the context of misogyny, this highlights that more subtle forms of degradation, often expressed as crude chauvinistic humour, are more dominant than open hate. Most misogynistic memes draw on common gender stereotypes between men and women (21%), depict women as sexual objects (17.7%), or portray them as stupid (16.2%). Although these forms of representation dominate the data set, we also identified more explicit forms of misogyny. For example, 5.5% of misogynistic memes trivialise (physical) violence against women and 6% deny their self-determination.

Figs. 8.5, 8.6 and 8.7 Misogynistic memes depicting women as sexual objects.

Body features are overtly sexualised or women are presented to the viewer—who is apparently assumed to be a heterosexual male—as freely available sexual fantasies. For example, one meme shows a young woman with bare legs lying next to a rubbish bin in the street. The text reads: "Why would you throw something like that away? It still looks good!!!!"[4] (Fig. 8.5). Another meme shows a young woman opening a flat door from the inside. She is naked below the waist and waves an imaginary visitor away: "Gas bill? Can you please come later, I'm just paying the electricity!" (Fig. 8.6) In addition to portraying the woman as a sex object, this also conveys a message of denied self-determination by implying that women have no money of their own and can only 'pay' with sexual services (6%). This example also shows that memes can convey a misogynistic message even if it is not their main message but rather as a side effect that is supposed to entertain the viewer. For example, this meme seems to mainly allude to rising gas and electricity prices in 2022 and the indignation felt by many consumers in Germany.

Even without explicit nudity, memes can degrade women by treating them as sex objects, for example, when beautiful women are oversexualised and women's bodies that deviate from the norm are devalued. Here, for example, is the famous film scene of a laughing Marylin Monroe with her dress caught by the wind and her legs exposed, next to Green Party politician Ricarda Lang, who is also wearing a dress. The caption reads: "Let's hope it stays windless". Although this motif of devaluation based on appearance is less common (16%) than that of oversexualisation, it conveys a similar message: women are supposed to be 'eye candy' for the male viewer. However, in addition to this sexist interpretation, there is also the possibility that the devaluation relates solely to body shape, i.e. it is 'only' fatphobic. There is therefore a degree of ambiguity which, coupled with the humorous wink, can be perceived differently by different recipients. At the same time, this gives an opportunity for

---

4   All quoted texts in this section are translated by the authors and are written in German in the original memes. All memes being shared here are graphically edited to avoid uncritical reproduction and to give anonymity to the people who are depicted.

disseminators to deny misogyny. In principle, however, physical devaluation is a widespread form of misogyny, and women are disproportionately affected by fatphobic hostility.

Elements, rhetoric, and style of hate memes

While deciphering narratives requires a great deal of interpretation, it is even more unclear what exactly is depicted in these memes that evokes different perceptions and attributions of meaning and allows for broad receptivity. In order to better understand how the resonance of memes works, we have also coded individual visual elements such as people, objects, animals, or symbols. This makes it possible to describe images as systematically and objectively as possible, and can help to contextualise visual carriers of devaluation and identify implicit patterns of persuasion. In this regard, studies show that the frequency of certain elements provides clues to the argumentative structure of memes (Bogerts and Fielitz 2019).

The distribution of image elements across the analysed hate categories initially reveals predictable patterns. For instance, in racist and anti-Muslim memes, the most frequently classified visual element is a non-white man (11% and 20% in each category). Antisemitic memes predominantly depict economically influential individuals (12%) or celebrities (8%), while misogynistic memes overwhelmingly feature women (20%).

However, a closer look reveals less obvious visual elements that provide a deeper understanding of ideological dynamics. In the LGBTQ category, for example, it is notable that political logos that stand for a political movement, such as the pride flag, are just as common (9%) as depictions of visibly trans/non-binary persons (8%). This may indicate that the visual discourse in this category is partly transphobic, but also targets the movements advocating for diversity, queer feminism, or queer politics. This ambiguity and ambivalence makes it difficult to distinguish between a critique of progressive politics and explicit transphobia. The intent of the creator remains blurry, as it is unclear in which context a specific meme was first shared.

This highlights a central characteristic of memes: they rarely convey clear messages and almost never construct arguments, but play with ambiguity and work associatively (Shifman 2013). In the case of LGBTQ hostility, this means that memes often exist in undefined grey areas or border zones. The frequency of certain image elements also shows that these memes often represent not only the target group itself, but also other social groups. For example, the frequent appearance of white women and children in memes related to racism (7% and 5%) and LGBTQ hostility (8% and 7%) suggests that these categories increasingly include threat scenarios in their messaging. In this case, racialized migrant men are portrayed as a threat to white women and LGBTQ persons as a threat to children and the traditional institution of the family.

The contextualisation of hate memes must also include the means of persuasion—in particular, characteristics within each category in terms of the rhetoric used. For instance, the rhetoric of 'outrage 'is more pronounced in anti-Muslim memes (22%) than in other hate memes, and racist memes use the rhetoric of ethnic superiority and pride (16%) more than in other hate categories. The prevalence of humour within the categories is particularly striking. Both LGBTQ hostility (52%) and misogynist memes (70%) use humour more often than other categories, while humour seems to play a comparatively very small role in antisemitic memes (12%).

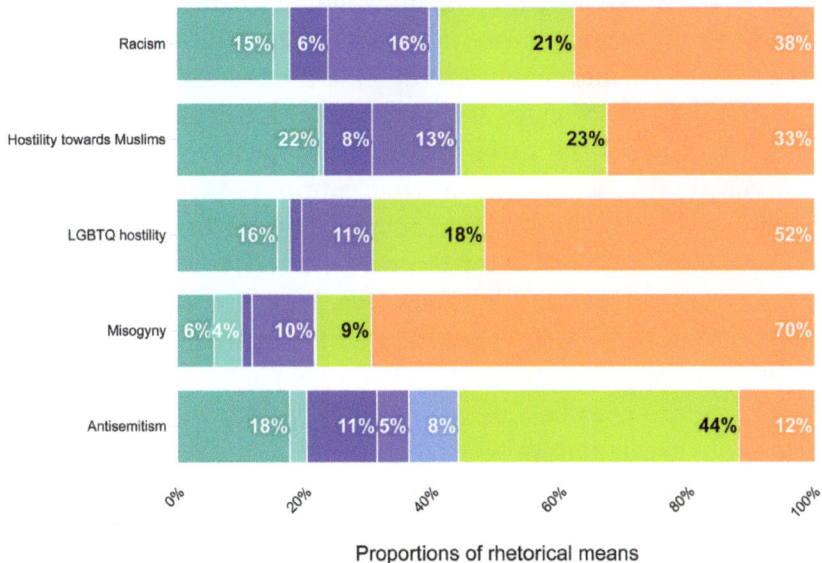

Proportions of rhetorical means

Fig. 8.8 Rhetoric of hate categories segmented by percentage.

It is noticeable that antisemitic memes mainly try to convince with alleged facts (44%). This rhetorical style is by far the most common in this category. This is in line with theoretical approaches in antisemitism research, as the phenomenon is primarily understood as a "rumour about the Jews" (Adorno 2005: 110). Conspiracy myths and ideologies are often an integral part of modern antisemitism when they provide a model for explaining the complexity of the modern world (Rathje 2021). Antisemitism has a long tradition of being expressed through visual imagery (Kirschen 2010), which has adapted its form over time and can be seen in today's digital cultures (Zannettou et al. 2018).

Particularly recurrent images are those that became especially well known in the course of the protests against the COVID-19 measures, such as images of software billionaire Bill Gates or investor Georg Soros. These individuals were repeatedly accused of having secret plans, ranging from alleged 'population replacement' to remote control by chip via vaccination. An example of this is the meme below. It shows a cartoon-like depiction of the economist and president of the World Economic Forum (WEF), Klaus Schwab. The word "reset" can be read as a possible allusion to the conspiracy narrative of the Great Reset. This is an initiative of the World Economic Forum that aimed to introduce economic reforms in the face of the COVID-19 pandemic. The conspiracy theory interpretation of the project, however, sees a secret alliance of elites behind it, who would have invented a pandemic to enslave the population and achieve global power. The conspiracy theory combines and continues existing narratives such as "The Great Replacement" and "New World Order". The pop-cultural iconography of the meme suggests a connection to John Carpenter's 1988 film *They Live*, in which the protagonist discovers that many of the world's authority figures are actually malevolent aliens controlling ordinary people for their own ends. While memes require a certain level of literacy to decipher, they leave interpretation to their recipients. Whether the Schwab meme is a pop-cultural and consumer-critical allusion, or whether it is intended to portray him as a manipulative string-puller who subjugates the world's population, is in the eye of the beholder.

Fig. 8.9 Meme about the conspiracy theory of the "great reset" with antisemitic connotation

Antisemitism is often expressed in coded language or metaphorically, not least because the accusation carries particular weight after the Holocaust, and its expression is considered taboo in large parts of German society. Whereas, in the 19th century, the term "anti-Semite" was freely chosen by open enemies of the Jews as a self-description, today hardly anyone openly admits to this resentment. At the same time, we can see that antisemitism is used in different ways in our stakeholder groups. Neo-Nazi channels, for example, dispense with humour and use the rhetoric of superiority to devalue Jews (and alleged Jews), while conspiracy theory channels deal with alleged facts in a more abstract way and are much more coded. Open threats of violence are very rarely expressed in antisemitic memes on Telegram, which is probably related to the possibility of legal consequences (in Germany).

Measuring virality through regression analysis

Moving away from the concrete composition of visual content, we were interested in measuring if (and which) hate memes go viral on Telegram. The analysis is based on 2,158 messages. For comparison, a random sample of 6,474 messages from 322 channels where memes were also shared was used as a reference dataset, resulting in a combined total of 8,632 messages. Two models were developed for this analysis. The first regression model (first row of Fig. 8.11) shows that the independent variable meme/no meme has almost no effect on sharing between channels. The second regression model (below the first row of Fig. 8.11) shows that hate categories as an independent variable has only a small effect on sharing. Specifically, misogynistic memes are shared less on average, while antisemitic memes are shared more than memes in other hate categories.

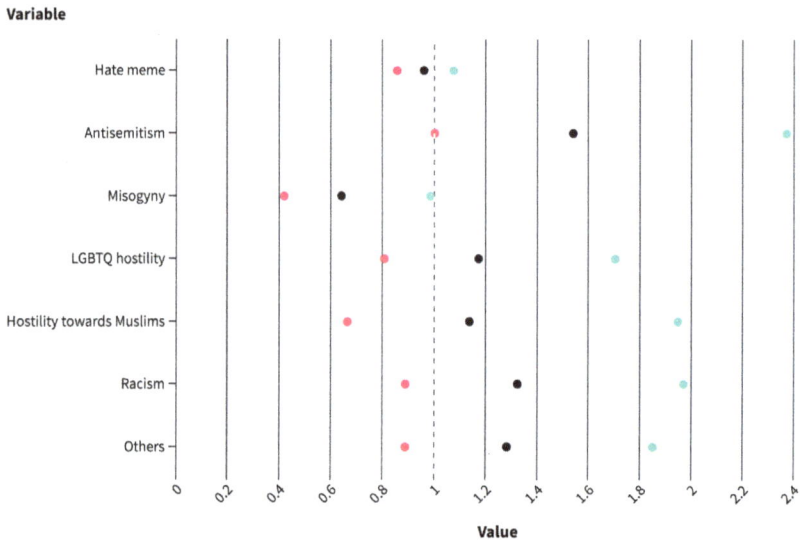

Fig. 8.10 Negative binomial regression on the influence of meme type on the number of shares[5]

At first glance, these results seem counterfactual: while we have seen that women are particularly targeted by memetic hate communication, the results of the calculated regression models indicate that misogynistic memes spread less in the analysed Telegram channels than memes of other hate categories. One possible explanation is that these memes are so ubiquitous and

5   Negative binomial regression models with fixed-effect estimation and varying intercepts for 322 channels; baseline model (above red line) only includes hate meme; full model (below red line) includes all types of memes; all models are controlled for number of subscribers.

familiar that there is little incentive to forward such messages. On the contrary, antisemitic memes are forwarded more often than other hate memes, even though they are much less present in the dataset overall. This may be due to the fact that antisemitic memes have a certain newsworthiness that distinguishes them from the derogatory everyday humour of most hate memes.

Discussion

The analysis has shown that the visual representation of group-focused hate is multifaceted and opens up new facets for thinking about image-based forms of far-right "politics from below". 5.3% of the analysed images were classified as derogatory against one or more of the predefined groups. The results of the regression analysis suggest that content conveying group-related hate rarely goes viral. One reason for the limited spread of hate memes in the German Telegram sphere may be the design of the platform. Communication via the channels is one-to-many, which excludes members from a collaborative process of meme creation. In addition, the target and user groups on Telegram are likely to be significantly different from those on platforms considered to be meme hubs, such as 4chan, imgur, or 9GAG. As a text-specific hybrid medium, Telegram does not reward images as much as platforms with algorithmically organised news feeds. Instead, the frequent, attention-grabbing posting encourages the DIY mentality inherent in participatory forms of image production. This means that images are created and shared according to one's own standards.

This aspect is reinforced by a lot of banal content with primitive forms of jokes and rude humour. The visual content on this instant messaging service is more likely to address borderline areas, associated with chauvinistic everyday humour, and less likely to promote explicitly extremist world views. If we take the example of online misogyny and LGBTQ hostility, we often find subtle expressions of discrimination and hate in the form of gender stereotyping. Many of these memes operate in a grey area, as they can be understood both as a critique of gender and sexual identity policies and as a devaluation of the people to whom these policies apply. This ambiguity or diversity of interpretation allows for the activation of multiple trigger points in an emotionally charged debate, particularly around the right to gender self-determination. Hence, group-related enmity is often used as a pretext to criticise liberal democracy as a whole.

Conclusion

This exploratory study has examined the memetic communication of group-focused hate as a form of everyday discrimination, but also of far-right politics. In our multilevel analysis, we found that the target groups of these memes are addressed differently in terms of frequency, rhetoric, and use of visual elements.Most of the imagery we analysed contains subtle forms of hatred and discrimination, and not explicit threats against marginalized persons, e.g. with (physical) violence, as one might expect. On the one hand, this may be due to the format of memes as a truly ambiguous form of communication, allowing for different interpretations and thus appealing to different audiences. On the other hand, the alternative right-wing Telegram scene in Germany is subject to a much stricter penal system than, for example, in the US, which is why public communication is much more coded than elsewhere. This said, we are aware that such offences are shared anonymously on other platforms such as less moderated imageboards. In light of this, our findings must be understood in the context of a specific platform culture.Furthermore, we need to acknowledge natural biases in the interpretations of the memes. Although coders are trained to be as objective as possible, many of the coding decisions are influenced by individual sensitivity to a form of degradation, prior knowledge, and political beliefs. Therefore, the results must always take into account how an academically socialised audience reads the memes. In addition, our material is a reflection of the time period we studied. It began after the coronavirus protests had died down in the winter of 2021/22, and extended until the beginning of the Alternative für Deutschland's (AfD) breakthrough beginning in the summer of 2023, which created a much more hostile political climate. As memes relate to current events, our findings therefore only provide insights into an episode of memetic communication of group-based enmity on a particular platform at a particular time. A similar snapshot of what happens on other platforms would presumably be different.

Nevertheless, by comparing not only statistical data but also qualitatively contextualising the elements of visual discourse, our study offers comparative insights into the narrative packaging of memes, as well as the rhetorical and aesthetic means used to communicate group-based enmity. This calls for further research on comparability across different time periods and political milieus in order to better understand the specificity of memes as a form of far-right mobilisation.

References

Adorno, Theodor W., 2005. Minima Moralia: Reflections on a Damaged Life. London/New York: Verso.

Askanius, Tina, 2021. "On Frogs, Monkeys, and Execution Memes: Exploring the Humor-Hate Nexus at the Intersection of Neo-Nazi and Alt-Right Movements in Sweden". Television & New Media, 22 (2), 147–165. https://doi.org/10.1177/1527476420982234.

—, and Nadine Keller, 2021. "Murder fantasies in memes: fascist aesthetics of death threats and the banalization of white supremacist violence". Information, Communication & Society, 24 (16), 2522–2539. https://doi.org/10.1080/1369118X.2021.1974517.

Bell, Philip, 2004, "Content Analysis of Visual Images". In: T. van Leuwen and C. Jewitt (eds), The Handbook of Visual Analysis. London: Sage, 10–34.

Beran, Dale, 2019. It Came from Something Awful: How a New Generation of Trolls Accidentally Memed Donald Trump into the White House. New York: St. Martin's Press.

Beyer, Jessica Lucia, 2014. Expect Us. Online Communities and Political Mobilization. Oxford: Oxford University Press.

Bogerts, Lisa, 2022. The Aesthetics of Rule and Resistance. Analyzing Political Street Art in Latin America. New York: Berghahn Books Incorporated.

—, and Maik Fielitz, 2019. "'Do You Want Meme War?'. Understanding the Visual Memes of the German Far Right". In: Maik Fielitz and Nick Thurston (eds), Post-Digital Cultures of the Far Right. Online Actions and Offline Consequences in Europe and the US. Bielefeld: Transcript, 137–153.

—, and Maik Fielitz, 2023. "Fashwave. The Alt-Right's Aesthetization of Politics and Violence". In: Sarah Hegenbart and Mara Kölmel (eds), Dada Data. Contemporary Art Practice in the Era of Post-Truth Politics. London: Bloomsbury Visual Arts, 230–245.

Brodie, Richard, 2009. Virus of the Mind. The New Science of the Meme. Seattle: Hay House.

Buehling, Kilian and Annett Heft, 2023. "Pandemic Protesters on Telegram: How Platform Affordances and Information Ecosystems Shape Digital Counterpublics". Social Media + Society, 9 (3), Article 20563051231199430. https://doi.org/10.1177/20563051231199430.

Cicchetti, Domenic V. and Sara A. Sparrow, 1981. "Developing criteria for establishing interrater reliability of specific items: applications to assessment of adaptive behavior". American Journal of Mental Deficiency, 86 (2), 127–137.

Crawford, Blyth and Florence Keen, 2020. "Memetic irony and the promotion of violence in chan cultures". Centre for Research and Evidence on Security Threats, London.

Dawkins, Richard, 2006. The Selfish Gene. 30th Anniversary edn. New York: Oxford University Press.

Dafaure, Maxime, 2020. The "'Great Meme War': the Alt-Right and its Multifarious Enemies". Angles. New Perspectives on the Anglophone World, (10), 1–28.

Doerr, Nicole, 2021. "The Visual Politics of the Alternative for Germany (AfD): Anti-Islam, Ethno-Nationalism, and Gendered Images". Social Sciences, 10 (1), 20. https://doi.org/10.3390/socsci10010020.

Donovan, Joan, Emily Dreyfuss and Brian Friedberg, 2022. Meme Wars. The Untold Story of the Online Battles Upending Democracy in America. New York: Bloomsbury Publishing.

Gagnon, Audrey, 2023. "Far-right virtual communities: Exploring users and uses of far-right pages on social media". Journal of Alternative & Community Media, 7 (2), 117–135. https://doi.org/10.1386/jacm_00108_1

Galip, Idil, 2024. "Methodological and epistemological challenges in meme research and meme studies". Internet Histories, 1–19. https://doi.org/10.1080/24701475.2024.2359846

von Gehlen, Dirk, 2020. Meme. Muster digitaler Kommunikation. Berlin: Verlag Klaus Wagenbach.

Grundlingh, L., 2018. "Memes as speech acts". Social Semiotics, 28 (2), 147–168. https://doi.org/10.1080/10350330.2017.1303020.

Hokka, Jenni and Matti Nelimarkka, 2019. "Affective economy of national-populist images: Investigating national and transnational online networks through visual big data". New Media & Society, August. https://doi.org/10.1177/1461444819868686

Jost, Pablo and Leyla Dogruel, 2023. "Radical Mobilization in Times of Crisis: Use and Effects of Appeals and Populist Communication Features in Telegram Channels". Social Media + Society, 9 (3), Article 20563051231186372. https://doi.org/10.1177/20563051231186372.

Kirschen, Yaakov, 2010. "Memetics and the Viral Spread of Antisemitism Through 'Coded Images' in Political Cartoons". Institute for the Study of Global Antisemitism and Policy.

Landis, J. Richard and Gary G. Koch, 1977. "An Application of Hierarchical Kappa-type Statistics in the Assessment of Majority Agreement among Multiple Observers". Biometrics, 33 (2), 363–74.

Macklin, Graham, 2019. "The Christchurch Attacks: Livestream Terror in the Viral Video Age". CTC Sentinel, 12 (6), 18–29.

Marwick, Alice, 2013. "Memes". Contexts, 12 (4), 12–13.

McSwiney, Jordan, Michael Vaughan, Annett Heft and Matthias Hoffmann, 2021. "Sharing the hate? Memes and transnationality in the far right's digital visual culture". Information, Communication & Society, 1–20. https://doi.org/10.1080/1369118X.2021.1961006.

Miller-Idriss, Cynthia, 2020. Hate in the Homeland. The New Global Far Right. Princeton: Princeton University Press.

Mortensen, Mette and Christina Neumayer, 2021. "The playful politics of memes". Information, Communication & Society, 24 (16), 2367–2377. https://doi.org/10.1080/1369118X.2021.1979622.

Nowotny, Joanna and Julian Reidy, 2022. Memes – Formen und Folgen eines Internetphänomens. Bielefeld: Transcript.

Phillips, Whitney, 2015. This is Why We Can't Have Nice Things. Mapping the Relationship Between Online Trolling and Mainstream Culture. Cambridge: MIT Press.

Rathje, Jan, 2021. "'Money Rules the World, but Who Rules the Money?' Antisemitism in post-Holocaust Conspiracy Ideologies". In: Armin Lange, Kerstin Mayerhofer, Dina Porat and Lawrence H. Schiffman (eds), Confronting Antisemitism in Modern Media, the Legal and Political Worlds. Berlin/Boston: De Gruyter, 45–68.

Regier, Darrel A., William E. Narrow, Diana E. Clarke, Helena C. Kraemer,, S. Janet Kuramoto, Emily A. Kuhl and David J. Kupfer, 2013. "DSM-5

Field Trials in the United States and Canada, Part II: Test-Retest Reliability of Selected Categorical Diagnoses". American Journal of Psychiatry, 170 (1), 59–70.

Rose, Gillian, 2016. Visual Methodologies. An Introduction to Researching with Visual Materials. 4th edn. London: Sage.

Schmid, Ursula Kristin, 2023. "Humorous hate speech on social media: A mixed-methods investigation of users' perceptions and processing of hateful memes". New Media & Society, Article 14614448231198169. https://doi.org/10.1177/14614448231198169.

—, Heidi Schulze and Antonia Drexel, 2023. "Memes, humor, and the far right's strategic mainstreaming". Information, Communication & Society. https://doi.org/10.1080/1369118X.2024.2329610.

Schulze, Heidi, Julian Hohner, Simon Greipl, Maximilian Girgnhuber, Isabell Desta and Diana Rieger, 2022. "Far-right conspiracy groups on fringe platforms: a longitudinal analysis of radicalization dynamics on Telegram". Convergence: The International Journal of Research into New Media Technologies, 28 (4), 1103–1126. https://doi.org/10.1177/13548565221104977.

Shifman, Limor, 2013. "Memes in a Digital World: Reconciling with a Conceptual Troublemaker". J Comput-Mediat Comm, 18 (3), 362–377. https://doi.org/10.1111/jcc4.12013.

—, 2014. Memes in Digital Culture. Cambridge: MIT Press.

Thorleifsson, Cathrine, 2021. "From cyberfascism to terrorism: On 4chan/pol/ culture and the transnational production of memetic violence". Nations and Nationalism (28), 286–301. https://doi.org/10.1111/nana.12780.

Tuters, Marc, 2019. "LARPing & Liberal Tears. Irony, Belief and Idiocy in the Deep Vernacular Web". In: Maik Fielitz and Nick Thurston (eds), Post-Digital Cultures of the Far Right. Online Actions and Offline Consequences in Europe and the US. Bielefeld: Transcript, 37–48.

Winter, Aaron, 2019. Online Hate: "From the Far-Right to the 'Alt-Right' and from the Margins to the Mainstream". In: Karen Lumsden and Emily Harmer (eds), Online Othering. Exploring Digital Violence and Discrimination on the Web. Cham: Springer, 39–63.

Zannettou, Savvas, Tristan Caulfield, Jeremy Blackburn, Emiliano De Cristofaro, Michael Sirivianos, Gianluca Stringhini and Guillermo Suarez-Tangil, 2018. "On the Origins of Memes by Means of Fringe Web Communities". arXiv:1805.12512.

Zick, Andreas, Carina Wolf, Beate Küpper, Eldad Davidov, Peter Schmidt and Wilhelm Heitmeyer, 2008. "The Syndrome of Group-Focused Enmity: The Interrelation of Prejudices Tested with Multiple

Cross-Sectional and Panel Data". Journal of Social Issues, 64 (2), 363–383. https://doi.org/10.1111/j.1540-4560.2008.00566.x.

Zidani, Sulafa, 2021. "Messy on the inside: internet memes as mapping tools of everyday life". Information, Communication & Society, 24 (16), 2378–2402. https://doi.org/10.1080/1369118X.2021.1974519.

9. Studying soft hate speech online: Synthesising approaches from multimodality research and argumentation theory

Dimitris Serafis and Janina Wildfeuer

Abstract

In this chapter, we analyse the reasoning that underlies implicit forms of hate speech in online communication. Focusing particularly on the multimodal complexity of particular news items, we aim to identify soft manifestations of hate speech in visual-verbal combinations. To achieve this aim, we provide an integrative, multi-layered approach that includes analytical tools from both multimodality studies and argumentation theory. This helps us to build a semantic representation of the multimodal artefact, interpreting this semantic representation with regard to the aim of delimiting contextual ambiguity, and, finally, showcasing the argumentative structure of the news item to make the inferential reasoning explicit.

Keywords: *hate speech, soft hate speech, inference, multimodality, argumentation*

https://doi.org/10.11647/OBP.0447.09

Introduction

The focus of this chapter lies on the analysis of the reasoning underlying implicit forms of hate speech (what we will later call "soft hate speech", following Assimakopoulos, Baider and Millar 2017). We grant the premise that implicitness is one way that hate infiltrates online communication environments today (see Assimakopoulos 2020).

Hate speech has been defined by the United Nations as "any kind of communication in speech, writing or behaviour, that attacks or uses pejorative and discriminatory language with reference to a person or a group on the basis of who they are, in other words, based on their religion, ethnicity, nationality, race, colour, descent, gender or other identity factor" (United Nations 2019: 2). Notably, this definition refers to the phenomenon as something spoken or written, and does not explicitly include visual forms of expression. Nevertheless, in this chapter, we want to address hate speech as a multimodal phenomenon, in most cases constructed by a variety of different expressive forms, i.e. semiotic modes (e.g. Hauser and Janáčová 2021), including images, emojis, GIFs and animations, among others. It is crucial to take into consideration all these semiotic modes, their intersemiotic interplay, and their meaning potential when analysing the reasons and justifications for hate speech. With this, we follow the overall trend in the humanities to consider communication as inherently multimodal, and our main claim in this chapter is that the analysis of the reasoning that justifies hate in society should equally and crucially be founded on a rigorous multimodal-analytic approach.

It is indeed more than a truism nowadays that hate speech is widely spread online, due (among other reasons) to the new technological developments and affordances with which digital environments provide their users (see Kopytowska 2017, KhosraviNik and Esposito 2018). This extensive diffusion constitutes one of the most hazardous phenomena that European Union (EU) member states seek to ban by enforcing their legal systems (see Alkiviadou 2017). At the same time, hate speech has achieved intense scholarly attention from different disciplinary lenses (see

Waldron 2009, Sellars 2016, Assimakopoulos, Baider and Millar 2017, Baider, Millar and Assimakopoulos 2020). However, there seems to be a lack of agreement on all-encompassing definitions of hate speech, especially when it comes to manifestations in public communication. Identifying this gap, Assimakopoulos, Baider and Millar (2017: 4, original emphasis) distinguished between "two different categories of hate speech. On the one hand, there is what could be called *hard* hate speech, which comprises prosecutable forms that are prohibited by law, and on the other, there is *soft* hate speech, which is lawful but raises serious concerns in terms of intolerance and discrimination."

According to the authors, hate speech can be realised in its illegal and prosecutable forms where a public incitement to violence and hatred against (members of) groups with protected characteristics (such as race, sexual orientation etc.) is witnessed (i.e. "hard" hate speech) as well as in forms that do not explicitly and publicly incite hatred and violence, but can still promote hatred and discrimination on the basis of which aggression may be justified (i.e. "soft" hate speech). Despite being labelled as "soft", this latter variety of hate speech is even more hazardous, not only because it does not explicitly manifest as a public incitement to hatred and violence against minority groups (Assimakopoulos 2020) and therefore passes under the (legal) radar, but most importantly, because it may subtly infiltrate public online discourse, and thus desensitise the general public that is exposed to such discursive articulations (Soral, Bilewicz and Winiewski 2017). Our focus in this chapter is on this soft variety of hate speech.

Specifically, when it comes to discussion about soft hate speech, recent research argues that relevant studies should focus on several public discriminatory discourses (e.g. xenophobic and/ or racist discourses) with a view to investigating the reasoning that (often implicitly) underlines and justifies hatred in society (see Serafis, Zappettini and Assimakopoulos 2023, Serafis and Assimakopoulos 2023, Serafis and Boukala 2023). This is precisely because hate speech, especially in its soft variety, "does not simply state that somebody is to be hated but [...] crucially, provides an underlying rationale in support of the purported discriminatory hatred" (Serafis 2022: 323). We, therefore, adopt an argumentative perspective for the analysis of the justification of soft manifestations of hate speech—and we focus on those manifestations that appear online, i.e. in multimodally complex communicative situations (Kress 2010, Bateman, Wildfeuer and Hippala 2017). Digital communication in online news magazines, forums, and on social media platforms facilitates the emergence of (soft) hate speech multimodally, i.e. by using not only verbal language but also visuals in the form of photographs, emojis, videos, or animations. These complex forms of hate, which are not only instances of speech, must be analysed carefully in order to identify the different aspects of the phenomenon and its underlying dynamics, while also countering a wider variety of possible forms of multimodally expressed hate speech.

In this chapter, we will therefore present an integration of approaches from multimodality studies and argumentation theory, and demonstrate the strengths and advantages of such a combination, in order to further support the development of the multimodal argumentative study of soft hate speech online. We particularly focus on the specific interplay of written text and photos as one example of the multimodal complexity of soft hate speech. In our analysis, we will demonstrate how our approach facilitates the description and evaluation of this and other forms of intersemiotic interplay, in order to go one step further in analysing the rationale of soft hate speech. Previously, approaches have often focused on individual expressive forms only, i.e. written or spoken language through several analytical lenses (see e.g. Brindle 2016, Assimakopoulos and Baider 2019, Jaki et al. 2019, Baider and Constantinou 2020, Carvalho et al. 2023, Serafis and Boukala 2023). In our analysis, we stress the importance of taking all resources into consideration, following the overall trend towards a comprehensive view of multimodal language and communication.

A methodological synthesis

In the following, we will illustrate our combined methodological endeavour with an analysis of an online news article from the news portal of the prestigious, right-wing Greek newspaper *Kathimerini*, given in Figure 9.1. We will study the interplay between the verbal and visual modes appearing in the news article, namely the headline "Κύμα εισροών στο Ανατολικό Αιγαίο" ["Waves of inflows in Eastern Aegean"], the accompanying photo, as well as the caption, which reads "Στον Καρά-Τεπέ, 4.000 πρόσφυγες απέκλεισαν τον δρόμο διαμαρτυρόμενοι για την έλλειψη τουαλετών" ["In Kara-Tepe, 4,000 refugees blocked the street, protesting against the lack of toilets"].

Using this analysis as an example, we aim to provide a systematic approach to the analysis of online forms of soft hate speech that is also generally applicable to other forms of (online) communication. Most of the frameworks and tools we will use have been developed for the analysis of several forms of multimodal and/or argumentative communication, usually not focusing on a particular genre or medium (see e.g. Wildfeuer 2014, Bateman and Wildfeuer 2014, Wildfeuer and Pollaroli 2017, 2018, Wildfeuer and Stamenkovic 2021, Serafis 2022, 2023). Most importantly, we will demonstrate the three steps of the analysis that lead to a comprehensive understanding of the multimodal reasoning. All of these steps can of course be adjusted for specific media forms, genres, and/or communicative contexts.

These communicative contexts are a crucial starting point for our analysis: we assume that the respective context in which a particular communicative artefact (such as the news article given in Figure 9.1) is embedded motivates specific argumentative inferences (cf. Wildfeuer and Pollaroli 2018, Serafis et al. 2020). Multimodal communication, in particular, usually demands from recipients a dynamic construction of hypotheses about its meaning and its argumentative patterns. In order to be able to reconstruct these inferences, we require an approach that describes both the semantic reconstruction of the overall meaning constructed in the artefact, and the argumentative structure. For the former, in this chapter we will make use of a 'discourse semantics' approach to multimodal analysis (Wildfeuer 2014, 2018) as well as employing the interpretative categories provided in the realm of social semiotics (van Leeuwen 2008). For the latter, we will draw on

Pragma-Dialectics (van Eemeren 2018) and the Argumentum Model of Topics (AMT, Rigotti and Greco 2019).

Κύμα εισροών στο Ανατολικό Αιγαίο

1' 15" χρόνος ανάγνωσης   Ακούστε το άρθρο

Στον Καρά-Τεπέ, 4.000 πρόσφυγες απέκλεισαν τον δρόμο διαμαρτυρόμενοι για την έλλειψη τουαλετών.

Fig. 9.1 Screenshot of the online news article under analysis (*Kathimerini*, 10 July 2015).[1]

Discourse semantics

The discourse semantics approach within multimodality research has been introduced mainly as one specific configuration of semiotic modes, in order to characterise how "regularities in material relate to their contextuali[s]ed interpretations" (Bateman 2020: 39). Within the Batemanian approach to multimodal analysis, discourse semantics plays a crucial role as the stratum of a mode that determines the intended range of interpretations that a semiotic mode might have (see e.g. the definition of a semiotic mode in Bateman et al. 2017: 112–138). The main aim of any analysis of multimodal discourse semantics is therefore to

---

1   Original article available online at: http://www.kathimerini.gr/822961/ article/epikairothta/ellada/kyma-eisrown-sto-anatoliko-aigaio

make more explicit the recipients' abductive inferences during the meaning construction and interpretation process. The basis for this kind of approach stems from both formal and functional discourse-analytical approaches to verbal discourses, e.g. other forms of speech and written discourses, that offer comprehensive approaches to meaning with diverse description parameters that have proven useful for an application to multimodal artefacts. In multimodality research today, there are several dimensions of discourse semantics that are analysed for several genres and media: discourse systems or regions and formal representations of the discourse; discourse relations and coherence; discourse structures (see Wildfeuer 2021: 7–8).

One particular framework, also known as the "logic of multimodal discourse interpretation" (Wildfeuer 2014), operates on all these dimensions and aims to describe the basic semantics of multimodal artefacts. As argued above, this first analysis of the foundational meaning of the discourse is necessary to examine, in a further step, the argumentative structure building on it. The logical analysis does so by building formal representations, so-called logical forms, of events, actions, and states in a multimodal artefact and relating these representations via discourse relations to each other to reconstruct the overall discourse structure of the artefact. Presenting these logical forms, and the discourse relations, makes the recipients' inferential reasoning about the content of the multimodal artefact explicit and reconstructable. For the news item in Figure 9.1, this kind of analysis can, for example, build three logical forms, given in Figure 9.2.

Each box represents one major event or action represented in the item, either on the level of the written language or on the level of the image. While gives a formal representation of the headline "Waves of inflows in Eastern Aegean", represents what is shown in the image: several refugees sitting and waiting outside. then gives a representation of the caption: "In Kara-Tepe, 4,000 refugees blocked the street, protesting against the lack of toilets". In each box, the main (either verbally or visually) represented participants are listed, as well as the specific setting, if available, and technical features such as the fact that the image is taken as a long shot. All these details are crucial for the inferences to be made and count as so-called discourse referents. In the last line of each box, therefore, those referents are listed that are necessary to come to the inferential conclusion of the respective event or action. While, for the verbal aspects of the news item, it is more or less straightforward to build these representations, it is more challenging for the image-only aspect in which meaning is less explicit.

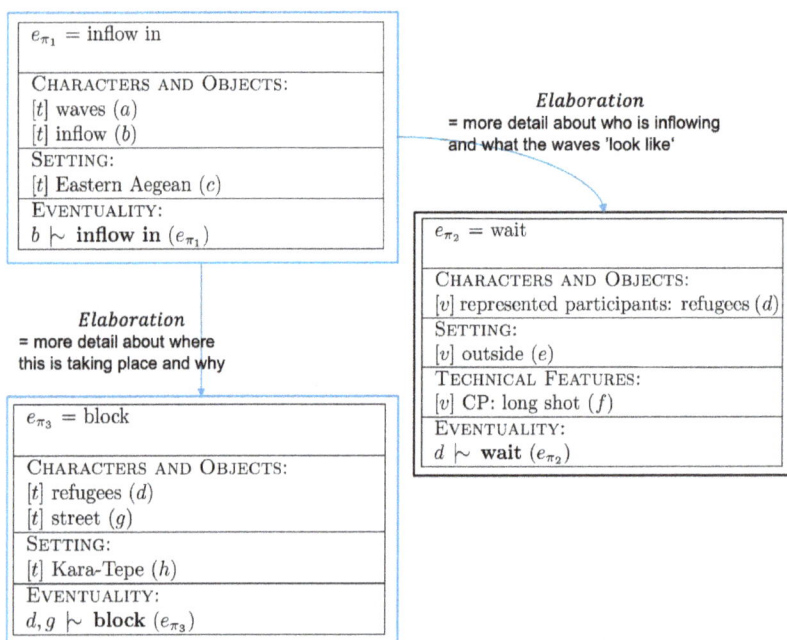

e_{π_1} = inflow in

CHARACTERS AND OBJECTS:
$[t]$ waves (a)
$[t]$ inflow (b)
SETTING:
$[t]$ Eastern Aegean (c)
EVENTUALITY:
$b \mathrel{\vdash}$ **inflow in** (e_{π_1})

Elaboration
= more detail about who is inflowing
and what the waves 'look like'

e_{π_2} = wait

CHARACTERS AND OBJECTS:
$[v]$ represented participants: refugees (d)
SETTING:
$[v]$ outside (e)
TECHNICAL FEATURES:
$[v]$ CP: long shot (f)
EVENTUALITY:
$d \mathrel{\vdash}$ **wait** (e_{π_2})

Elaboration
= more detail about where
this is taking place and why

e_{π_3} = block

CHARACTERS AND OBJECTS:
$[t]$ refugees (d)
$[t]$ street (g)
SETTING:
$[t]$ Kara-Tepe (h)
EVENTUALITY:
$d, g \mathrel{\vdash}$ **block** (e_{π_3})

Fig. 9.2 Logical forms built as semantic representations of the main events and actions described in the news item in Figure 9.1.

The second step of the analysis is then to relate the logical forms to each other via discourse relations. The framework provides a concise set of predefined relations for narrative or exploratory texts, which include basic logical processes such as Narration, Elaboration, or Explanation, for example, but also text-structuring relations such as Parallel or Contrast. In the news item, the three events are related to each other via Elaboration relations that, with each new piece of information, give more details about the formerly introduced content. for example, specifies the 'inflow' in further by exemplifying and visually representing those who inflow. expands on this further by specifying these visual representations as refugees in a specific place. By identifying the relations holding between the logical forms, we also describe the overall coherence of the different elements of the news item and its discursive structure, which also makes the intersemiotic interplay of the different modes explicit. This is particularly relevant in the context of news items, because often in these image-text constellations the semantic gap between the content of the headline and the content presented visually is quite large (cf. Otto et al. 2019).

With this analysis, we identify, formalise, and visualise the logical processes that are necessary for the understanding of the news item. Notably, we do not only focus on the verbal aspects of the constructed discourse, but we build an abductive interpretation from all of the resources involved as well as their interplay. Such an analysis builds a strong and important basis for all further steps of interpretation towards the argumentative reconstruction, but also for other forms of analysis of the multimodal complexity of communication.

Social semiotics

On the basis of the formal semantic analysis, we then draw on a social semiotic perspective to unveil the "meaning potential" (Halliday 1978) that the multimodal artefact under scrutiny realises in its actual and broad social context of use. Following Halliday's systemic functional grammar (Halliday and Matthiessen 2004), the social semiotic approach to multimodality—as, firstly, developed by Kress and van Leeuwen (1996) in their "grammar" of visual and multimodal texts—studies the ways in which the interplay of verbal and visual modes contribute to the representation of social reality (see Halliday's "ideational metafunction") and the construction of social relations (see Halliday's "interpersonal metafunction") in different texts (see Halliday's "textual metafunction").

Furthering this line of research, van Leeuwen (2008) studied the ways in which the representation of certain elements in multimodal texts (such as social actors/action) meaningfully constructs social practice. In the examined news item, we can associate these constructions to each of the logical forms identified in step 1: firstly, in $e_{\pi 1}$, migrant populations are "impersonalised/abstracted" via the use of the dehumanising metaphor "waves of inflows" in the headline, since these are construed as forces "whose meaning do not include the feature 'human'" (van Leeuwen 2008: 46). As underlined by van Leeuwen (2008: 47) "the qualities abstracted from their bearers serve, in part, to interpret and evaluate them". In the particular discursive context of the item, this choice construes migrant populations "as a threat and thus assigns a special sense of urgency to the situation" (Serafis et al. 2021: 570 and references therein). Moreover, the impersonalised migrant populations are "activated" by "circumstantialisation" (see van Leeuwen 2008: 36) through the use of the prepositional phrase "in Eastern Aegean". In this sense, the threat/emergency (see "waves of inflows") appears to occur at Greek-Turkish borders. It is worth mentioning that this last prepositional nominal phrase triggers contextual knowledge, advancing the sense of urgency given the fragile two-sided state relations (see Serafis et al. 2020: 552; see also Way and Serafis 2023). When it comes to the press photo, the relevant populations are "assimilated/collectivised" (van Leeuwen 2008: 37), since their individual characteristics are not visually evident and therefore a portrayal of a solid mass that stands on Greek soil is facilitated. This is also advanced by the long shot adopted in the photo and explicitly identified in $e_{\pi 2}$, which creates distance with the audience and accelerates the 'othering' of the portrayed population. All in all, these representational choices give rise to a construction of migrant populations as an active and massive threat/emergency for/in Greece.

As recent research on multimodal texts maintains (see Wildfeuer and Pollaroli 2018, Serafis 2023, Serafis and Tseronis 2023), representations of social practices, such as those previously analysed, can inferentially give rise to implicit micro-argumentative moves that finally justify the relevant constructions of reality. In our case, the inferential reasoning could bring about a claim in favour of the prevention of migration. This claim is based on the construction of migrant populations as a threat to the host country. Following pragma-dialectics, this move could be reconstructed as the following standpoint 1, which is supported by the argument 1.1:

1. migrants/migration in Greece must be stopped

1.1. migrants/migration constitute a threat/emergency for Greece

To unveil this micro-argumentative inferential dynamic further, in Section 2.3, we adopt the "quasi-Y" reconstruction of "argumentative inferences", offered by Rigotti and Greco's (2019) Argumentum Model of Topics (AMT). We will also showcase how this can be fertilised by the multimodal synthesis illustrated in this section and the previous section.

The Argumentum Model of Topics (AMT)

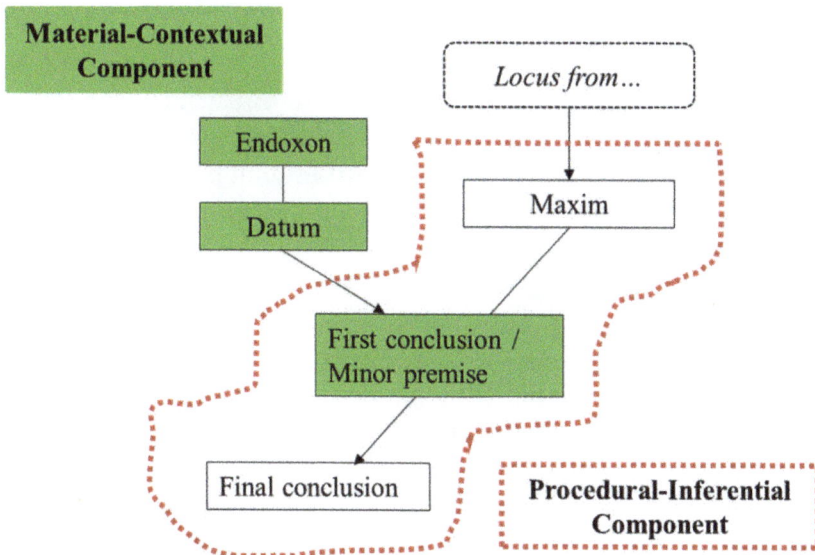

Fig. 9.3 The interplay of the "procedural-inferential component" and the "material-contextual component" of the AMT (adapted from Rigotti and Greco 2019: xiv).

The AMT belongs to a set of studies in argumentation theory that examine argumentation as being closely related to the notion of "inference" (see Pinto 2001, Rigotti and Greco 2019). Under this premise, the AMT seeks to reconstruct the argumentative inference that leads to the defence of a standpoint by an argument. This is done by integrating (a) the logical premises of an argumentative move in its "procedural-inferential component" as well as (b) the contextual premises in its "material-contextual component" (see Fig. 9.3).

Specifically, the first component is governed by the "locus", that is, the (onto)logical basis on which an argumentative inference emerges when combined with certain inferential principles, which are denoted in terms of the "maxim". For example, in an argumentation from analogy, which could be summarised under the "locus from analogy" (Rigotti and Greco 2019: 261–262), a related "maxim" could be 'if X similar to Y is doing A, then Y is expected to do X'. The second component encompasses a reinterpretation of the Aristotelian concept of "endoxon", which outlines the dominant values and knowledge in context and then connects endoxon with a "factual premise" that is the "datum", which in its turn corresponds to the text and its meaning potential in context. The endoxon-datum combination leads to a "first conclusion/minor premise" that, when combined with the inferential principle (i.e. "maxim"), leads us to the "final conclusion" that is the inferentially defended standpoint (see for more details Rigotti and Greco 2019: 207–246).

Based on a representation of migrant populations as a massive and active threat/emergency in Greek context—as emerged in the multimodal analysis in the previous two sections—we may reasonably assume that a claim in favour of the cessation of migration may inferentially arise. In that, the multimodal analysis can crucially illustrate the elements included in the material-contextual component (see Serafis, Mădroane and Lalér 2024, Stöckl 2024). In particular, the discourse-semantic analysis can provide us with insights on how the different modes logically connect, enabling the development of specific inferences in a specific context. Then, the semantic combination can pave the way to show

how the multimodal representation projects coherent meaning potential in context, when seen through the social semiotic lens. Thus, our approach can unveil the ways in which different modes participating in the creation of a cohesive and coherent multimodal text in context interrelate (see also Stöckl and Pflaeging 2022) and thus set light to the "datum" of the inferential configuration. It can also provide us with hints about the "endoxon" sustained in this particular case (see also Stöckl 2024).

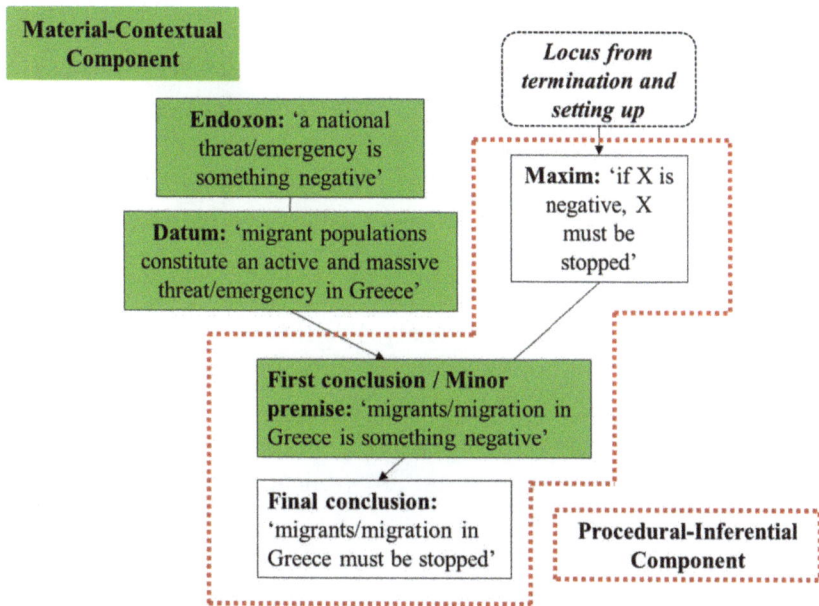

Fig. 9.4 The AMT quasi-Y reconstruction of the argumentative inference.

Specifically, the datum in this case can be verbalised as follows: 'migrant populations constitute an active and massive threat/emergency in Greece' and interrelate with an endoxon such as the following: 'a national threat/emergency is something negative', leading to a first conclusion/minor premise: 'migrants/migration in Greece is something negative'. The logical lines that govern this inference are, in our case, based on a "locus from termination and setting up" (Rigotti and Greco 2019: 263) and realised by the maxim: 'if X is negative, X must be stopped'. They lead to the final conclusion 'migrants/migration in Greece must be stopped', which corresponds to the inferentially defended standpoint (Fig. 9.4). This argumentative inference showcases a line of reasoning that constitutes soft hate speech. Intolerance and discrimination against the relevant minority group are rationalised and argumentatively justified, although there is no explicit incitement to hatred and violence against them (see Assimakopoulos, Baider and Millar 2017: 4.

Concluding remarks

In this short chapter, we presented a methodological synthesis and triangulation of analytical tools that offer a step-by-step multimodal argumentative reconstruction of instantiations of multimodal soft hate speech online. Following relevant research from both the area of multimodal analysis as well as argumentation theory, we grant the premise that the harm of soft hate speech lies in its potential to argumentatively create the necessary conditions for a justification of hatred in society. For this, we provide a broad multimodal argumentative perspective applied to a single example case. This example, however, is just one out of many cases of the public communication of hatred and, building on several other previous analyses, we think that an application of our framework to the many other cases is possible.

Our focus in this chapter lies mainly in the fact that these cases, and public communication in general, are inherently multimodal and that any detection of such forms of (soft) hate speech requires a comprehensive and combined approach that takes into account several layers of analysis and interpretation. We see this approach as working bottom-up, building a semantic representation of the multimodal artefact first and identifying specific semiotic modes as well as their interplay, interpreting this semantic representation with regard to the meaning potential of the respective modes and with the aim of delimiting contextual ambiguity, and, finally, showcasing the argumentative structure to make the inferential reasoning explicit.

Our endeavour is a tentative methodological one, and we do not mean to generalise our findings. However, we maintain that future analysis following the outlined proposal can, on the one hand, profit from the effective triangulation of approaches from two different and only partly connected disciplines. Only by combining the different steps of analysis can more knowledge about the particular multimodal argumentative construction of hate speech be gained. On the other hand, this analysis allows us, at the same time, to focus on larger sets of data going beyond individual examples. Even though the analysis is seemingly fine-grained and extensive, it offers at the same time a strong basis for more empirical analyses in search of generalisable evidence. Following the recent trend towards more empirical multimodality research (see Pflaeging et al. 2019), this would then also involve comprehensive comparisons of several media and genres used for the reproduction of soft hate speech and therefore for the subtle dissemination of hateful ideological beliefs.

References

Alkiviadou, Natalie, 2017. "Regulating hate speech in the EU". In: Assimakopoulos Stavros et al. (eds), *Online Hate Speech in the European Union: A Discourse-Analytic Perspective*. Cham: Springer, 6–10.

Assimakopoulos, Stavros, 2020. "Incitement to discriminatory hatred, illocution and perlocution". *Pragmatics and Society*, 11 (2), 177–195. https://doi.org/10.1075/ps.18071.ass?locatt=mode:legacy

—, and Fabienne H. Baider, 2019. "Hate speech in online reactions to news articles in Cyprus and Greece". In: Maria Chondrogianni, Simon Courtenage, Geoffrey Horrocks, Amalia Arvaniti and Ianthi Tsimpli (eds), *Proceedings of the 13th International Conference on Greek Linguistics*. London: University of Westminster, 398–406.

—, Fabienne H. Baider and Sharon Millar (eds), 2017. *Online Hate Speech in the European Union: A Discourse-Analytic Perspective*. Cham: Springer. https://doi.org/10.1007/978-3-319-72604-5

Baider, Fabienne H. and Maria Constantinou, 2020. "Covert hate speech: A contrastive study of Greek and Greek Cypriot online discussions with an emphasis on irony". *Journal of Language Aggression and Conflict*, 8 (2), 262–287. http://dx.doi.org/10.1075/jlac.00040.bai

—, Sharon Millar and Stavros Assimakopoulos (eds), 2020. "Hate speech: Definitions, interpretations and practices". *Pragmatics and Society*, 11 (2), 171–335. https://doi.org/10.1075/ps.11.2?locatt=mode:legacy

Bateman, John and Janina Wildfeuer, 2014. "A multimodal discourse theory of visual narrative". *Journal of Pragmatics,* 74, 180–208. https://doi.org/10.1016/j.pragma.2014.10.001

—, Janina Wildfeuer and Tuomo Hippala, 2017. *Multimodality: Foundations, Research and Analysis – A Problem-Oriented Introduction.* Berlin: De Gruyter. https://doi.org/10.1515/9783110479898

Brindle, Andrew, 2016. *The Language of Hate: A Corpus Linguistic Analysis of White Supremacist Language.* New York/London: Routledge.

Carvalho, Paula, Danielle Caled, Cláudia Silva, Fernando Batista and Ricardo Ribeiro, 2023. "The expression of hate speech against Afro-descendant, Roma, and LGBTQ+ communities in YouTube comments". *Journal of Language Aggression and Conflict.* https://doi.org/10.1075/jlac.00085.car

Halliday, Michael A. K., 1978. *Language as Social Semiotic: The Social Interpretation of Language and Meaning.* London: Arnold.

—, and Christian M. I. M. Matthiessen, 2004. *An Introduction to Functional Grammar.* 3rd edn. London: Arnold.

Hauser, Jakub and Eva Janáčová (eds), 2021. *Visual Antisemitism in Central Europe: Imagery of Hatred.* Berlin: De Gruyter. https://doi.org/10.1515/9783110616415

Jaki, Sylvia, Tom De Smedt, Maja Gwóźdź, Rudresh Panchal, Alexander Rossa and Guy De Pauw, 2019. "Online hatred of women in the Incels. me forum: Linguistic analysis and automatic detection". *Journal of Language Aggression and Conflict*, 7 (2), 240–268. https://doi.org/10.1075/jlac.00026.jak

KhosraviNik, Majid and Eleonora Esposito, 2018. "Online hate, digital discourse and critique: Exploring digitally-mediated discursive practices of gender-based hostility". *Lodz Papers in Pragmatics*, 14 (1), 45–68. https://doi.org/10.1515/lpp-2018-0003

Kopytowska, Monika, 2017. "Introduction". In: Monika Kopytowska (ed.), *Contemporary Discourses of Hate and Radicalism Across Space and Genres.* Amsterdam: John Benjamins, 1–12. https://doi.org/10.1075/bct.93.001ed?locatt=mode:legacy

Kress, Gunther, 2010. *Multimodality: A Social Semiotic Approach to Contemporary Communication.* London: Routledge.

—, and Theo van Leeuwen, 1996. *Reading images: The Grammar of Visual Design.* London: Routledge.

Pflaeging, Jana, Janina Wildfeuer and John A. Bateman (eds), 2021. *Empirical Multimodality Research: Methods, Evaluations, Implications.* Berlin: De Gruyter. https://doi.org/10.1515/9783110725001

Pinto, Robert C., 2001. *Argument, Inference and Dialectic: Collected Papers on Informal Logic.* Dordrecht: Kluwer.

Rigotti, Eddo and Sara Greco, 2019. *Inference in Argumentation: A Topics-Based Approach to Argument Schemes.* Cham: Springer. https://doi.org/10.1007/978-3-030-04568-5

Sellars, Andrew, 2016. *Defining Hate Speech.* Berkman Klein Center Research Publication No. 2016–20. Boston University School of Law. https://dx.doi.org/10.2139/ssrn.2882244

Serafis, Dimitris, 2022. "Unveiling the rationale of soft hate speech in multimodal artefacts". *Journal of Language and Discrimination,* 6 (2), 321–346. https://doi.org/10.1558/jld.22363

—, 2023. *Authoritarianism on the Front Page: Multimodal Discourse and Argumentation in Times of Multiple Crises in Greece.* Amsterdam: John Benjamins. https://doi.org/10.1075/dapsac.99

—, and Stavros Assimakopoulos, 2023. "'Let's send them to desert islands': Right-wing populist argumentation and hatred against migrants in Greece". In: Bjørn Hamre and Lisa Villadsen (eds), *Islands of Extreme Exclusion.* Leiden: Brill, 83–103. https://doi.org/10.1163/9789004688520_005

—, and Salomi Boukala, 2023. "Subtle hate speech and the recontextualisation of antisemitism online: Analysing argumentation on Facebook". In: Eleonora Esposito and Majid KhosraviNik (eds), *Discourse in the Digital Age.* London: Routledge, 143–167. https://doi.org/10.4324/9781003300786-10

—, Sara Greco, Chiara Pollaroli and Chiara Jermini-Martinez Soria, 2020a. "Towards an integrated argumentative approach to multimodal critical discourse analysis: Evidence from the portrayal of refugees and immigrants in Greek newspapers". *Critical Discourse Studies,* 17 (5), 545–565. https://doi.org/10.1080/17405904.2019.1701509

—, Sara Greco, Chiara Pollaroli and Chiara Jermini-Martinez Soria, 2020b. "Multimodal arguments in the mainstream press: Illustrating portrayals of migration". OSSA12 Conference 2019, 1–14.

—, Irina Diana Madroane and Theodor Lalér, 2024. "Critical reconstructions of populist multimodal argumentation: Illustrations from right-wing parties' Facebook posts on the Russo-Ukrainian refugee issue". *Journal of Argumentation in Context* 13 (2), 232–259. https://doi.org/10.1075/jaic.00029.ser?locatt=mode:legacy.

—, Carlo Raimondo, Stavros Assimakopoulos, Sara Greco and Andrea Rocci, 2021. "Argumentative dynamics in representations of migrants and refugees: Evidence from the Italian press during the 'refugee crisis'". *Discourse & Communication*, 15 (5), 559–581. https://doi.org/10.1177/17504813211017706

—, and Assimakis Tseronis, 2023. "The front page as a canvas for multimodal argumentation: Brexit in the Greek press". *Frontiers in Communication*, 8, 1230632. https://doi.org/10.3389/fcomm.2023.1230632

—, Franco Zappettini and Stavros Assimakopoulos, 2023. "The institutionalization of hatred politics in the Mediterranean: Studying corpora of online news portals during the European 'refugee crisis'". *Topoi*, 42 (2), 651–670. https://doi.org/10.1007/s11245-023-09890-w

Soral, Wiktor, Michał Bilewicz and Mikołaj Winiewski, 2017. "Exposure to hate speech increases prejudice through desentization". *Aggressive Behavior*, 44, 136–46. https://doi.org/10.1002/ab.21737

Stöckl, Hartmut, 2024. "Fresh perspectives on multimodal argument reconstruction". *Frontiers in Communication*. https://doi.org/10.3389/fcomm.2024.1366182

—, and Jana Pflaeging, 2022. "Multimodal coherence revisited: Notes on the move from theory to data in annotating print advertisements". *Frontiers in Communication*, 7, 1–17. https://doi.org/10.3389/fcomm.2022.900994

United Nations (2019). *United Nations strategy and plan of action on hate speech*. https://www.un.org/en/genocideprevention/documents/advising-and-mobilizing/Action_plan_on_hate_speech_EN.pdf

van Eemeren, Frans H., 2018. *Argumentation Theory: A Pragma-Dialectical Perspective*. Cham: Springer. https://doi.org/10.1007/978-3-319-95381-6

van Leeuwen, Theo, 2008. *Discourse and Practice*. Oxford: Oxford University Press

Waldron, Jeremy, 2012. *The Harm in Hate Speech*. Cambridge: Harvard University Press

Way, Lyndon and Dimitris Serafis, 2023. "Scroll culture and authoritarian populism: How Turkish and Greek online news aggravate 'refugee crisis' tensions". *Critical Discourse Studies*, 20 (6), 643–664. https://doi.org/10.1080/17405904.2022.2156568

Wildfeuer, Janina, 2014. *Film Discourse Interpretation. Towards a New Paradigm for Multimodal Film Analysis*. London: Routledge.

—, 2018. "It's all about logics?! Analyzing the rhetorical structure of multimodal filmic text". *Semiotica,* 220, 95–121. https://doi.org/10.1515/sem-2015-0139

—, and Chiara Pollaroli, 2017. "Seeing the untold. Multimodal argumentation in movie trailers". In: Tseronis Assimakis and Charles Forceville (eds), *Multimodal Argumentation and Rhetoric in Media Genres.* Amsterdam: John Benjamins, 189–215. https://doi.org/10.1075/aic.14.08wil?locatt=mode:legacy

—, and Chiara Pollaroli, 2018. "When Context Changes: The Need for a Dynamic Notion of Context in Multimodal Argumentation". *International Review of Pragmatics,* 10(2), 179–197. https://doi.org/10.1163/18773109-01002003

—, and Dušan Stamenković, 2021. "An empirical multimodal approach to open-world video games". In: Jana Pflaeging, Janina Wildfeuer and John A. Bateman (eds), *Empirical Multimodality Research: Methods, Evaluations, Implications.* Berlin: De Gruyter, 259–279. https://doi.org/10.1515/9783110725001-011.

10. Analysing deepfakes: A discourse-semiotic approach

Marcus Scheiber

Abstract

Manipulated communicates in the form of altered images and/ or videos—so-called deepfakes—threaten to fundamentally undermine belief in the authenticity of visual artefacts (online). Deepfakes allow the face of a person in an image to be transferred to the face of another person, or to depict actions that a person has never taken in order to spread forms of disinformation, as well as hate and conspiracy ideologies. As advancing technologies in the field of AI have made deepfakes more accessible and easier to use, and, in many cases, users no longer recognise them as fakes, deepfakes can act as a catalyst for echo chambers.

Even though AI-based solutions already exist that have made enormous progress in recognising deepfakes, they are often trained on isolated contexts and are unable to capture the complexity of visual practices (of digital communication), or incorporate the semantic nuances of implicit patterns into their identification processes. The construction of meaning of visual artefacts is always embedded in social contexts of action, which are both prefigured by collective knowledge and entail certain practices of use. Within this context, this chapter aims to present a qualitative approach that promises to complement the existing quantitative AI-based approaches with a discourse-semiotic perspective.

https://doi.org/10.11647/OBP.0447.10

Keywords: *deepfakes, image analysis, qualitative analysis, hate speech, social semiotics, discourse analysis, discourse semiotics, digital culture, multimodality*

Deepfakes within an image-centered culture

"The ability to make images characterises people perhaps even more fundamentally than the ability to use language, if one understands the use of language as a specific variant of image-making" (Köller 2004: 41). In the context of a linguistically centered society, this statement may initially seem strange, or at least surprising. Although imagery is the older cultural practice from a historical perspective, language is usually given primacy over visual action in everyday life: conversations with friends or partners, shopping in the supermarket, and reports on the annual family holiday are all coordinated primarily through verbal sign actions. At the same time, what all these everyday actions have in common is that it is not only the verbal signs used that fulfil the function of constituting meanings, but that all semiotic modalities are used for this purpose: a conversation involves gestures and facial expressions; finding a free parking space is realised via the visual instructions commonly used for this purpose in the form of signs; and stories about the last holiday must, in principle, be accompanied by photos. As basic as Köller's statement may appear at first glance, the epistemic claim that it makes is nevertheless very serious. It is a claim that is based on the realisation that processes of knowledge formation are not solely the result of the use of verbal sign actions, but also always take place via non-verbal sign processes. Within a certain (social) context of use, images also actualise a potential for meaning that accesses the discursively fixed knowledge of a society and is made communicatively usable.[1] While language prototypically enables

---

1   Human life presents itself as a network of semiotic practices, insofar as both symbolic representation and the constitution of knowledge take place via sign processes: "Insofar as all knowledge is objectified, typified and transmitted with the help of signs of different types, all knowledge formation also has a social background, since every formation of perceptual

a "flexible reference and the representation of logical connections […], the image is suitable for the feature-rich representation of objects in space" (Klug and Stöckl 2016: 248), insofar as it refers to something "that is not directly accessible to direct […] perception for current or fundamental reasons" (Köller 2004: 42).

Although pictorial signs also present themselves as a perspectivised section of a socially constituted reality, they are considered to have a significantly greater authenticity than language in being able to depict this reality faithfully. The reason for this is that in their basic cognitive nature, "('representational') pictorial signs are understood as signs that are particularly close to perception, which […] are more easily conceptualised and memorised" (Klug 2016: 173), as their semantic richness enables an immediate and simultaneous understanding of the image: the image of a cow always and immediately shows a cow and never a hippopotamus, which all people can identify as just that due to their visual organs.[2]

At the same time, the epistemic value of images has been contested by the manipulation of images since people have been using pictorial sign acts.[3] However, while this used to be in the hands of a few experts, digital technologies now allow any user to manipulate images or generate deepfakes by using "AI and DL algorithms to generate highly realistic synthetic media, including images, videos, audio, and text" (Chong et al. 2023: 206). There are multiple manipulation options available to users: face swaps can be used to transfer the face of one person (on a picture) to the face of another person. Lip syncs can be used to match or adapt the lip movement in a visual artefact with other words to be spoken; or puppeteerings are used to imitate body movements (Manjula et

---

perspectives presupposes an implicit or explicit consensus formation" (Köller 2004: 249).

2   This sign-theoretical approach to image analysis is opposed by a phenomenological approach that negates the sign character of images and attempts to grasp the quality of imagery solely through perceptual processes (Abel 2005: 17). However, such a view ignores the fact that images fundamentally fulfil a representational function and can therefore function as sign acts or be interpreted as such by social actors.

3   Consider Hippolyte Bayard's self-portrait as a drowned man, the first (known) photo manipulation.

al. 2022: 29). Deepfakes are therefore able to manipulate existing images as well as depict events or make people carry out actions that never took place: "Using deep-learning approaches, it is possible for the computer to learn both the source and target human faces and then to infer what a human face would look like in a particular position, with particular lighting and a specific human expression" (Seymour et al. 2023: 60). Related techniques can go even further and generate new images that have never existed.

At the same time, deepfakes do not represent a new epistemic threat. Images were already being manipulated digitally before deepfakes appeared. As a result, users are often sceptical about images in digital communication.[4] Nevertheless, the extent of image manipulation can erode social cohesion: if images no longer function as a referential, fact-based, safe haven of collective knowledge due to the large number of potential deepfakes, and if any use of images online is fundamentally questioned, then trust in authorities and political discourse as such is lost:

> As deepfakes become more prevalent, it may be epistemically irresponsible to simply believe that what is depicted in a video actually occurred. Thus, even if one watches a genuine video of a well-known politician taking a bribe and comes to believe that she is corrupt, one might not know that she is. Moreover, in addition to causing false beliefs and undermining justification for true beliefs, deepfakes can simply prevent people from acquiring true beliefs (Fallis 2021: 625).

Given the risk of ascribing authenticity to deepfakes, users therefore often remain in their restricted information bubble, as this—despite its epistemic isolation—offers a sense of security (of the selective and subjective experiences of each user). However, this poses the risk that existing hate ideologies are legitimised and reinforced, as the plurality of opinions (that run counter to these hate ideologies) do not even reach the respective users or are immediately dismissed by them as possible deepfakes, which

---

4   This scepticism sometimes goes so far that images are completely denied their authenticity and legitimacy—despite evidence to the contrary. Consider, for example, the fact that the visual depiction of the moon landing is still being questioned in parts of society today.

can lead to a radicalisation of these users. The epistemic deficiency opened up by deepfakes in digital communication thus reinforces existing echo-chamber effects.[5]

At the same time, users are generally not passively exposed to these deepfakes, as pictorial signs are not simply consumed, but rather users carry out actions with images, or the images open up certain possibilities for action for the user. After all, viewing an image is not the same as grasping its intended meaning: even if a depicted cow can always be recognised as a cow and never as a hippopotamus, the intended meaning of the pictorial action in a concrete communication situation does not necessarily have to be directly apparent. For example, the illustration of a cow in a cookbook realises different meanings than the use of the same illustration in a children's book. Imagery thus represents "not a raw but an institutional fact" (Scholz 2005: 67), insofar as images only attain their status by being "embedded in socially regulated [...] patterns of action" (Scholz 2005: 67) and are used within them:

> An image is use-dependent because there is no intrinsic quality that makes an object an image. No image is an image by itself, rather it only becomes an image when we use it in a certain way [...]. This dependence on utilisation means that the meaning of an image can only ever be determined relative to a corresponding system of signs and rules and the respective framework of action or conditions of perception" (Sachs-Hombach 2003: 81).

The constitution of the meaning of pictorial signs therefore cannot be derived exclusively from the composition of the image or its perception, but takes place along the existing knowledge of the recipients about its use, which current algorithms do not (yet) take into account in the generation and identification of deepfakes.[6] For instance, it has been shown that human coders perform

---

5   Even though the concept of echo chambers is being increasingly criticised (Arguedas et al. 2022), several researchers continue to postulate their existence (Matuszewski and Szabó 2019, Wolleback et al. 2019).

6   This is particularly evident in culturally specific practices and their interpretation in relation to gestures and facial expressions—such as the different variants of head-shaking within Indian culture, which can express different degrees of approval.

significantly better than AI in the identification of deepfakes, provided that images shown include a possible context and the coders can apply their corresponding knowledge (Groh et al. 2022: 9).[7] Although the manipulation of images in the form of deepfakes has taken on a new dimension in terms of both quality (technical precision) and quantity (distribution and accessibility), users are still able to identify them (to some extent) if they can draw on their experience. Consequently, a discourse-semiotically oriented analysis of deepfakes promises to be a profitable, complementary perspective to previous AI approaches, insofar as it focuses on the "identification of culturally shaped knowledge and image patterns [...] as well as their scope for visual [...] designability to fulfil certain communicative purposes" (Große 2011: 17).

AI as the origin—AI as the solution?

The ongoing development of new technologies in the field of AI now makes it possible for users without the relevant expertise to easily generate deepfakes using neural rendering technologies (NR).[8] This is because NR technologies go beyond previous generative machine-learning (ML) approaches in that they enable controlled image generation:

> The ability to direct the rendering process with some control makes the range of possible techniques wide and enables novel view synthesis, semantic photo manipulation, facial and body re-enactment, relighting, and free-viewpoint video. This allows for a broad range of use cases, from the widely discussed image manipulation (deep fakes) to the creation of photorealistic

---

7   Algorithmically generated tweets use significantly fewer 'mentions' (i.e. direct references to other accounts) than tweets created by humans, as a result of which the former can be recognised more frequently as deepfakes, since Twitter (now X) is designed for interaction, which also manifests itself in the usage of tweets (Chong et al. 2023: 205).

8   "NR techniques are defined as deep image or video generation approaches that enable explicit or implicit controls of scene properties such as illumination, camera parameters, pose, geometry, appearance, and semantic structure" (Seymour et al. 2023: 58).

avatars for virtual reality (VR) and augmented reality (AR), virtual telepresence, and digital assistants (Seymour et al. 2023: 58).[9]

In view of these developments, numerous approaches for identifying image manipulation or deepfakes are also based on ML, i.e. the same quantitative approaches are used and differentiated that were originally responsible for the emergence of deepfakes. These AI-based approaches are able to achieve deepfake detection rates of 95% (Manjula et al. 2022: 1) or 88.3% (Chong et al. 2023: 205). Although these are impressive detection rates, these approaches have several problems: these high detection rates can be attributed to the fact that the respective ML methods were trained on specific forms of deepfakes, and they only achieve such rates with regard to these forms and are not applicable to other forms of deepfakes: "AI models can also be trained on the visual data of a single individual to produce a digital human that resembles that individual. However, the digital human is bound by the training data. For example, if the training data does not include the back of the individual's head, the digital human cannot turn around" (Seymour et al. 2023: 61). Consequently, AI models (both with regard to the generation and identification of deepfakes) can only perform to the extent that the training data provided in advance allows them to do so:

> Newer solutions improve on many aspects of earlier software but are still dependent on good training data. For example, even footage with matching lighting, resolution, and camera angles can still produce inadequate results if the training data includes motion blur or facial occlusion. Algorithms are improving constantly, but automatic occlusion in the target video remains only a partially solved problem and often requires ML segmentation-based image correction and compositing (Seymour et al. 2023: 61).

On the other hand, these ML methods consistently work with isolated contexts, as a result of which the pictorial sign acts that are used prove to be semantically underdetermined and thus do not

---

9 "While NR techniques do not yet allow for a full range of complex movements, the level of realism achieved has proven to be often equal to, or to exceed, that of more traditional approaches" (Seymour et al. 2023: 60).

do justice to an authentic or natural use of images (online). Images are never used in semiotic isolation—as the examples of everyday life listed at the beginning of this chapter clearly demonstrate—but every human action is a combination of several sign modalities (Klug and Stöckl 2016: 243), which are subject to certain rules of social reality, i.e. linked to communicative expectations and conventionalised usage patterns.

The fundamental process of interpreting pictorial sign acts does not therefore consist of simply observing the composition of the image, but of recognising types of images and assigning them to functional patterns, i.e. categorising and interpreting them with regard to their recurring (social) contexts of action (Stöckl 2011: 45). Previous quantitative methods neither include the production conditions nor the reception possibilities of the digital sphere in their evaluation. However, these are both definitive and selective in their semiotic representation as well as in the specific participation possibilities, meaning that certain practices of use and semiotic patterns of action (in the form of a limited use of images) are forced on the one hand and restricted on the other. In other words: the use of a specific (technical-social) context determines which pictorial signs or deepfakes are generated in which way with regard to the recipients' expectations, in order to imitate authentic image use or to spread disinformation via deepfakes.

Discourse-semiotic analysis framework

The previous sections have made it clear that, with regard to the theoretical and methodological basis of a framework for identifying deepfakes, a qualitative approach is required that complements the previous AI-based approaches by comprehensively reflecting the possibilities and conditions of image use (online) in its technical, socio-pragmatic and semiotic aspects.[10] A discourse-semiotic

---

10 However, digital communication is characterised by such a heterogeneity of social interaction spaces, fast pace, and different forms of communication (wikis, social networks, gaming, online shopping) that an exhaustive list of characteristics or specific description of all aspects is simply not within the scope of this chapter.

approach that generates an analytical framework for prototypical image use and contrasts this with non-authentic image use (in the form of deepfakes) in order to highlight the differences between them promises to fulfil these criteria. Such an approach is aware that the use of signs—and thus also the use of images (online)—is not to be understood as one-sided channelled consumption, but rather as meaning-creating interaction between sign modalities on the one hand and users as social actors on the other. A discourse-semiotic approach to the use of signs or images understands the potential for meaning-making in such usage, and realises that it is not an invariable parameter of reference: sign modalities are defined as a resource that is subject to the epistemes of the respective discourse and which users utilise in order to constitute meanings within these discourses. As a result, meaning reveals itself as a socially negotiated good, as a result of ongoing negotiation, recognition, and rejection of knowledge in discursive practice (Spitzmüller and Warnke 2011: 41). Knowledge proves to be a relative entity and not an ontological fact: the way in which reality is perceived, interpreted, and experienced is always contextualised against the background of practices and collective knowledge that have developed as socially traditional patterns of interpretation in certain cultures (Spitzmüller and Warnke 2011: 8): "Discourses are socially constructed knowledges of (some aspect of) reality. By socially we mean that they have been developed in specific social contexts, and in ways which are appropriate to the interests of social actors in these contexts" (Kress and van Leeuwen 2006: 4). Therefore, the knowledge on which an entity is predicated was, in turn, negotiated in the course of a social practice and was able to establish itself in society in the form of valid propositions. Hence, knowledge is subject to the normativity of epistemic (semiotic) practices and consequently to the institutional production and reception conditions of social communities. The way in which a pictorial sign is used (online) depends therefore on the interpretative practice of its systematic use within concrete (digital) contexts in a specific (discursive) community of knowledge (Wildfeuer and Bateman 2018: 12), as knowledge is not orientated towards truth, but solely towards the validity of propositions within a discourse:

"In a social-semiotic account of meaning, individuals, with their social histories, socially shaped, located in social environments, using socially made, culturally available resources, are agentive and generative in sign-making and communication" (Kress 2010: 54).

In order to understand the image of a concrete pictorial sign action, an interpretative effort is required, which takes place along a social practice of the use of signs, i.e. along practices that have established themselves through corresponding contexts and in whose shaping the recipients themselves were inextricably involved (as participants of the discourse). This interpretative effort is expressed, for example, in the knowledge of, or the appropriate interpretation of representational conventions, or the semiotic framework of action of a particular place of reception. The (realistic) image of a cow is usually interpreted as the same animal, even though the cow is located as a three-dimensional entity, while the image is only able to exploit two dimensions. At the same time, the image of the cow is ascribed the status of a work of art as soon as it is exhibited in a museum or labelled as an artistic work by means of language.[11] The fact that appropriate interpretations arise regardless of a missing dimension or solely through semiotic contextualisation is due to a "perceptual schema that has become a convention" (Geise and Müller 2015: 20), which is based on the knowledge of precisely those discursively consolidated practices of pictorial perception: "Like linguistic structures, visual structures point to particular interpretations of experience and forms of social interaction" (Kress and van Leeuwen 2006: 2).[12]

---

11 This raises the question of how sign users generate the sign action appropriate to the context of use when the choice of possible sign actions is vast. However, this problem is quickly solved, as the selection falls on those actions with which a user has been socialised, so that typical and atypical interpretations can be distinguished. What is generally attributed to a context of use subsequently manifests itself as a conventional interpretation.

12 The possibilities of cultural and historical variation within the perceptual system could be negated in favour of an anthropological constant in perception. However, the proof of such a constant is extremely difficult or even impossible to obtain, so that a usage-related determination of perception seems more plausible (Sachs-Hombach 2005: 21).

However, assessing the status of pictorial signs exclusively in terms of their usage or reducing them to their contexts ignores the fact that "pictoriality and pictoriality [genuinely] represent optical properties of graphic constellations (form, contour, surface, colour, etc.) as well as certain syntactic and semantic aspects of visual signs" (Stöckl 2004: 54). Although pictorial sign acts must necessarily be realised within concrete contexts (Klug 2016: 168), their significance is not limited to this fact alone. For in their interplay of "sign carrier, context of action and mode of reference" (Felder 2007: 193), images can be characterised as sign complexes that appear as holistic-simultaneous entities due to their internal structural arrangement and semantic constitution (Stöckl 2004: 94). Accordingly, a discourse-semiotic approach must also be aware of these specific qualities of imagery, so that the three dimensions of form, content, and discourse are incorporated into the analytical framework:

1. Form: this category describes the spatial-visual organisation of pictorial sign acts and their actualised semiotic potential in a concrete pictorial action.

2. Content: this category describes the prototypical interpretation (collective knowledge) of the previous category (form) against the background of a concrete social context, which contains or evokes certain communicative as well as cultural-epistemic dispositives.

3. Discourse: this category describes the institutionalised practices of use, which, as discursively transmitted patterns of interpretation, underlie every pictorial action or are expressed in them.

Although these categories are not absolute, but should be understood as heuristic approaches, they nevertheless open up a framework that allows us to gain an understanding of the semiotic processes and discursive procedures of a pictorial action (or at least to hint at them) in order to reveal inconsistencies in the use of deepfakes, i.e. non-authentic pictorial action. Decoding a pictorial action and identifying any deepfakes involves the following steps within this analytical framework and in the subsequent analysis: firstly, the reconstruction of the spatial structure of an image. Secondly, the identification and categorisation of the optically perceptible visual units by synchronising them with the known reality and attributing prototypical functions to them. Thirdly, the contextualisation of the pictorial action within a social practice and drawing possible implications for action.

Not all pictorial actions are the same: Contesting deepfakes

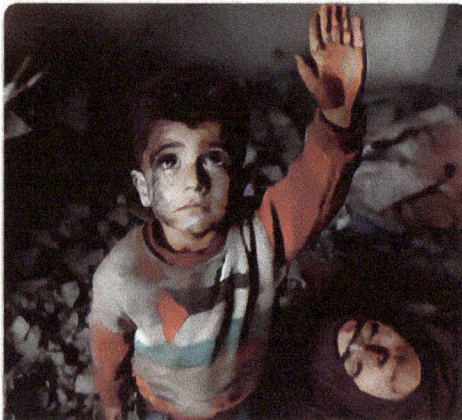

Fig. 10.1 Deepfake Gaza.

The microstructure of the image in Figure 10.1[13] already places demands of the most complex kind on users, since they must first identify the semiotic components of the text-image structure before they can assign them a meaning within their mutual integration and decode the emergent meaning. The integration of

---

13   https://amimagazine.org/2023/12/13/dastardly-digital-deception/.

pictorial and verbal sign modalities is characterised as a context-sensitive comprehension process that aims to "match visual elements with lexemes and statements, [...] to [reveal] nominations and predications, to recognise deictic and pronominal references from the text to the image [and from the image to the text as well as] syntactic, information-related or rhetorical-argumentative connection patterns" (Stöckl 2011: 54). Hence, the verbal parts of the artefact generate a frame, within which the contents offered in the image are arranged in a communicative logic of action and linear time axis, i.e. they are localised in a situational reality—the current conflict in Gaza:

Meanwhile, the arrangement as text-image structure corresponds to the users' expectations regarding the communication format in recourse to the existing knowledge about the prototypical realisation possibilities of the same: tweets are prototypically multimodal. In the selective sensory reception of information, the individual pictorial signs are focused on first, since the pictorial parts of a text-image relationship claim a higher relevance in cognitive processing, and only secondly does the user turn to the verbal sign acts (Geise and Müller 2015: 97). With regard to the dimension of form, it should be emphasised that the arrangement of the individual visual elements on the surface is subject to a deliberate composition. Within this, spatial positionings reveal themselves as constitutive of meaning or are interpreted as carrying meaning by a recipient who is conditioned to attribute meaning to them in the course of his semiotic and medial socialisation. This becomes apparent in the attribution of relevance to individual elements in relation to the categories of foreground and background or absolute and relative size: in the centre of the image, a person is depicted, whom the viewer interprets as the central motif of the image due to their positioning and size, and which the user identifies as a male child expressing a performative act of appeal by means of the positioning of the hand. The interpretation of the physical movements shown as that specific gesture refers to a specific cultural framework of knowledge, which is applied in the reception, insofar as the recipients must have knowledge of that type of representation in order to understand the pictorial action. The same applies to other elements used, which refer to specific, socially traditional, visual action patterns: the incidence of light and the dark background suggest a gloomy, threatening scene. The static frontal shot creates an emotional involvement in what is happening in the image. At the same time, the person is not looking directly into the camera, which means that they do not establish a direct relationship with the recipient, and the viewer is asked to follow their gaze. Where the gaze is directed remains unclear, as it refers to an entity outside the image, which can imply a religious dimension: by identifying the boy as a Palestinian child through the verbal contextualisation, it can be assumed that he is of Muslim faith, so that the appeal can also refer to a divine appeal (as the gaze is directed upwards (towards the sky), where prototypical religious entities are located.

Moreover, the strong colour saturation of the depicted child's clothing emphasises its relevance in contrast to the other elements in the image, including the background, which is less complex and blurred. This gives rise to the assumption at the formal level that the image has been edited. The reason for this is that a natural image usually does not have such saturation. The fact that this is not an authentic image, but in fact a deepfake, becomes evident at the form level, as the person depicted has more than five digits on their left hand, which is not typically the case with humans and recipients are aware of this.

At the level of content, it becomes apparent that the text "Raise your hand if you STAND with palestine" clarifies the gesture of the raised hand as a request for solidarity, which in turn is justified by the visual elements: on the one hand, this is articulated in the depiction of a child, who supra-culturally receives special protection as a vulnerable group, but this is not guaranteed in the depicted scene. The red spots on the child's face, his hand and the face of the person depicted in the lower edge of the picture suggest the interpretation—although other interpretations are possible in principle, even if discursively absurd—that these red spots are blood in each case. It can therefore be assumed that the child is in an unsafe environment or is injured. This interpretation is reinforced by the spatial proximity of the other person in the bottom right-hand corner of the image: by interpreting this person first as female due to the burqa they wear (and thus again via a cultural-knowledge framework) and then (by virtue of inferences based on natural law) as the mother of the same child, who is interpreted as dead due to the closed eyes, the stains on her face and the current context of the situation in Gaza, she can no longer fulfil her function to protect the (her) child from harm.

On the other hand, the justification for the demand of solidarity is manifested in the colour of the boy's clothing, insofar as it refers to the Palestinian flag. This activates—just like the intrasemiotic reference to the verbal part of the multimodal communication ("Gaza")—knowledge about the conflict, in light of which the entire pictorial action is interpreted. The flag thus associates both the boy and the woman as belonging to a specific group, to which implicit collective reference is made: it is not (exclusively) the depicted boy and his mother who are experiencing suffering, but they are representative in the sense of a *pars pro toto* for the entire Palestinian population, and the recipients know that they are experiencing suffering (at the time of publication of this chapter). Since there is a social proposition to avert possible suffering of people (and especially children), the individual pictorial actions culminate in a visual argument to support the textual call to action to comply with a statement of solidarity with Palestine.

The fact that this is not an authentic image, but a deepfake (or at least a manipulated image), is also evident at the content level, insofar as it runs counter to the prototypical behaviour of a child in such a situation: wounded and emotionally shaken in the face of the likely violent death of their own mother, no child would perform such a pose or make such a gesture.

With regard to the level of discourse, it can be said that the multimodal communication portrays Israel—although neither pictorially nor verbally referenced, but only inferred—as EVIL through discursive perspectivisation. Israel is blamed for the mass murder of a vulnerable group by generalising the Palestinians collectively as the victims. The motif of collective innocence in relation to the Palestinian side manifests itself in the mutual integration of the verbal and pictorial aspects, insofar as the prototypical qualities of a child ("innocence") are amalgamated with the collective ("Gaza"), resulting in an equation of the two. At the same time, the depiction of the suffering of a particularly vulnerable group (children) implies that Israel is not doing enough or anything to prevent this suffering. Moreover, it implies an intention to harm innocents in general and children in particular, alluding to connotations of malevolence and bloodthirst, and thus the idea of blood libel, which has existed for many centuries and is updated in this context: blood libel implies that the deaths of children in conflict are not accidental, but rather that their killing is deliberate and calculated. Within this discursive framing, i.e. in the juxtaposition of Israel as an entity that intentionally causes suffering and the Palestinians as an innocent collective, the Israeli side is identified as the sole perpetrator in the conflict and sole guilt is ascribed to Israel. Ultimately, the text-image structure reveals itself to be a discursive self-positioning that, on the one hand, establishes a certain claim to validity and, on the other hand, asks recipients to agree to this claim to validity: The individual elements may not be perceived as antisemitic on their own, but in combination the image generates the argument of ascribing traditional antisemitic stereotypes such as evil, blood libel and blaming Israel alone for the conflict, so that this image is used as an antisemitic positioning to normalise antisemitic ideas within the discourse.

The fact that this is not an authentic image use but a deepfake (or at least a manipulated image) is also evident at the discourse level. After all, users are aware of the fact that, within a conflict, every party tries to shift validity claims with regard to their own discourse position. They are also aware of the fact that the Arab-Israeli conflict is not monocausal, but extremely complex, so that this tweet can easily be recognised as simplistic propaganda. The qualitative analysis thus reveals on all three levels (form, content, discourse) that the image is a manipulated image that has been generated using deepfake technologies in order to spread a certain antisemitic perspective in relation to Israel in the discourse.[14]

---

14   This also undermines the actual suffering of the civilian population and
     it may create opposition to (or some uncertainty about the grounds for)
     decisions to help those affected if some portrayals of suffering in Palestine
     are understood to be deepfakes.

However, it is not always that simple: in order to avoid automated moderation and social stigmatisation, users often fall back on implicit patterns of pictorial actions that can be generated just as easily with the help of deepfake technologies. These implicit patterns of image use can only be accessed via inferences and thus via knowledge that is not (necessarily) apparent in the pictorial act, but is reserved for an insider community. Consider the following example:[15]

Fig. 10.2 Happy Merchant Rats.

At the form level, the above image (initially) shows shapes against a dark background that are interpreted as the central element of the image due to their size and positioning: these shapes are identified as rats in a rubbish bin. At the content level, these are prototypically qualified as unpleasant, dirty, and carriers of diseases in the context of a specific cultural knowledge framework, which is reinforced by the depiction of the rubbish bin, insofar as these negative qualities are also attributed to rats. At the discourse level, various calls to action and self-positioning can be derived, which are dependent on

---

15   https://comment-cdn.9gag.com/image?ref=9gag.com#https://img-comment-fun.9cache.com/media/aq2Nq57/apzxNP2Q_700w_0.jpg.

the context in which the image is used: the characterisation of rats as pests and the (implicit) call to action to avoid or even eradicate them as a result, for example, refers to a specific social practice that is rooted in the Neolithic revolution.[16] However, what applies to all text-image structures is particularly true in implicit pictorial patterns of this kind: the whole represents more than the sum of its parts. Although the previous analysis of the image is by no means inaccurate, such deepfakes evoke yet another level of meaning by utilising the divergence between visual perception and the experience-based act of image interpretation. If the recipients are aware of the so-called 'Happy Merchant' meme, this very motif can also be recognised in the combination of the individual elements. The Happy Merchant meme is composed of conceptual elements that are charged in an antisemitic way: the basic visual pattern with its curved nose, the bulging lips, the crooked posture, and the label of 'merchant' (which, according to antisemitic readings, attributes to Jews the qualities of harming other non-Jewish people through financial and other activities, which makes them happy), are all typical elements of antisemitic beliefs (Scheiber, Troschke and Krasni forthcoming). The activation of knowledge about the figure situates the image in an antisemitic reality. By oscillating back and forth between the Happy Merchant meme and the depiction of the rats, the constitution of meaning of the pictorial action amalgamates the prototypical qualities of rats with Jews. This results in an equation of the two and refers to the practice of dehumanising Jews, which has existed for many centuries. Since such implicit patterns can only be decoded by a specific community, such seemingly harmless images can also diffuse into discursively moderate milieus.[17] As deepfake technologies also contribute to the normalisation of antisemitism within the digital sphere in this way, holistic approaches to identifying deepfakes, both quantitatively and qualitatively, are more urgent than ever.

---

16   Due to the lifestyle of settlement and agriculture, rats were only culturally identified as pests.

17   For a differentiated analysis of the implicit Happy Merchant Memes, see the chapter by Lev Topor in this volume.

Conclusion

"For decades, algorithmic advances and simulations have aimed to better emulate reality with ever more accurate simulation models" (Seymour et al. 2023: 58), which now allows any user without special expertise to manipulate images or generate deepfakes. Although there are many applications for deepfakes that can be useful and have an impact on everyday life,[18] the dangers that arise from the ease of access to and use of deepfake technologies cannot be ignored: the multitude of potential deepfakes erodes the epistemic value of images (online). Deepfakes allow the relevant actors to spread their hate ideologies in the digital sphere via seemingly authentic image use, which is not always easily recognised as manipulation, thereby reinforcing existing echo-chamber effects.

In order to counter these developments, existing algorithms are constantly being developed further, which—rather like a cat-and-mouse game—attempt to identify the progressively more precise deepfakes. However, the improvement of current technologies in the AI sector alone is not enough to completely eliminate the misuse of deepfakes—even if they are able to drastically reduce them— but a qualitative approach is also required. After all, AI-based approaches do not include the social practices of image use in the identification process of deepfakes, meaning that implicit patterns and ambiguities are not recognised: AI-based approaches operate solely on the compositional surface of the pictorial signs. In this way, they are not able to take into account complex, semantically nuanced forms of image use, which is particularly prevalent in the dissemination of hate ideologies, as the relevant actors attempt to avoid automatic recognition and therefore often resort to implicit patterns. The qualitative analysis framework presented here promises to include these forms of deepfakes and to complement the AI-based approaches by integrating the possibilities and conditions of image use (online) with their technical, socio-pragmatic and semiotic aspects into the identification process of deepfakes.

---

18   Consider the use of deepfakes in marketing, historical didactics or film productions.

References

Abel, Günther, 2005. "Zeichen- und Interpretationsphilosophie der Bilder". In: Stefan Majetschak (ed.), *Bild-Zeichen. Perspektiven einer Wissenschaft vom Bild*. München: Wilhelm Fink, 13–29. https://doi.org/10.1515/9783110522280-049.

Chong, Alicia Tsui Ying, Hui Na Chua, Muhammed Basheer Jasser and Richard T. K. Wong, 2023. "Bot or Human? Detection of DeepFake Text with Semantic, Emoji, Sentiment and Linguistic Features". Shah Alam: IEEE 13th International Conference on System Engineering and Technology (ICSET), 205–210. https://doi.org/10.1109/icset59111.2023.10295100.

Fallis, Don, 2021. "The Epistemic Threat of Deepfakes". *Philosophy & Technology*, 34 (4), 623–643. https://doi.org/10.1007/s13347-020-00419-2.

Felder, Ekkehard, 2007. "Von der Sprachkrise zur Bilderkrise. Überlegungen zum Text-Bild-Verhältnis im Paradigma der pragma-semiotischen Textarbeit". In: Friedrich Müller (ed.), *Politik (Neue) Medien und die Sprache des Rechts*. Berlin: Duncker und Humblot GmbH, 191–219.

Geise, Stephanie and Marion G. Müller, 2015. *Grundlagen der visuellen Kommunikation*. München: UVK Verlagsgesellschaft. https://doi.org/10.36198/9783838524146.

Groh, Matthew, Ziv Epstein, Chaz Firestone and Rosalind Picard, 2022. "Deepfake Detection by Human Crowds, Machines, and Machine-informed Crowds". *Proceedings of the National Academy of Sciences*, 119 (1), 1–11. https://doi.org/10.1073/pnas.2110013119.

Große, Franziska, 2011. Bild-Linguistik. Grundbegriffe und Methoden der linguistischen Bildanalyse in Text- und Diskursumgebungen. Frankfurt am Main: Lang.

Klug, Nina-Maria, 2016. "Multimodale Text- und Diskurssemantik". In: Nina-Maria Klug and Hartmut Stöckl (eds), *Handbuch Sprache im multimodalen Kontext*. Berlin: De Gruyter, 165–189. https://doi.org/10.1515/9783110296099.

—, and Hartmut Stöckl, 2016. "Sprache im multimodalen Kontext". In: Nina-Maria Klug and Hartmut Stöckl (eds), *Handbuch Sprache im multimodalen Kontext*. Berlin: De Gruyter, 242–264. https://doi.org/10.1515/9783110296099.

Köller, Wilhelm, 2004. *Perspektivität und Sprache. Zur Struktur von Objektivierungsformen in Bildern, im Denken und in der Sprache*. Berlin: De Gruyter. https://doi.org/10.1515/9783110919547.

Kress, Gunther and Theo van Leeuwen, 2006. *Reading Images. The Grammar of Visual Design.* London: Routledge. https://doi.org/10.1075/fol.3.2.15vel.

—, 2010. *Multimodality. A Social Semiotic Approach to Contemporary Communication.* London: Routledge. https://doi.org/10.1080/10572252.2011.551502.

Manjula, A.K., R. Thirukkumaran, K. Hrithik Raj, Ashwin Athappan and R. Paramesha Reddy, 2022. "Deep Fakes Image Animation Using Generative Adversarial Networks". Chennai International Conference on Advances in Computing, Communication and Applied Informatics (ACCAI), 1–6. https://doi.org/10.1109/ACCAI53970.2022.9752506.

Matuszewski, Paweł and Gabriella Szabó, 2019. "Are echo chambers based on partisanship? Twitter and political polarity in Poland and Hungary". *Social Media + Society*, 5 (2). https://doi.org/10.1177/2056305119837671.

Sachs-Hombach, Klaus, 2003. Das Bild als kommunikatives Medium. Elemente einer allgemeinen Bildwissenschaft. Köln: Herbert von Halem.

Scholz, Oliver Robert, 2005. "Bilder: konventionell, aber nicht maximal arbiträr". In: Stefan Majetschak (eds), *Bild-Zeichen. Perspektiven einer Wissenschaft vom Bild*. München: Wilhelm Fink, 63–76.

Seymour, Michael, Kai Riemer, Lingyao Yuan and Alan R. Dennis, 2022. "Beyond Deep Fakes". *Communications of the ACM*, 66 (10), 56–67. https://doi.org/10.1145/3584973.

Stöckl, Hartmut, 2004. Die Sprache im Bild – Das Bild in der Sprache. Zur Verknüpfung von Sprache und Bild im massenmedialen Text. Konzepte. Theorien. Analysemethoden. Berlin: De Gruyter. https://doi.org/10.1515/9783110201994.

—, 2011. "Sprache-Bild-Texte lesen. Bausteine zur Methodik einer Grundkompetenz". In: Hajo Diekmannshenke, Michael Klemm and Hartmut Stöckl (eds), *Bildlinguistik. Theorien. Methoden. Fallbeispiele*. Berlin: Erich Schmidt, 45–70.

Spitzmüller, Jürgen and Ingo Warnke, 2011. Diskurslinguistik. Eine Einführung in Theorien und Methoden der transtextuellen Sprachanalyse. Berlin: De Gruyter.

Wildfeuer, Janina and John A. Bateman, 2018. "Theoretische und methodologische Perspektiven des Multimodalitätskonzepts aus linguistischer Sicht". *IMAGE. Zeitschrift für interdisziplinäre Bildwissenschaft*, 28 (14), 5–46. https://doi.org/10.25969/mediarep/16402.

Wollebæk, Da, Rune Karlsen, Kari Steen-Johnsen and Bernard Enjorlas, 2019. "Anger, fear, and echo chambers: The emotional basis for online behavior". *Social Media + Society*, 5 (2). https://doi.org/10.1177/2056305119829859.

Index

About the Team

Alessandra Tosi was the managing editor for this book.

Lucy Barnes proof-read and indexed this manuscript.

Jeevanjot Kaur Nagpal designed the cover. The cover was produced in InDesign using the Fontin font.

Cameron Craig typeset the book in InDesign and produced the paperback and hardback editions. The main text font is Noto Serif and the heading font is Californian FB. Cameron also produced the PDF edition.

The conversion to the HTML edition was performed with epublius, an open-source software which is freely available on our GitHub page at https://github.com/OpenBookPublishers.

Jeremy Bowman created the EPUB.

Laura Rodríguez was in charge of marketing.

This book was peer-reviewed by an anonymous referee. Experts in their field, our readers give their time freely to help ensure the academic rigour of our books. We are grateful for their generous and invaluable contributions.

This book need not end here...

Share

All our books — including the one you have just read — are free to access online so that students, researchers and members of the public who can't afford a printed edition will have access to the same ideas. This title will be accessed online by hundreds of readers each month across the globe: why not share the link so that someone you know is one of them?

This book and additional content is available at:
https://doi.org/10.11647/OBP.0447

Donate

Open Book Publishers is an award-winning, scholar-led, not-for-profit press making knowledge freely available one book at a time. We don't charge authors to publish with us: instead, our work is supported by our library members and by donations from people who believe that research shouldn't be locked behind paywalls.

Why not join them in freeing knowledge by supporting us:
https://www.openbookpublishers.com/support-us

We invite you to connect with us on our socials!

BLUESKY
@openbookpublish
.bsky.social

MASTODON
@OpenBookPublish
@hcommons.social

LINKEDIN
open-book-publisher

Read more at the Open Book Publishers Blog
https://blogs.openbookpublishers.com

You may also be interested in:

For Palestine
Essays from the Tom Hurndall Memorial Lecture Group
Ian Parker (Ed.)

https://doi.org/10.11647/obp.0345

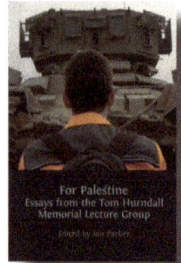

Introducing Vigilant Audiences
Daniel Trottier, Rashid Gabdulhakov, and Qian Huang (Eds)

https://doi.org/10.11647/obp.0200

Peace and Democratic Society
Amartya Sen (Ed.)

https://doi.org/10.11647/obp.0014

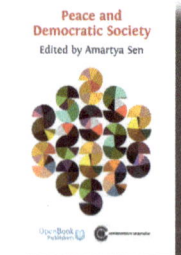

www.ingramcontent.com/pod-product-compliance
Lightning Source LLC
Chambersburg PA
CBHW040148270326
41929CB00025B/3419